# The  Great Unfrocked

# THE GREAT UNFROCKED

## Two Thousand Years of Church Scandal

## Matthew Parris

### Assistant Editor: Nick Angel

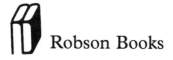 Robson Books

This paperback edition published in 1999 by
Robson Books, 10 Blenheim Court, Brewery Road,
London N7 9NT.

First published in Great Britain in 1998 by Robson
Books Ltd.

**British Library Cataloguing in Publication Data**
A catalogue record for this title is available from the
British Library

ISBN 1 86105 263 4

Typeset in Plantin by FSH Print & Production Ltd,
London
Printed in Great Britain by St Edmundsbury Press Ltd,
Bury St Edmunds, Suffolk

This book is dedicated to the memory of the
Reverend Harold Davidson,
Rector of Stiffkey until he was unfrocked,
who was unfortunately savaged by a lion

# Contents

# ACKNOWLEDGEMENTS

This book has been a joint effort and thanks are due to my small team.

My Assistant Editor, Nick Angel, has provided all the legwork and a good deal of the brainwork, too. He has helped choose our subjects and gathered much of the evidence. His energy and ingenuity in particular in tracking down obscure, contemporaneous and sometimes ancient pictures and records – documents of whose existence we could only guess – has stamped this anthology with a personality it might have lacked. For 18 months he has bounded around like a terrier, sniffing, scrabbling, digging and following scents. Nick has been working *ad hoc* and so his work is over now. If anyone wants a brilliant researcher and drafter they should contact me soon.

My full-time researcher, Julian Glover, has managed the whole project as well as helping with original research. Without Julian's resourcefulness and steadiness I would have despaired. He has kept Nick on some kind of leash, so far as this is possible. He has kept lines open to our publisher's editor, Kate Mills, whom all three of us would like to thank for her patience and thoughtful help throughout.

I would also like to thank David Prosser, who came up with the idea for this book at Buenos Aires airport, did much of the preliminary research and worked on several chapters; Nicholas Garland for drawing a splendid cover; Martin Rawson at the *Guardian* for his cartoon of Roddy Wright; Ruth Gledhill at *The Times*; Dr Christopher Tyerman; the British Library; Lambeth Palace Library; the John Rylands Library, Deansgate, Manchester; the Beinecke Library, Harvard; Christ Church College, Oxford; the Somerset Record Office; the Norfolk Record Office; the

Northumberland Record Office; the Public Record Office, Kew; Ian Montgomery at the Public Record Office of Northern Ireland; Lord Roden; Andrew McCarthy; Dr Deborah Vess from Georgia State University for permission to quote from *Magistra*; the Reverend Canon D. Price; Ollie Jennings at Shamtown Records for permission to reproduce the Saw Doctors' lyrics; Mrs George Reynolds, Stiffkey for permission to reproduce her cartoon by the Reverend Harold Davidson; and William Heinemann for permission to quote from Peter Stanford's *The She-Pope*.

I could never have found time to work on *The Great Unfrocked* had I not been able to rely on my Secretary, Mrs Wright, to organise the rest of my life. My thanks, as ever, to dear Eileen.

# INTRODUCTION

Many of the people in this book went to Oxford and a large number of them were hanged. Nearly all were ordained priests or ministers, many were bishops, some were archbishops and one may have been Pope. Some were formally unfrocked by Church authorities, others less ceremoniously disgraced. Most died ignominiously, or in the Reverend Harold Davidson's case, savaged by a lion in Skegness.

All became, at least for a while, famous. Almost all did exist – with the possible exception of St George, Pope Joan and the Reverend Jane Davison who may in fact have been a Mr T. Heppel.

But what of the author? Am I a believer? According to what criteria have I selected the stories which follow? You ought to ask, for if an author has what it is now the fashion to call a hidden agenda, his readers are entitled to know; this field is certainly vulnerable to an editor with a selective eye and an axe to grind: there is unlimited material to choose from and it will be as plain to you as it fast became to me that an anthology of Church scandal could run into more volumes than the *Encyclopaedia Britannica*. So what was I looking for?

I have no religious faith myself: I am an unbeliever. But faith fascinates me, and I hope I am capable of distinguishing good men from bad among the ranks of believers. Who would not be moved by the dedication Tristan Garel-Jones recently caused to be inscribed on the foundation stone of a chapel he built in Spain for his Spanish (and Roman Catholic) wife, Catalina: 'a believer', he wrote, 'in whom he, a non-believer, believed'.

*Esta capilla la mando construir TGJ un no creyente para Catalina*

*Garrigues Cornier una creyente en quien el cre.*

Although on these pages I have a little fun at the expense of embarrassed church authorities who repeatedly insist that the personal failings of those who profess a faith are not an argument against the faith itself, I do accept that their insistence is fundamentally right – or how could I remain a Tory! I have not chosen these stories in order to undermine the Church, and suspect that churchgoers may enjoy them as much and understand them a little better than the rest of us.

On what basis, then, have I chosen?

Sheer caprice. If I had been able to find a tale (I have not) into which the punchline 'as the actress said to the Bishop' could reasonably have been introduced, I would have chosen it for that alone. Whim has been my guide. You will seek unifying principles in vain. Our searchlight has not been confined to any one era or any particular type of sin nor to the British Isles alone.

But, that said, a preponderance of my subjects are English and their preponderant sins were Greed and Lust – with a little Sloth, Pride, Avarice and Gluttony thrown in. When it comes to memorable sin there is such richness to be found among our own clergymen that it was hardly necessary to look abroad. This anthology's trips overseas are only a sample. Irish church scandal could fill a library; vice in the Vatican is a subject in itself; and Latin American clerical corruption forms its own branch of South American history. I could not begin to do these justice.

So accuse me, if you will, of caprice: I plead guilty without contest.

You may notice, too, that this book is not crammed with child-abusers, mutilators, flashers, the grossly indecent and the clerical victims of mental breakdown. We do not, in these pages, spend too long in public lavatories. A ten-year archive of the inside pages of the *Daily Mail* or the *News of the World* provides a lifetime's supply of such wretched news items. Be assured that, though a short peep at a two-paragraph snippet about an adulterous vicar, frolics with a lissom Sunday-school teacher or peek-a-boo games with choirboys in the vestry – buried among 'Other News' in the *Daily Telegraph* – may be good for a giggle over the Weetabix, more than a few pages of this stuff is repetitious beyond belief.

So I have kept it to a few pages. Under the chapter-heading 'Other News' we offer a sort of 'And finally...' reprise of Sunday scandalsheet snippets: a tombola-full of those silly-season stories for whose sub-editors the fact that 'vicar' rhymes with 'knicker' is daily a reason to thank Providence. These are just samples: there are thousands more where they came from and you don't want to read them all believe me: we have.

This survey also offers only a glance in the direction of those cases – serial abusers of little boys or girls in church orphanages, for example – where clerics who have become festering sores within their Church occasionally hit the press, and investigation uncovers a story so truly depraved as to lower the spirits without teaching us anything more useful than that the Church, like any big employer, has her share of human monsters. A serious journalist would take me to task for omitting Father Brendan Smyth, a Catholic priest who abused hundreds of children over several decades in institutions all over the British Isles and whose scandal brought down the Irish Taoiseach but I must come clean with you. I simply did not want to write about such people and I doubted whether you cared to read about them either.

Instead I have gone for tales with something of the bizarre or exotic – and often something humorous too. There is more fruitcake here than gristle. I have preferred the colourful clergyman who is larger than life to those quivering pieces of human wreckage whom doorstepping reporters seek out to torment. Many of the characters who step from the following chapters are rather lovable.

Others of my *dramatis personae* (like Titus Oates) are included for their importance in history, or for the sensation they caused at the time, my hope being that this book will often surprise, on the whole amuse, but also occasionally instruct.

To venture, as I do, the shy boast that this book turned out as rather better history than it deserved to be, is to admit I have relied on nearly eighteen months' labour by an excellent historical researcher, my Assistant Editor Nicholas Angel (whom I have asked to write an 'Afterthought'). I began with the idea of trawling through the press-cuttings and religious encyclopaedias and coming up with a few score jolly scandals. Nick ignored my instructions and headed for the British Library and the Bodleian, and then set off around Britain on a series of visits to cathedral chapters, county record offices and parish churches – and even the Bull Hotel in Peterborough, in one of whose rooms xvi The Great Unfrocked

Archdeacon John Wakeford stayed (or did he?) with a mysterious woman who was not his wife. Nick came back with some real surprises.

The result is an anthology of reports which include – certainly – some famous and well-documented ecclesiastical disgraces, but which also finds space for new, long-forgotten or scarcely-published material. There is little-trodden ground to be found out there among the court records and local newspaper archives.

Why is any of this interesting? Why should a collection of stories about wicked bishops and naughty vicars be a more obvious idea for a book than stories about (shall we say) sinful shipping clerks or errant grocers?

For centuries there has been a standard answer to this question, and I do not accept it. Most recently the answer was offered me by the Editor of the *Sunday Mirror*, whom I had asked to account for the fact that newspaper editors were not spied upon or giggled about by journalists as vicars are.

'Vicars preach,' he replied. As if editors don't.

This is the familiar 'public interest' defence for wanting to publish (and wanting to read) stories about scandal in the Church. It is hardly new. The thought was expressed in vigorous language in 1823 by William Benbow, who emerged from a spell in prison among convicted clergymen to write a book: *Crimes of the Clergy*. In the introduction to his book, Benbow says:

We have political, puritanical, proud, gambling, drunken, boxing and fox-hunting parsons in abundance, who blazon their deeds to the world; but how few are really devout ministers, who act upon the doctrines laid down by our blessed Redeemer?...It will be a painful task to record many, who are lovers of themselves, covetous, boasters, proud, blasphemers, without natural affection, truce-breakers, false accusers, incontinent, fierce despisers of those that are good, lovers of pleasure more than lovers of God; having the form of godliness, but denying the power; led away with diverse lusts, men of corrupt minds, and reprobates concerning the faith; but who, nevertheless, are priests after the order of Melchisedeck, in their own estimation, and really do exercise the divine right to take tithes of all we possess.

...Solitary instances of back-sliding parsons are not now

quoted with sorrow; they thicken, they swarm like locusts in the field, they are a pestilence visibly destroying by day, and a meteor consuming by night.

In short: these are public men and this is a public disgrace. Such people set themselves up in moral authority above us; we have a right to know if they say one thing from the pulpit yet do another in secret. According to this view we both ought to read about the sins of vicars, and are entitled to enjoy reading about them, for – hah! – the mighty are fallen, the pleasure is pure *schadenfreude*, and fair enough, too.

But just how mighty is the modern parson? How high has a bicycling urban priest reached, from which to fall? And can most readers of the *Sunday Mirror* honestly claim that the vicar they giggle at – or indeed any vicar at all – preaches to *them*? Only a tiny minority of our countrymen today are practising Christians, while the clergy have little power, hold or authority over the rest; yet still the godless majority feel entitled to take as gleeful and absorbed an interest in the sins of an obscure parson as in those of a Cabinet Minister. If we British no longer acknowledge the authority of the Church, what right have we to ask our newspapers to keep a watchful eye on the private lives of those who serve it? In Benbow's time the Church did retain real power – and could, for instance, exact tithes from parishioners. Benbow's outrage at the sinfulness of parsons was at least plausible. But now?

Besides, the modern Church of England takes so permissive a view of the sins of the laity that she might reasonably ask the laity to take a tolerant view of the sins of the clergy. Increasingly it is the case that the clergy do not 'preach' at the readers of the *News of the World*; it is the Editor of the *News of the World* who preaches at the clergy. True, the Roman Catholic Church still exerts quite a grip on the lives of millions; for them honest outrage at the sins of the priesthood might be understandable. But is that justification open to the lager-swilling reader of the Sunday tabloids, giggling on the sofa with his common-law-wife at reports of another vicar caught drink-driving? He is probably being paid more than the vicar.

Exposing or satirising drunks and fornicators among the clergy used to be the weapon of the radical in a time when bishops were the fat cats of their day and when the rural population was oppressed by an iniquitous tithe system. Outrage over the Bishop of Clogher (pp144–157) was caused by more than news of his private misbehaviour with a soldier; what infuriated the public was the fact that he had previously abused his authority by having another man flogged almost to death, and imprisoned, for accusing him of the same offence. Bishop Atherton (see p157), who was hanged for buggery, would probably never have been charged had he not been a vicious tithe-collector.

But today the Church – or at least the Anglican Church – can hardly be called oppressive or corrupt. Her bishops enjoy the sort of modest salary a middle-manager in Woking might hope to collect, and live in cramped annexes to palaces they can scarcely afford to heat. And yet the clergy seem as open to ridicule and public scandal as in a previous age. The *News of the World* is as packed as ever with stories of Spunky Monks, Naughty Nuns, Kinky Canons, Romeo Reverends, Dirty Deans, Filthy Fathers and Beast Priests. For the modern journalist, the naughty vicar remains as much a stock-in-trade as the Lottery Love-Rat or the 'Top Tory in Sex Shame' has become. Why?

The answer, I believe, is no longer to be found – if it ever was – in pompous moralising about wickedness in high places. The 'public interest' defence won't wash any more. The truth is that, like darts, exposing scandalous clergymen has become a national sport. The game predates football, cricket, snooker and politician-baiting: indeed it predates the popular press. Perhaps (as I discuss in my epilogue) it is the incipient sense of guilt in us all which prompts us to turn every paradigm of virtue into a pantomime figure, and throw blotting-paper pellets at it? Perhaps when we lampoon a flesh-and-blood parson we are lampooning, too, an effigy of piety: an effigy of our own construction? Mingled with our shocked amusement at the fall of a cleric is a quiet satisfaction that, if we are no better than we ought to be, well, nor were they either. It's rather reassuring, in its way.

And how ancient is the sport! In 1744 a writer was moved to publish his 'Vindication of Christianity from Gross Misrepresentation thrown upon it by general apostasy of its own Clergy'. In 1647 Thomas Colyer published a pamphlet, 'A brief discovery of the corruption of the ministry of the Church of England'. Henry VIII instructed his agents to dig up scandal in the cloisters so as to justify the dissolution of the monasteries. In the eleventh century so many clerics kept concubines, to such general hilarity, that Pope Gregory VII was obliged to pass the celibacy rules which in October 1996 were to cause the Bishop of Argyll (see p182) such difficulty.

And if vicar-bashing has become a national sport it cannot be said that the clergy have failed, since time immemorial, to offer us ammunition. Even in what was supposedly the golden age of the Church, the age of St Augustine and the century when the Emperor Constantine converted to Christianity, we find no less a figure than the Bishop of Jerusalem, St Jerome, embarrassed by tongue-wagging about those 'who only seek the office of presbyter and deacon that they might be able to visit women freely'. He goes on:

These fellows think of nothing but dress; they must be nicely scented, and their shoes must fit without a crease. Their hair is curled and still shows traces of the tongs; their fingers glisten with rings; and if there is wet on the road they walk across on tiptoe so as not to splash their feet. When you see these gentry, think of them rather as potential bridegrooms than as clergymen. Indeed, some of them devote their whole life and all their energies to finding out the names, the households, and the characters of married ladies.

Jerome could have been describing the fashionable clergymen of the Eighteenth Century – perhaps Dr Dodd (see p66), who powdered his face, wore a diamond ring and a lavish wig, was forever writing *billets doux* to other men's wives, and was eventually hanged at Tyburn, though for financial, not sexual, impropriety.

Which brings me to my final question. If (as I suggest) there is a time-honoured human enthusiasm for the pricking of clerical balloons, and if the bangs are secretly pleasing to us, has the Church shown a corresponding propensity to offer us brightly-coloured balloons to prick? Is there something about the priestly vocation which attracts a fellow of exotic or extravagant inclinations – or turns him that way after he is ordained?

I'm afraid I think there is. I cannot believe that a study of the sins of shipping clerks would have yielded as rich a harvest as we offer you here. In my book *Great Parliamentary Scandals* I found the personal failings of politicians to be rather humdrum even though their consequences were often profound. But the sins of the clergy are not humdrum. Many of the characters who unfold in the pages ahead are really quite extraordinary people: gifted, original, headstrong, volatile and as various in their virtues as they are inventive in their vices, these are birds of bright plumage. Political sinners are starlings beside them.

Such churchmen were all, in their ways, leaders – and they form a distinct category, to which I return in a moment. Henry Ward Beecher and Dr Dodd are examples.

But there is another category. Especially in times past, the Church has raised up and sheltered men who are hardly original but whose distinguishing characteristic is really no more than self-indulgence. Such clergy have not so much led as wallowed, and the sheltering privileges of the Church have in the past left them to wallow, their weakness undetected – or at least unpunished. A man such as the Bishop of Clogher (though the circumstances of his discovery were theatrical) had no religious vocation at all. 'Bishop' was engraved on the silver spoon placed at birth in the young aristocrat's mouth. He hardly preached a sermon.

This second category – the prodigiously weak – is easily explained. Any profession with privileges which place it almost above the law will produce members who abuse those privileges. If plumbers were elevated and cocooned as parsons once were, then the trade of plumbing too would stew in its own greed and concupiscence, as parts of the Church once did. Corruption on this scale is a thing of the past in the Church of England, though elsewhere in the world the Catholic Church still shelters a few miscreants. But, as to the past, there is no more mystery about why some clergymen misbehaved than about why dogs lick their balls: because they could!

The first category are more interesting. Dodd was a genuinely fine preacher, moving whole congregations to tears. Beecher was a liberal crusader of real courage and vast influence. The power of Bishop James Cannon's personality (see p200) was an engine of the Prohibition movement in the United States. Titus Oates, for all his unmitigated wickedness, must have been a livewire and persuader of great force and cleverness. The Reverend Henry James Prince (see p127) persuaded the movement he founded that he was the Second Coming. Surprisingly often the word 'spellbinding' finds use in describing such men, and their talent to communicate and inspire. I think of them in company with great actors, hypnotists, witchdoctors, magicians.

I wonder whether the power to cast a spell over other human beings corrodes the moral faculties of its possessor? To have crowds and individuals in the palm of one's hands – a sensation you, perhaps, (and I certainly) will never know – may nurture a sense of invulnerability. The power to bless, and the suspicion that one is oneself blessed, are strangely tangled.

# AN ORIGINAL SIN

## THE NUN OF WATTON

## Then the Affair was Turned Over to the Virgins

The story which follows – involving adultery, genital mutilation and (perhaps) abortion, all in a monastic context – was related by Aelred of Rievaulx, and produced not to horrify or amuse but to demonstrate the strength of religious fervour in the nunnery of Watton, a newly reformed Gilbertine house in Yorkshire in the twelfth century.

St Matthew wrote that 'there are eunuchs made so by human agency and there are eunuchs who have made themselves so for the sake of the Kingdom of Heaven'. One Gilbertine monk, thus mutilated, had the nuns of Watton to thank for choosing this way of assisting him on his path to righteousness. Sin became impossible.

The woman whom succeeding ages would only ever know as the Nun of Watton was entrusted to the care of the monastic house in the village when aged just four, at the request of Archbishop Henry of York. Like many girls who were dumped in nunneries because there was no other place for them, she had little appetite for things spiritual. Aelred – whose account surviving in just one Latin manuscript is all we have – reports that she was lazy, frivolous, unruly and unresponsive either to verbal or physical correction. As soon as she had passed the age of infancy and entered the years of girlhood, 'she put on the looseness of girls', he records. No love for religion nor respect for order nor fear of God had any effect upon her. She always had a roving eye and an indecent tongue.

One day, in about 1160, a group of lay-brothers from the adjoining house came over to carry out some repair work.

'He anticipated fornication while she, as she later said, thought only of love.'
But their affair came to a messy end.

'Wherefore, she considering, approached, more curiously contemplating their faces than their work. Among them was an adolescent who was fair of face and clean of body. And the miserable girl thrust herself before his eyes and he turned them upon her,' says Aelred. First there was a nod ... then, breaking silence they exchanged sweet words of love. They ignited one another and sowed together the seeds of lust, incentives and desire.

'He anticipated fornication while she, as she said later, thought only of love.' Ah, it was ever thus.

The two met at night, and it was arranged that the man would throw a pebble onto the roof of the nun's accommodation to attract her attention. Heartlessly lured, she went out and soon was caught like a dove in the hawk's claws. She was thrown down, her mouth gagged lest she cry out. First her mind and then her flesh were corrupted. Having experienced it, she must repeat the wicked pleasure. When they had done this often, the sisters, who wondered at the noise they often heard, began to suspect some fraud.

The girl was summoned by wiser matrons. Zeal stiffened their bones. Looking at one another, they fell upon her with their hands. The veil was torn from her head and while some threw it on the flames, others excoriated her life. And some wanted her punished with a stick or burnt with coals. But the matrons checked the fervour of the adolescents.

Finally, she was stripped, stretched out and mercilessly subdued by the whip. She was bound and thrust into a prepared prison. Shackles ringed each foot, into which chains of no small weight were inserted, one of which was fixed to an immense tree trunk by a key and the other drawn through a hole was closed outside the bar to the door. She was kept alive on bread and water and daily covered with shame. Meanwhile, her swelling uterus displayed the foetus.

What to do? The nun was tricked into summoning her lover one more time. The sisters had persuaded her that she would be allowed to run off with him. The monk, unaware that he had been rumbled, turned up as arranged. 'His beloved was waiting, veiled and aflame with desire, as soon as he spied the veil, he threw himself like a brainless horse or mule upon her.'

Instead of a kiss, he received a mighty whack where it hurts. The veiled object was not the nun of Watton, but a monk in disguise; hidden about him was a band of fellow monks who set on him with sticks, and extinguished that fever at its source.

Worse was in store. As Aelred puts it, ominously, 'Then the affair was turned over to the virgins.' Horrors! Anything but the virgins!

> Soon some of them, full of zeal for God though not guided by knowledge, desiring to take revenge for the injury to their virginity, asked that the youth be turned over from the brothers to them for a little while, as they would learn some secret from him. They took him up and he was laid out and bound. She who was the cause of all the evils was brought forth as to a spectacle.
>
> His instrument was placed in her hand and she was unwillingly compelled to amputate the man with her own hands. Then one of the women standing there seized what had been taken and thrust it all stinking with blood into the mouth of the sinning woman.

The nun prepared to give birth. But the night before her child was due, reports Aelred, 'she saw a woman bearing the child all covered in white linen going away... and she felt that she was delivered of the weight in her belly. In the morning, her custodians found her uterus no longer swollen and her face maidenly, not to say virginal... All was healed, all was fair.'

But more was to come. The nun, still bound in chains, had a second vision the following night in which two men released her. She awoke unchained. 'Though they marvelled at the disappearance of the chain, the other sisters in the monastery wanted to shackle her once more until the holy father arrived, to announce that many things worthy of eternal memory had been told, through which we were clearly intended to understand God's benevolence to them that fear him and hope for his mercy.' The nun of Watton was finally left alone.

# COSTUMERY

## CROSS-DRESSING CLERICS

## Frock Shock for Flock

The *Sun* headline in December 1996 broke the news that a Church of England clergyman had resigned his living to change sex. A vicar from near Bournemouth announced that from now on he was to be known as Georgina.

I see no need to name the vicar, for the affair was no scandal. But it did come as a surprise – a 'Frock Shock for Flock' as the *Sun* put it. Perhaps it should not have been. It has long occurred to cooler observers of the ecclesiastical scene that exchanging a cassock for a skirt is for some only the final step in a journey which begins at theological college. Bishops 'are chiefly known among the people by their grotesque attire,' remarked John Wade, the author of the *Black Book, or Corruption Exposed* in 1820. 'They are the only men (save exquisites) who continue to dress in imitation of the female dress.' Sydney Smith understood as much when he wrote that there are really three sexes: 'men, women and curates.'

Pope Joan is probably the most famous cross-dresser in the history of the Church. Naturally Continental observers have decided she must have been English. Supposedly ruling under the name John VIII for 25 months between 855 and 858, Joan's subterfuge was only discovered (the story goes) when she gave birth in the middle of a papal procession.

The fact that she almost certainly never existed has hardly diminished her legend. Indeed, Mr Peter Stanford, a former editor of the *Catholic Herald* who should know better, has recently come out as an enthusiastic supporter for Joan's existence. His book *The She-Pope*, an engaging, cleverly argued historical investigation, *almost* convinces – and is worth reading for the ride,

if not the destination. Just about everything anyone 'knows' about
Pope Joan is contained in the fifteenth-century historian
Bartolomeo Platina's *Lives of the Popes*:

> John, of English extraction, was born at Metz and is said to
> have arrived at Popedom by evil art: for disguising herself as
> a man, whereas she was a woman, she went when young with
> her paramour, a learned man, to Athens and made such
> progress in learning under the professors there, that, coming
> to Rome, she met with few that could equal, let alone go
> beyond her, even in the knowledge of the scriptures; and by
> her learned and ingenious readings and disputations, she
> acquired so great respect and authority that upon the death
> of Leo by common consent she was chosen Pope in his room.
>
> As she was going to the Lateran Church between the
> Colosseum Theatre and St Clement's her travail came upon
> her, and she died upon the place, having sat two years, five
> months and four days, and was buried there without any
> pomp.

Other versions call her Agnes, or Gilberta, and some add the
more grisly ending that on being discovered her feet were bound,
she was tied to a horse's tail and dragged through Rome for half
a league while people stoned her to death. A kinder version has
her placed in a nunnery. One hopelessly optimistic account elects
her child Pope.

Given the vast improbability of the events – Benedict III
(855–858) was Pope at the time 'John VIII' is supposed to have
ruled – and the fact that the story only began circulating in the
thirteenth century, it has gained a remarkably wide currency. So
eager was the desire to authenticate Joan's existence that one
mysterious hand tampered with early histories of the Papacy held
in the Vatican and inserted a passage about Joan, to make it look
as though a contemporary had witnessed the events described.
The story became a stick with which to beat the Papacy. Most of
those who have taken the closest interest in this story have had an
axe to grind or a penny to turn.

Jan Hus cited Joan as evidence of the moral dissolution of the
Papacy at the Council of Constance (1414–18); he was declared
a heretic and burned at the stake. During the Reformation

Protestant pamphleteers gleefully trawled through the rumours and published titles such as *The History of Pope Joan and the Whores of Rome*. In the nineteenth century a Greek with a fierce belief in Joan's existence, Emmanuel Royidis, wrote up her story as a best-selling novel. In this century, Joan has been claimed by feminists as their own.

The myth spawned another, even more fantastic: that after Joan's disgrace all subsequent pontiffs were obliged to undergo a humiliating inspection of their genitals to ensure that a woman could never again be installed as Pope. The inspection (rumours say) was an integral part of the ceremony of enthronement. The throne upon which the Pope-elect sat had a hole in it, through which the most junior dean present would stick his hand and grope until satisfied that the incumbent was male. This done (according to Felix Haemerlein, writing in 1492) 'the person who feels them shouts out in a loud voice, "He has testicles!" And all the clerics reply, "God be praised!".' They then proceed joyfully to the consecration of the Pope-elect.'

It was this that really clinched it for Mr Stanford, for in an obscure corner of the Vatican Museum he discovered a chair... with a hole in it, just right for groping papal goolies. Proof! Being ushered round the museum's Mask Room one day he took advantage of his attendant's brief absence:

> With a glance behind me, I plonked myself down. It felt like a desecration...Pulse racing, white-faced, I leant back and back and back. As I'd thought, this could not be a commode. The angle of the back was more like a deck-chair. But the keyhole shape, I noticed as I brought my spine vertical, was in precisely the right place for the test.

We will leave Mr Stanford in this somewhat undignified pose for a moment. Naturally the Vatican has always denied there was ever any gender test, and on balance I believe the Vatican here – although the Swedish traveller Lawrence Banck in 1644 described such a ceremony, and included a lively illustration in his *Roma triumphans seu actus inaugurationem* (see end of chapter). Another explanation for the Vatican's chair is that it was a birthing chair, indeed used by popes at their consecration, but symbolising the papacy as the mother church.

What other evidence is there for Joan? It is pointed out that subsequent papal processions avoided the Vicus Papissa, scene of the terrible event. Why would they do that if the story was untrue, her defenders ask? Indeed the very name, Vicus Papissa, can be translated as 'street of the woman pope', and visitors there, including Martin Luther, report that there was once a statue depicting the fatal birth. The indefatigable Stanford, raised from his throne and resuming his enquiries, inspected the area and found hope in 'the sharpness of the climb and descent, sharp enough to bring on a birth'. In Siena Cathedral there was long rumoured to be a bust of Joan, now vanished. Better still, in St Peter's itself Bernini executed a series of faces, contorted apparently to depict the   stages of a woman in labour. Commissioned by Pope Urban VIII, Bernini (Stanford suggests) 'was dropping a dark hint about a tale his employers had done their best to sweep under the carpet'. But this was in the mid-seventeenth century and hardly *proof*.

It is all rather nebulous. I think the story of Joan is an exotic fancy, and remarkable evidence of what people will believe of the papacy.

The Roman Church is not alone in being rumoured to have mistaken the sex of its clergy – but the Methodists seem to have made the opposite mistake over their preacher, Jane Davison. The story is recorded in just one (not always reliable) source – William Benbow's *Crimes of the Clergy* – and may have originated in the ale-house. Unlike Joan, Davison has inspired no great traditions in Northumberland, the scene of her or his activities, and inspired no extensive historical sleuth work, save for my own efforts which yielded one tantalising grain of verifiable historical fact.

If we are to believe Benbow, in 1793 an itinerant female Methodist preacher began evangelising her way through the north of England and Scotland. Unsurprisingly she had a particular talent for claiming women's souls for the Lord. Settling in Alnwick in Northumberland in 1794, she was taken into the house of another Methodist minister, Mr Hastings, who had two unmarried daughters.

Jane Davison stayed there for four months before mysteriously absconding – when, to universal horror, it was discovered that both of Mr Hastings's daughters were pregnant. 'Jane Davison', it transpired, was in fact a man, Mr Thomas Heppel, who had not only seduced both daughters without either realising it, but actually arranged to elope with the pair. Benbow tells us that each sister was waiting in a different part of Alnwick, prepared for romantic flight. Both were stood up, and Heppel ran off with the contents of their wardrobes. For such a man, it seems, ladies' clothes came in handy. Buying them himself might have proved embarrassing.

Reader, I find this as improbable as you may. And yet, and yet...I have been able to confirm that, living in Alnwick – a small town (but with a cathedral), the seat of the Earl of Northumberland – there *was* at this time a Mr David Hastings married to a lady named Grace with two daughters, Ann and Sophia, aged 15 and 22. Was this family rent asunder by a rogue cross-dressing minister? Or were the pregnant Ann and Sophia just unusually inventive in explaining their condition? I offer a small reward to any reader who can offer documentary proof that Heppel existed.

As for Heppel's fate, in Benbow's account he flees to York and is arrested for stealing corpses. After the trial (Mr Hastings attends as a witness) Heppel is transported to Australia and no more is heard of him. Perhaps this is all true, though transportation to Australia is a useful device for imaginative would-be historians who need to round off a story in a manner proof against checking. Well, I have checked transportation records, without success. Benbow calls his tale *The Dexterous Fornicator; an account of T HEPPEL – Methodist Preacher, better known in the Northern Counties by the name of Miss Jane Davison.*

I admit that my first two stories – Pope Joan and Miss Davison – are of dubious provenance. But the third, though brief, has a more reliable source: Gregory, Bishop of Tours, who records it in his *History of the Franks.*

An unseemly squabble appears to have arisen between the Frankish princess Clotild and the abbess of the nunnery of the Holy Cross in Poitiers. Clotild made a variety of allegations against this woman – ranging from her unholy habit of playing backgammon every night, to the (undisputed) fact that a great number of the nuns in her care were pregnant. But the accusation which most rankled was that the abbess kept in the convent a male lover disguised in women's clothes.

After a good deal of unseemly wrangling the charges were heard before a council of Frankish bishops, including Gregory. In the course of the hearing Clotild produced dramatic evidence to support her claims: the man himself. 'There he stands yonder,' said Clotild, pointing at him. And, writes Gregory, 'There, in truth, he stood, in the face of all present, wearing women's clothes.' The man was asked to speak, and explained that he only wore women's clothes because he was impotent. This improbable defence seems to have satisfied the bishops, for they found the abbess not guilty of the charge and reinstated her, but advised that in future she should restrain herself when it came to backgammon.

Thus arises a pleasing continuity between sixth-century France and late twentieth-century Bournemouth. From 'Bishops Shun Nun Fun' to 'Frock Shock for Flock', tradition runs deep in the Church.

*Sedes marmorea Pontificis in Basilica Lateranensi.*

# BUTCHERY

## JAMES HACKMAN

## I Could Murder a Sandwich

Fashion has altered over the last two centuries. Today a younger vicar might contemplate becoming a soldier in order to impress a woman. In the late eighteenth century one young soldier took holy orders in the hope of winning his beloved heart. The strategy failed.

On 7 April, 1779, the Reverend James Hackman, Vicar of Wireton, shot dead Martha Ray, the mistress of the Earl of Sandwich, as she emerged from the theatre in Covent Garden. Fewer than two years after the execution of Dr Dodd (see p66) another clergyman was dragged along thronged streets to Tyburn. But whereas Dr Dodd had married a mistress of the Earl of Sandwich, Hackman had murdered one. Both were hanged.

The murder caused a sensation and passed into romantic folklore. A year after the event a collection of fictitious love letters, purporting to be between Hackman and Martha Ray, was published by an enterprising clergyman, Sir Herbert Croft. It was still in print a century later. Ballads were composed celebrating a doomed love. And earlier this century, the tawdry saga was turned into a novel.

Yet Hackman and Ray were no Romeo and Juliet. How far they had been lovers at all became a matter of minor controversy after both were dead, with 'friends of Martha' and 'friends of Hackman' entering conflicting claims in various collections of letters.

Handsome James Hackman had met comely Martha Ray eight years earlier, at an army recruiting party at Lord Sandwich's country house in Huntingdonshire. He was a soldier, just turned 20. Ray was 35, a former dressmaker's assistant, and had been Sandwich's mistress for nearly a decade. This was a competitive

THE REV.ᴰ JAMES HACKMAN.
*From the Original Drawing by M.ʳ Dighton*

Miſs. MARTHA REAY.
Publiſhd, June 7 1779.

*James Hackman and Martha Ray, from contemporary pamphlets*

position, for Lord Sandwich was a renowned roué ('She is a fine woman who you debauched very young', recalled one of Sandwich's friends, Lord Loudon, of Martha Ray).

At the party Hackman was immediately smitten. There is no evidence that Ray was impressed in return, but, in the hope that they might marry, he quit the army in December 1778 to take holy orders – 'hoping,' wrote a characteristically waspish Horace Walpole, that 'a cassock would be more tempting than a gorget.' Hackman found a living in Wireton, Norfolk and proposed to his intended in April 1779. To his dismay, Ray refused.

This rejection – accompanied by a request that their relationship end immediately – led Hackman to write to his brother-in-law, Frederick Booth, on the morning of 7 April, 1779. It was a suicide note, bleak, succinct and touching.

When this reaches you I shall be no more, but do not let my unhappy fate distress you too much. I strove against it as long as possible, but it now overpowers me. You know where my affections were placed; my having by some means or other lost hers (an idea which I could not support) has driven me to madness. The world will condemn, but your heart will pity me. God bless you, my dear Frederick!

There is no evidence in this letter of any plan to murder Martha Ray. In fact, Hackman concludes with the hope that Booth will take care of her.

That same evening he went to the Covent Garden Theatre, where Ray was attending an opera, *Love in the Village*. Towards the end of the performance he positioned himself outside the theatre. He was armed with two loaded pistols. As Ray came out, Hackman saw another man helping her into her coach. Perhaps this was the final straw.

He approached her, tugged at her cloak and as she turned fired one of the pistols directly into her forehead. Ray slumped to the ground, dying but not at this point dead. Hackman then took the other pistol and tried to shoot himself in the head. Remarkably, he was only grazed. Falling to the ground he tried to finish the job by dashing the pistol's butt against his temples. According to a nearby fruit-seller he was shouting 'Kill me! Kill me! Kill me!'

Disarmed, he was taken with Martha's body to a nearby pub, the Shakespeare Head Tavern. Ray was pronounced dead. Hackman was arrested. In his pocket was a letter he had sent to Ray and she had returned, begging her to leave Lord Sandwich and marry him.

Martha Ray's murder was a terrible blow for Sandwich. The two were effectively man and wife (Sandwich's wife was insane) and they had had five children together. On hearing the news of her death (wrote a friend) 'his Lordship stood, as it were, petrified; till suddenly seizing a candle he ran upstairs and threw himself on the bed, and in an agony exclaimed, "Leave me for a while to myself – I could have borne anything but this".'

The tragedy could not have happened at a worse time for Sandwich. The war against the rebel American colonies was going badly, and, as first Lord of the Admiralty, the Earl of Sandwich was under fire. A mob had recently attacked Admiralty House and torn off the gates. Critics questioned not only his naval strategy but also his morals. They attacked him for taking bribes and distributing patronage in a manner brazen even by the standards of the eighteenth century. Sandwich was an effective administrator, but he spent more time at the gambling table than at the Admiralty. He is credited with inventing the sandwich during one 24-hour session in 1762.

At the news of Ray's murder the press displayed characteristic magnanimity and twisted the knife. The *London Evening Post* (an ancient enemy of Sandwich) summed up his ghastly situation, made it clear that the murder of someone he loved was on the whole what he deserved, and wondered why the public had ever given way to 'a strange kind of sympathy, whilst they shed tears of condolence for the vilest of men, to alleviate his distress for the loss of his mistress'. For good measure he was also described as 'the man, who, by his voice and counsel, has drenched whole provinces [of America] with murdered blood'. The implication was that the murder of his mistress by a vicar somehow avenged the New World.

Hovering at the time above the whole episode was the ghost of Dr Dodd, of recent memory (see p66). 'Dishonour, shame and wretchedness, if not an untimely end, seem to be the portion allotted by Providence to the friends and companions of [Sandwich],' sniffed the *Evening Post*. The cases of Hackman and Dodd bore convenient superficial similarities for journalists: one publisher, with an eye to economy, was able to recycle the woodcut of a clergyman hanging on a rope he had used to illustrate Dr Dodd's execution.

The law moved quickly against the vicar of Wireton. After a few wretched days in prison where he did little but lament the fact that he had failed to kill himself he came up for trial at the Old Bailey on Friday, 16 April. The public were charged a guinea to enter. James Boswell, who had taken a particular interest in the case, reported for the *St James's Chronicle* and described the trial as 'one of the most remarkable that has ever occurred in the history of human nature'.

Throughout the proceedings the court was in tears. Hackman had been persuaded by his sister to plead not guilty on the grounds of temporary insanity. He did this without conviction. The trial lasted just an hour and a half. Hackman was found guilty and sentenced to hang the following Monday.

Hopes had been raised that Sandwich might intervene at court to spare Hackman and thereby 'gain the esteem of thousands',

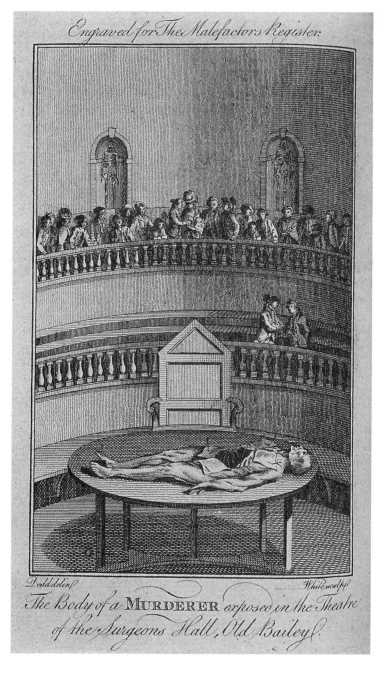

The 1778 Newgate Calendar depicts the body of a murderer being dissected in
Surgeon's Hall. Angelo's visit there to see Hackman's corpse put him
off pork chops for the rest of his life.

although Hackman hardly seemed interested in living. So the execution proceeded, attended by Boswell who apparently found it insufficiently dramatic. 'Saw the execution quite well,' he recorded in his journal. 'Little affected in comparison of what might have been expected.' Henry Angelo, a fencing master and the Nigel Dempster of his era also attended, and the next day went to Surgeon's Hall where the corpse had been taken for dissection. This, he wrote, put him off pork chops for life.

Thus ended the life of James Hackman, a winsome soldier-turned-clergyman whose sin had been (in the words of Othello) to love 'not wisely, but too well'. As it happened, the Covent Garden Theatre chose the evening of Hackman's execution to stage not *Othello* but *Romeo and Juliet*. Hackman's story, short, brutal and sad, lacks the sentimentality which pervades that other tragedy.

# GEORGE ABBOTT

## 'An angel might have miscarried in that sort'

That George Abbott killed someone only by accident did not quite excuse the offence in the eyes of seventeenth-century England. It was simply not the sort of thing Archbishops of Canterbury did. Abbott went hunting and, instead of killing a stag, killed a gamekeeper. A huge personal tragedy for Abbott (and a setback for the gamekeeper), the Archbishop's misguided arrow proved a boomerang. His enemies seized on the scandal to try to topple him.

But for the killing, George Abbott would be considered one of the less notable archbishops in English Church history. Had he better exemplified the qualities of mercy or tolerance in his own person he might have hoped for a little more of both from others. However, described by Hugh Trevor-Roper as 'simply indifferent, negligent, secular', George Abbott was distinguished mainly by his Calvinism and prickly self-importance.

Once as Vice-Chancellor of Oxford he sent 140 undergraduates to prison for failing to take their hats off in his presence. Owing his appointment to James I he was zealous in protecting his patron. A Somerset clergyman, Edmund Peacham, who criticised the King in a sermon which was never published or even preached, found himself manacled and (it is said) tortured on the archbishop's instructions.

Abbott also persecuted many heretics. An obsessive anti-Catholic, he spent much of his ministry trying to promote war with Spain. A characteristic contribution to Anglo-Spanish relations was when he imprisoned the Spanish Ambassador's guests, among them Donna Luisa de Carrajal, a benefactor of English Catholic causes.

On 24 July 1621 Abbott joined a hunting party at Bramshill

Park in Hampshire. Guests were always warned to give the archbishop a wide berth: he was famous for his clumsy archery. But one of the gamekeepers, Peter Hawkins, got in the way. 'The fame of this man's death flew faster than the Arrow that killed him,' recorded the chronicler, Thomas Fuller. A coroner recorded a verdict of 'death by misfortune and his own fault' – Hawkins's fault, that is. The reasoning was that an archbishop with a bow and arrow was so obvious a danger that anyone who failed to steer clear could be regarded as the author of his own misfortune. The King was sympathetic. 'An angel,' he said, 'might have miscarried in that sort.'

But Abbott had too many enemies for the matter to rest. Politics took over. The Spanish ambassador privately informed the Venetian Doge and Senate that the Spanish faction at court was doing its best to undermine Abbott's position. An apologist for Abbott (possibly Abbott himself) complained that the archbishop had become the subject of 'common gossip'. The scandal 'giveth opportunity to the enemies of religion of all kinds, to rejoice, to speak their pleasure, to fill their books and libels, within the realm, and perhaps, beyond the Seas...' In Paris the Sorbonne debated the case three times, and three times condemned the archbishop.

The most damaging censure, however, came from Abbott's fellow clergy, among whom he was unpopular. Accident or not, Abbott had committed homicide, and should have forfeited his estate and renounced his canonicals.

It happened that three newly-elected bishops, yet to be consecrated, were William Laud, Abbott's oldest enemy, who had been elected to the see of St David's, Dr Valentine Cary and John Williams, bishop-elect of Lincoln. These men disagreed with Abbott on a fundamental point of religion. While the archbishop was a straight-down-the line Calvinist who sympathised with European states which had abolished the episcopacy, Laud and his friends were followers of a new religious movement, Arminianism, inspired by the Dutch theologian Jacob Arminius. This put great weight on the role and status of bishops, and rejected the Calvinist belief that people were predestined to go to heaven or hell. In their view, men had free will, and their actions directed their fate.

A homicidal archbishop, therefore, would have seemed doubly terrible to Arminians: it disgraced an office of the church that they held particularly dear and it implied the man would go to hell. And they had another reason to object to Abbott. They all wanted his job, John Williams in particular. 'His majestie hath promised me...one of the best places in this Church,' wrote Williams to the King's favourite (and sometime lover) the Duke of Buckingham. To leave a man 'of blood' as 'primate and patriarke of all his Church,' he went on, 'is a thing that sounds very harshe in the old councels and canons of the Church.' All three refused to be consecrated by Abbott. The King was forced to set up a commission to settle the matter.

It was Abbott's bad luck that the Commission included the three men who had so much to gain from his disgrace: Laud, Williams and Cary. The King asked the commissioners to decide how Abbott's 'involuntary homicide' should be viewed, whether that fact might 'tend to scandal in a churchman' and whether and how it might be possible to rehabilitate the archbishop. On all questions the Commission was split. It effectively referred the matter back to the King, late in 1621.

King James pardoned Abbott completely. The three bishops-elect again refused to be consecrated by Abbott. Extraordinarily, the ceremony had to be conducted by the Bishop of London. Historians quibble about the religious history of early seventeenth-century England but it is clear that the King (in contrast to his son, later Charles I) was cautious about promoting individuals with strong Arminian beliefs, and sympathetic to elements of Calvinism. Perhaps this was why he pardoned his archbishop.

Sheltered by James I, Abbott might have been disgraced but could not be toppled. He continued as archbishop for another 12 years until his death in August 1633, in the reign of Charles I. He was succeeded by William Laud whose religious hot-headedness helped create tensions which led to the Civil War and then to his own beheading in 1645. Abbott, until his death, held a monthly fast on a Tuesday, the day on which Peter Hawkins had died. In his will he left the widow a generous annuity, to be continued until her own death. This, as one commentator put it in the cynical terms of the age, 'soon procured her another husband'.

Since then, no Archbishop of Canterbury has ever shot any of his countrymen, even by mistake – with pistol, rifle, or, indeed, bow-and-arrow.

# HENRY TIMBRELL

## Methodist Preacher Castrates Sleeping Apprentices

Newspaper reports are a bleak way of reaching the truth. The bare facts and legal details may be recorded, together with a handful of those more exotic highlights for which journalists down the ages have developed a keen eye, but the real character of the participants and their likely motivation frequently fail to emerge. What a person was really up to, and why, so often remains mysterious.

Such a mystery is provided by a short newspaper report from 1764, now filed in the British Library. It records the trial and conviction of one Henry Timbrell, a Methodist (or perhaps Anabaptist) preacher, who farmed on a small estate at Kemble, near Malmesbury, Wiltshire. Apart from this one eighteenth-century article, the story, as far as I can discover, has never been told.

Henry Timbrell was sent to the county gaol by the court at Salisbury for maiming and castrating two apprentices, one aged eight and the other sixteen. It is most unclear why he did this. 'He is a man,' says one report, 'who has assumed divers characters to support a life of indolence and laziness.' He continues:

Of late he made a practice of breeding up bastard children for a stipulated sum. Two of these little unfortunates, both boys, he had endeavoured to get rid of by throwing them in the way of small-pox; which not succeeding, his barbarity at length suggested to him an operation that might qualify them for singers at the opera, and by this means turn them to good account should they survive.

Accordingly he took an opportunity, when his children were in bed, to wicker them after the manner in which poor rams are treated. The boys, however, are living, and like to do well. This matter being soon noised abroad, the hard-hearted rascal was apprehended.

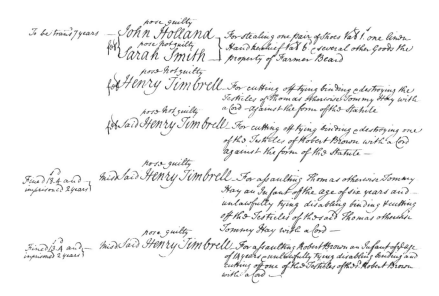

Detail the Wiltshire Circuit records, 1764, recording Henry Timbrell's conviction for castrating his apprentices

No account is offered of whether the lay preacher's money-making plan was really a practical one, or whether (as seems more likely) it was the rationalisation he offered for some deviant personal urge to castrate his fellow-sex. The court records for the Wiltshire Assizes of winter 1764 simply note the acts for which he was tried:

- For cutting off, tying, binding and destroying the testicles of Thomas, otherwise Tommy, Hay with a cord, against the form of the statute – Not Guilty

- For cutting off, tying, and binding and destroying one of the testicles of Robert Brown, with a cord, against the form of the statute – Not Guilty

- For assaulting Thomas, otherwise Tommy, Hay as an Infant of the age of six years and unlawfully tying, disabling, binding and cutting off the testicles of the said Thomas, otherwise Tommy Hay with a cord – found Guilty, Fined 13s 4d and imprisoned 2 years.

- For assaulting Robert Brown as an Infant at the age of 14 years and unlawfully tying, disabling, binding and cutting off one of the testicles of the said Robert Brown with a cord – found Guilty, Fined 13*s* 4*d* and imprisoned 2 years.

The crowds waiting outside the court cared little why Timbrell did it, being more interested in his sentence. A fine of 26 shillings and eightpence and a four-year gaol term evidently failed to satisfy them.

'This sentence was deemed by the female part of the mob so inadequate to his crime, that all the constables of that city, the javelin-men, and, in short, the whole civil power, were scarce sufficient to protect him from their rage.' The fascination and fury of the English populace at a disgraced preacher and the pleasure taken by the press in the details seem to have altered little from those days to our own.


# JOHN BALL

## The Mad Priest from Kent


For a small-time curate from Essex it is something of an achievement to gain the attention of the King, murder the Archbishop of Canterbury and end one's life by being hacked into pieces and distributed to the four corners of the Kingdom. Such were the passions engendered, even in the fourteenth century, by the community charge – or poll tax.

And such was the parabola of John Ball's remarkable career as clergyman, social revolutionary and finally martyr. Not everyone would agree that his story is one of personal disgrace. Credited with providing the intellectual support for Wat Tyler's peasant revolt of 1381, John Ball has been hailed by socialist historians as the first Marxist thinker. The claim owes much to his snappy ditty:

When Adam delved and Eve spun,
Who was then the Gentleman?

On the basis of this early demonstration of the efficacy of the memorable soundbite, Ball has been described by one progressive vicar as a 'mature political thinker'. Contemporaries were less kind. The chronicler Froissart described him as 'a mad priest from Kent'.

In the Church, John Ball never advanced beyond the position of parochial chaplain of St James's Colchester. He fell out of favour with the ecclesiastical powers as one 'who feared not to preach and argue both in the Churches and the Churchyards (without leave or against the will of the parochial authorities) and also in the markets and other profane places, there beguiling the ears of the laity by his invectives', said the Archbishop of Canterbury. Shortly after he imprisoned him.

The extreme move followed much provocation. John Ball travelled around the country preaching dangerous, levelling, doctrines. It was his belief that all lords, bishops, abbots, priors,

John Ball depicted in *Froissart's Chronicles*

monks and canons should be done away with – and that he should himself be enthroned as Archbishop of Canterbury. He was excommunicated in 1366 and in the years leading up to 1381 he was continually in and out of prison. The King banned his subjects from hearing Ball preach.

Then in 1381, Archbishop Sudbury, who had also been appointed to the Chancellorship as well as Canterbury by the fourteen-year-old King, Richard II, implemented England's first poll tax. When the consequent revolt broke out, Ball was already in archbishop's prison at Maidstone, Kent. Tyler and a group of other rebels arrived, sprung him from the gaol and proceeded to Canterbury where they stormed the Cathedral and demanded that John Ball be made archbishop.

By now the rebels numbered some 50,000 men and they made their way to London where Ball celebrated mass at Blackheath. They then continued to the Tower of London, burning down as much of the capital as they could *en route*. Archbishop Sudbury – who as the moving force behind the poll tax had good reason to be alarmed – went into hiding in the Tower. 'Where is the traitor to the Kingdom, where is the spoiler of the Commons?' a group of rebels led by John Ball demanded. Sudbury emerged. 'Here I am your archbishop – neither a traitor nor a spoiler,' Sudbury (reportedly) said before being decapitated by the mob. His head was placed on the parapet of London Bridge.

What followed is famous. Wat Tyler was tricked and executed by the Mayor of London in front of the King, with whom he had been trying to negotiate terms. John Ball fled to the Midlands but was captured in Coventry, tried and sentenced to be hanged, drawn and quartered. The sentence was carried out in the presence of Richard II on 15 July 1381. His body was divided into four pieces, and distributed to four towns across the country.

King Richard, who had earlier promised the peasants that many of their demands would be met backtracked. 'Serfs you have been and serfs you shall remain in bondage, not such as you hath hitherto been subjected to, but incomparably viler.' The politics of the fourteenth century had a marvellously robust quality.

# LECHERY

## GIACINTO ACHILLI

### 'A Profligate under a cowl'

Mid-nineteenth-century England was in the grip of one of her periodic fits of moronic zeal against Catholicism. No allegation against the Church of Rome, however lurid or absurd, was too far-fetched to be thought plausible. Prejudice ranged from the lowest to the highest in the land, from semi-literate pamphlets with sensationalist inventions of treasons, conspiracies and misdemeanour in the confessional, all the way up to Parliament and the judiciary. When Dr Newman – a former Anglican vicar in Oxford, the century's most eminent Catholic convert, a future cardinal, and the hero of this chapter – constructed a new religious house in Birmingham with a basement an MP seriously suggested that Newman's only possible reason for building underground cells was to murder Protestants. As Newman would soon discover, religious prejudice even extended to the country's courts of law.

It was ironic. England's grandest convert from Protestantism to Catholicism found as his antagonist England's most celebrated convert from Catholicism to Protestantism, Giacinto Achilli.

At the time, the trial of John Henry Newman for criminal libel in June 1852 seemed one of the most remarkable in decades. Rational opinion was shocked that in England it was possible for the law to be so blatantly bent to serve partisan religious prejudice. Not since the days of Titus Oates's lying accusations [see p213] had a Catholic been so monstrously failed by British justice.

In July 1851, Newman, against the background of an increasingly violent war of words between Catholics and Protestants, delivered a lecture on the 'Logical Inconsistencies of the Protestant View'. To illustrate his argument he singled out one man, Giacinto Achilli, who (so it was said) had recently escaped from the dungeons of the Roman Inquisition.

Achilli, a lapsed Dominican friar and convert to Protestantism, was touring the country denouncing, to packed public meetings, the brutality of the Inquisition and the depravity of Roman clergy. Such themes endeared him to English audiences. He was everywhere hailed as a popular hero of the Protestant cause.

Achilli had described his conversion to Protestantism as a slow, painful period of doubt over the doctrine of transubstantiation, leading to his final rejection of all Roman doctrine – and to his confinement by the Inquisition for heresy. Newman's version was rather different. Describing Achilli as a 'Profligate under a cowl', Newman denounced the hero.

'You are a priest; you have been a friar; you are, it is undeniable, the scandal of Catholicism, and the palmary argument of Protestants, by your extraordinary depravity.' He alleged a series of sexual offences which had led to Achilli's being deprived of all holy offices by the Inquisition, and which, even after his 'conversion' to Protestantism, had continued. Newman found it puzzling that a man who, he said, had either raped or seduced a string of women across Europe, sometimes as young as 15 and on several occasions in the sacristy of a church, should be used by Protestants as chief witness against Catholicism. Achilli, said Newman, was in himself a living, logical inconsistency of Protestantism.

It need not diminish our censure of the injustices which were to follow, but helps us understand them, if at this point we note that Newman's argument was both provocative and offensive. He did not limit himself to discrediting Achilli as a witness but, having described the Italian as a lying lecher, went on to insinuate that this sort of moral and intellectual corruption was somehow illustrative of the whole Protestant religion, and rooted in it. Using Achilli's case, he attacked Protestantism. Returning fire, Protestantism cornered itself into the foolish position of defending Achilli.

But Achilli was indefensible. The charges were not new: they had appeared more than a year before in Cardinal Wiseman's *Dublin Review*. Then, Achilli had kept prudently silent, leaving it to his Protestant sponsors to respond on his behalf. On informal advice from his solicitor Newman decided it would be safe to repeat the allegations.

A month later, Achilli announced that he was to sue for libel: the beginning of what Newman would later describe as 'the most trying event of my life'.

It took a year for the case to come to court, a period chronicled in Newman's letters. 'Say a Hail Mary for me now and then,' he wrote to a friend, 'for this miserable Achilli has the power of annoying me.'

Newman had hoped he might forestall a criminal trial by convincing the judge before it started that the accusations were justified. For this, he needed the official documents on which Cardinal Wiseman had based the first article. To Newman's despair, Wiseman had lost them. They were discovered – six hours too late. Newman had been committed to stand trial for criminal libel.

He had always suspected that if the case came before a jury he would 'be done for'. But he started gathering evidence none-theless, and this meant finding the women debauched or seduced by Achilli, located all across Europe, and persuading them to make the journey to England to testify. This was difficult. Newman deputed a friend to 'pounce on one woman at Naples, another at Viterbo, and forthwith to return with one in each hand'.

Many were found and some were persuaded, then brought to a secret location in Paris, away from the bribes of Achilli's agents. But once the crucial witnesses had been secured, Achilli's lawyers succeeded in postponing the trial (listed for February) until after Easter. They hoped the added costs might force witnesses to return home.

On 21 June 1852, the hearing began. From the outset Newman had noted that 'a Protestant bias pervades the whole court'. Part of the problem was the judge, Lord Chief Justice Campbell, a militant Protestant who seemed to believe it was his vocation to prevent any further incursions of Catholicism into England. The jury, Protestants to a man, were happy to assist. They were pushing against an open door for sitting on the bench near Campbell was the engagingly-named Sir Culling Eardley, founder of the extreme Protestant Evangelical Alliance – and the man who had brought Achilli to England and sponsored his tours. Quite how Sir Culling talked his way into court is unclear.

The trial was viewed nationally as a set-piece battle between Protestantism and Catholicism. Achilli and Newman were both ardent and famous advocates of the faiths they had adopted – 'two great champions of these contending churches,' as Sir Alexander Cockburn, Newman's counsel and a former Attorney General, put it in his opening remarks. Public interest was enhanced by the prospect of sensational and sordid sexual evidence. Three hundred years of European religious controversy lurked beneath the apparently simple question of whether a jury was to believe the testimony of an exotic miscellany of middle-aged Italian peasants and English maidservants.

The first Italian witness was Elena Giustini, by then 40 but aged about 17 when she had 'known' (as she put it) Achilli in Viterbo, where he had been a Dominican monk. One reporter called her 'sufficiently plain-looking now, [but] probably a comely girl at the time to which her testimony referred'. Giustini's evidence – often shocking, sometimes hilarious – set the tone for the rest of the trial. 'Dr Achilli deflowered me,' she stated bluntly. 'It was in the sacristy.' Asked if Achilli had given her any presents, her reply – 'he gave me a silk handkerchief, which was older than himself' – was greeted with roars of laughter from the court.

Asked if there were any other presents, she replied: 'Yes, and beautiful presents they were – three sausages! The sausages were given at the same time as the handkerchief.' He had also promised her an umbrella, she said, which never materialised.

Giustini grew fond of Achilli ('the first time he forced me, but after that he used the caresses which are usual to a woman'), and their affair continued a while. 'I have never mentioned it to anybody except my confessors, but once Salvatori Larosi, a chemist, asked me, "is it true that Father Achilli has deflowered you?" I answered, "who told you that?" and he said, "himself".'

Details like these posed anti-Catholics with a dilemma. They wanted to believe stories which described 'the church of Rome wallowing in a mire of abomination and pollution,' – but they also wanted to believe Achilli, who denied them. Many, however, contrived to believe both.

As the trial proceeded, an extraordinary picture emerged of this 'rapacious wolf in sheep's clothing' as Giustini's confession had described Achilli.

In 1834 Achilli had moved to Capua where, according to Newman, he had seduced two more women. In 1840 he was in Naples, where once again the sacristy was the scene of his seductions. By now, the court heard, the ecclesiastical authorities in Italy were stirring to action. Achilli was expelled from Naples and in June 1841 arrested by the Inquisition and suspended from the performance of Mass and from preaching. He was also ordered to spend three years' penance in a remote Dominican house in Nazzaro. Achilli spent only two weeks. Then he discharged himself, went to Corfu (then a British possession), and converted to Protestantism.

In Corfu he opened an Italian Protestant chapel. He also struck up a relationship with a certain Mrs Corriboni, married to a chorus singer and pimp. She supplemented her income by prostitution. To the court's amusement it was revealed that both Mr and Mrs Corriboni helped as servers at the Protestant chapel.

So far as Achilli was concerned Mrs Corriboni was a 'second Magdalen'. He showed his compassion by fondling her breasts and kissing her. All this was observed by the English customs officer for Corfu, Mr W.A. Reynolds, who lived opposite Achilli and could see straight into his top room. 'I have seen Dr Achilli put his hands on her shoulders and on her bosom, talking and laughing all the time. I have seen it several times. I kept my blinds down on account of my daughters, it being an improper sight for them.' Shocked by Achilli's behaviour, he demanded that the chaplain sack Mrs Corriboni. Achilli refused to comply, and the Reynolds family led an English exodus from Achilli's chapel. Not long afterwards Achilli considered it prudent to leave Corfu.

He was in England during 1847, with time to turn his attentions to Catherine Foreman, who subsequently testified that Achilli had repeatedly tried and failed to seduce her. Next he appeared in Malta where in 1847 he was appointed a professor at the Protestant College, whose head was the philanthropist Lord Shaftesbury. Achilli was sacked after he had connived in the escape of two errant members of the college, both former Catholic priests, under investigation for bringing prostitutes into the college. Lord Shaftesbury – himself no friend of Catholicism – testified to events at the college.

Achilli, the court heard, left Malta and returned to England, where this time he behaved himself; but on the outbreak of revolution in Rome in 1849 he went to the Eternal City. Here he married a Miss Heley. Then he was arrested by French secret agents involved in the Inquisition. After six months in prison he escaped and fled, with the help of the occupying French forces. Achilli was brought over to England by Sir Culling Eardley's Evangelical Alliance.

Even now, as he toured the country as a Protestant hero, Achilli could not keep his hands off maidservants. Their evidence followed a similar pattern. A 19-year-old, Sarah Wood, had been in Achilli's service, and was categoric. Achilli, she said, had grabbed her while his wife was out of the house, and thrown her onto a bed. 'I resisted with all my might,' she told the court. 'But I could not get away. He was intimate with me then against my will.' Another woman, Jane Legge, who had worked for Achilli for seven or eight months, described a similar story – and had become pregnant, the child dying later of smallpox.

These women witnesses came from many different parts of Europe. All told a similar story. Achilli's response was always the same. He rejected the stories absolutely, often disclaiming any knowledge of the female witness. His testimony – he appeared as a witness, although the proceedings amounted to a prosecution of himself – was the dramatic high point of the trial. Faced with four Italian and three English women as well as a wealth of corroborating evidence, he just denied the lot.

Occasionally the questions were easily susceptible to this approach: 'In the month of July, 1834, did you debauch, seduce and carnally know a woman whose name is unknown, and who was before chaste?'

'No.'

On other occasions Achilli squirmed. He was at his least impressive when Sir Alexander Cockburn pushed him to state, on oath, that he had ever been immoral. Asked, directly by Cockburn: 'Now can you state that, from the time you were professed in 1819, until you left in 1833, you had no intercourse with any woman whatever?'

Achilli merely smiled. Pressed again he replied: 'I could answer no.' Pressed further he finally said: 'Whether I have had intercourse with others I decline to answer.' The tortured apology his supporters found for this testimony was to see it as a noble example of his integrity. For others it suggested that, even if particular charges could not be made to stick, Achilli remained under a cloud of unspecified immorality.

But Achilli's critics expected no more of him. What infuriated Catholics was the conduct of the judge. Lord Campbell behaved like a minor demagogue; his defence of Protestantism brought foot-stamping from the gallery. 'I am not considering whether it is evidence under which Dr Achilli could be led out to be burnt alive, or to be imprisoned for life in the dungeons of the inquisitions, but merely whether it sustains the allegation in the plea. We must not be frightened at the word inquisition! Thank God the thing has no place in this country.' The cheering in court was so loud that he repeated the last phrase.

After two hours of deliberation, the jury returned with the inevitable Guilty verdict. The news was greeted with roars of approval, which Campbell did nothing to still.

The immediate reaction of the press was mixed. *The Times*, to Newman's immense surprise, was harsh in its criticisms both of the jury's decision and of Lord Campbell's behaviour. Such sentiments were echoed in the *Morning Chronicle*. But for the most part the verdict was seen as a vindication of Protestantism and a blow against English Catholics. Much of England found it possible to believe that the whole saga had been an international conspiracy organised from Rome. Before succumbing to disbelief, we should remember that much of England did believe in a Catholic plot to destroy Protestantism, and within such a view of the world it was not incredible that a string of foreigners might have been sent to England to offer false testimony against a leading Protestant.

For Newman the outcome was all he had expected. Several agonising months followed before sentence was passed. When he was finally sentenced in January 1853, he had packed a bag ready for prison, and settled his financial affairs. But the sentence suggested a certain sheepishness on the part of the Protestant establishment. Newman was fined £100. The public gallery, this time packed with supporters of Newman, roared their approval. This time the judge ordered them to be silent.

Whatever his immediate support, Achilli lost favour fast. Although he had cleared his name in law, his reputation was tarnished. He seems to have ended his life as carelessly as he lived it. After emigrating to America he had been charged with adultery in New Jersey. In 1860 he deserted the woman concerned, and his eldest son, in New York. He left what was apparently a suicide note.

From the written record Achilli never fully materialises as a character: some sort of dark and wayward spirit lies behind the disjointed accounts of his career. His writings were a concoction of half-truths and lies. Newman, with characteristic insight, guessed that Achilli had never wanted to bring the libel charge, and that he probably did not much care for his adoptive Protestant companions.

This, though in some ways a small and unusual story, was not a glorious hour in English history. It is hard in hindsight to explain it, lacking as we do any sense of the real fear of Continental Catholicism and its imagined designs which survived so long in England. Newman survived it, and in 1880 was created a cardinal.


# TOM TYLER


## A Case of Baggy Underpants


In 1963, in the wake of the Profumo scandal, in order to eliminate a Cabinet minister from his enquiry into the affair, the Master of the Rolls, Lord Denning, ordered the unnamed minister's penis to be examined in secret by a doctor. One of my distinguished predecessors on *The Times*, the columnist Bernard Levin was astonished...

> ...how it came about, almost exactly two-thirds of the way through the Twentieth Century, and in a country as advanced as Britain, that a judge should have been obliged to ask a doctor to examine the penis of a politician, is something so extraordinary, and in many ways so significant, that it

deserves examination as detailed as that which the Minister underwent.

Similar questions may have passed through the mind of Thomas Tyler, vicar of Henfield, Rural Dean of Hurst – or (as he was dubbed by the tabloids) 'Reverend Rat'. Nine-tenths of the way through the twentieth century, he found not only his penis but the colour of his pubic hair and the age and relative bagginess of his underpants paraded as evidence before a court. It is in the nature of sensational sexual trials that all the evidence, down to the smallest detail, should be scrutinised. Unfortunately for Tyler there was no shortage of witnesses prepared to help the court take this to remarkable lengths.

Tyler's was the classic 'frisky vicar' story, briefly enthralling both tabloids and the *Daily Telegraph* – and soon forgotten. Aged 50 and married with three grown-up children, Tyler had, by 1990, been vicar of Henfield for 25 years. For ten of them he had been conducting an affair with the wife of one of his church-wardens. Tyler's seduction techniques were not subtle: after a church service one day he had guided Mrs Sue Whittome's hand under his cassock, placed it on his erect penis and said, 'You see what an exciting girl you are.' In the years that followed they romped (there is no more suitable word) in the vicarage, at her home and in the back of the vicar's Ford Cortina. Of all the details which emerged, it was perhaps cruellest to bring to national attention the fact that the vicar possessed a Ford Cortina.

But Tyler, widely agreed to be an improbable Lothario (he looks uncannily like the Culture Secretary, Chris Smith), grew tired of Mrs Whittome and turned his attentions to 32-year-old Mrs Barbara Edwards. Mrs Edwards was pregnant when their affair began. Tyler was no more subtle in his advances. 'He lifted my dress and kissed my bulge,' Mrs Edwards said later. 'By then I just wanted him and we had sex standing up in the hall, it didn't last long.'

Mr Edwards, who shared with Tyler an interest in classic cars, grew suspicious. He confronted Mr Tyler in the vicarage. 'Have you been fiddling with my wife?' he challenged him. 'Have you been fiddling with my wife's breasts and got your penis out?' Edwards made Tyler swear on the Bible that nothing had been going on.

But it was when each woman learned of the other's existence

that Tyler was in serious trouble. Mrs Whittome approached the Bishop of Winchester and broke the story to him.

For only the second time in the history of the Church of England, one of its vicars found himself in a consistory court charged with 'conduct unbecoming a clerk in holy orders'. The case was heard in October 1990 in St George's Parish Hall, Winchester – normally the scene of nothing more dramatic than the city's annual pantomime. After hearing the opening cases from both sides, the judge, Quentin Edwards (the press were keen to point out that he sat in exactly the spot where Old King Cole had sat the previous Christmas) decided the case would 'injure public morals' if reported. Accordingly the media were excluded.

It was only from the final speeches for the defence and prosecution (which were given in open session) that the public were alerted to what we had been spared. Although both alleged lovers were agreed that Tyler was circumcised, there was no consensus when it came to the location of a pimple in his groin. As for Mrs Whittome's assertion that Tyler had 'ginger-grey' pubic hair, it was, said counsel for the defence, Judith Hughes, quite false. (How did she know?) Such inconsistencies failed to sink the prosecution, and Tyler was found guilty on all charges by a panel of five assessors. The Bishop of Winchester made it clear that, although Tyler would be deprived of his living, he would not be unfrocked.

Perhaps Tyler should now have called it a day. Although found guilty, the evidence had been heard behind closed doors, public morals remained uninjured, and – save for the Ford Cortina – embarrassment had been minimal.

Clergymen, when they fall, sometimes become fanatical. They see the prospect of disgrace not as the consequence of their own folly, but as the work of enemies in their parish. They seem able to convince themselves that the Devil himself, determined to interrupt God's work, has tripped them through the agency of bishops, deans, churchwardens and interfering laymen. Often the entire edifice of the church is blamed. The vicar's cause and God's cause are thus one and the same; attempts to clear the vicar's name become a holy war.

It would be wrong to suggest that Tom Tyler saw himself as the victim of a satanic conspiracy; but refusing to acknowledge any weakness in himself, he began to blame his downfall on the controversial style of his ministry, and the division and resentments this brought in his parish. He was adamant that the women were both lying. He successfully appealed for a new trial on the grounds that one of the assessors in the original hearing may have been biased.

This time there were no restrictions on the press. Mrs Edwards had already sold her story to the *Daily Mirror* for £10,000, posing in her underwear under the headline, 'How The Randy Vicar Bedded Me'. Millions of *Mirror* readers had demonstrated that the public was very ready to injure its own morals. The case proceeded.

The difficulty over pimples was never resolved. Only the charge concerning Mrs Edwards was considered this time and so there was no chance of disagreement between mistresses; but a new area of controversy opened up on the question of Tom Tyler's underpants. Mrs Edwards claimed that they were old and baggy. Mr Tyler insisted that they were tight, and white. And so Mrs Tyler was called as an expert witness.

'If I were to suggest to you that your husband had old underwear, would you accept that?' she was asked by the junior defence counsel. 'No,' replied Mrs Tyler. 'If I were to suggest to you that his underwear was baggy and worn, would you accept that?' she was asked. An indignantly houseproud Mrs Tyler replied that she would not accept that.

The second trial lasted a week. Once more Tyler was found guilty. The *Sun* was sympathetic. 'Admittedly he took the laying on of hands a bit far, but was it really necessary to deprive him of his living and his home?' the newspaper reasoned, adding that Mrs Edwards 'was comforted at least a dozen times in as many different positions'. Mr Edwards was less understanding. He punched the vicar in his much-discussed private parts, and narrowly avoided prosecution for assault.

To this day Tom Tyler insists that he is innocent. He wrote a book on the case, but never found a publisher. When last heard of he was living in Ipswich – with his wife. One often feels that the spouse is the only undisputed victim of such affairs.

# LUST, PRIDE, ANGER, ENVY AND GLUTTONY

## TELE-EVANGELISTS

## 'Where in the Bible does it say a church has to be non-profit?'

'God wants his people to go first class,' said Jim Bakker, perhaps the most notorious among the tub-thumping evangelists who swept American television in the 1980s with a noxious blend of hellfire, inch-thick make-up, tears and corruption. And first class is certainly how they travelled. A chapter which is not to run to hundreds of pages can only trawl through the record selecting at whim the occasional excess or grotesquerie which catches the author's eye. A comprehensive account would be impossible.

To anchor this story I have chosen Jim Bakker simply as one outstanding example of a phenomenon which was nationwide. Any reader tempted to dismiss the excesses of former centuries as exotic examples – remote in time – of the sort of thing which could never happen in the Church today, should study what follows: and keep in mind the knowledge that *all this is really true. It happened just a few years ago in one of the world's biggest, richest, most powerful, most advanced and best educated nations.*

At its height the US TV God business was worth the quite extraordinary figure of *$2 billion a year*, most of it won by Christian superstars with a con-man's art and a freephone number for credit-card donations in the corner of the screen.

They appealed for funds for pet giraffes, planned biblical roller-coasters, bought private jets and compared their churches with Citibank and Chase Manhattan. It could hardly last. By 1991 many of the self-made religious celebrities had joined the ranks of the great unfrocked. They destroyed themselves, falling foul of two of the commonest sins in this book – greed and lust.

Their victims were the 20 per cent of Americans who describe themselves as evangelical Christians – 45 million people. They are a blue-collar force to be reckoned with. Presidents vie for their votes. In 1979 Jimmy Carter summoned Jim Bakker on board Airforce One to pray for the release of Americans held in Tehran. When Ronald Reagan took office in 1981 his administration was presented with a report proving that television preachers were pocketing funds raised for good works. The report was shelved for fear of rasing the ire of the southern states.

And US evangelical Christians are not only powerful, they are also generous. Almost half pay tithes to their church out of their own income. Some of the individuals mentioned below – it is important to acknowledge this – are blameless. Much of the money is used reputably.

But not all. At his peak the podgy-faced Jim Bakker made a reported $150 million a year but (it was said) gave only $200,000 a year to his church. He spent the rest on himself and his Praise the Lord (PTL) organisation, one of six big groups which dominated TV proselytising. Its chief asset was Heritage USA, a 2,200 acre clean-living, Godfearing, no-smoking, no-boozing religious theme park in a pine wood in South Carolina, beaten in visitor numbers only by the Disney Corporation.

Now closed, Heritage USA's exhibits epitomised the brazen world of the tele-evangelists. 'A 21st-century Christian campground,' Jim Bakker called it. There was a re-creation of Billy Graham's boyhood home, a Walk of Faith leading to an air-conditioned replica of the 'top room' where the Last Supper was held, nightly passion plays, a Heavenly Fudge Shoppe and a Noah's Ark Toy Shoppe. When Bakker fell, fundraising was well underway for a $100 million copy of London's 1851 Crystal Palace.

There was a $10 million water park – denounced by a rival preacher as an insult to God – intended to keep children quiet while their parents took spiritual refreshment. Bakker even planned a saintly ghost train, rattling visitors through representations of Heaven and Hell built according to accounts in the Book of Revelations.

None of this seemed at all odd to the millions of middle-Americans who visited. 'Americans spend a lot of time every day reading their Bible and speaking to Jesus as a personal friend – we're not just speaking about crazy people, just the average American. That's why this place is so successful,' said Neil Eskelin, once vice-president of the park.

Jim Bakker, the founder of all this, started as just such a typical American; and he became a typical tele-evangelist. Brought up in a strict Pentecostal family (his grandfather denounced TV as 'hellvision') Bakker's first ambition was to join his brother selling shoes in a local store. But his weepy, ingratiating manner (practised with the aid of a tape-recorder) proved too good for footwear. Bakker broke out of blue-collar obscurity via a Bible college in Michigan where he developed flamboyant piety and sexual promiscuity in equal measure. At the college he met and married Tammy Faye LaValley. It was to prove a profitable partnership.

The couple hit the revivalist road in the early 1970s, living as itinerant preachers in the South and Midwest. In Portsmouth, Virginia they stood in for a local television evangelist, attracting notice with their little home-made puppets, their songs and melodrama. From then on they exploited America's booming cable TV industry, enriching themselves, enriching the company – PTL – which they established in Charlotte, North Carolina, and, of course, enriching the mascara industry while Tammy Faye dressed in fly-whisk eyelashes and pasted herself with make-up and eye-shadow. Both the Bakkers had an endless ability to cry *ad hoc* and *ad infinitum*. This was perhaps their closest approach to a real miracle. Tammy Faye Bakker designed her own waterproof mascara to cope.

With their hour-long daily syndicated show, on which Jim pleaded for money and Tammy Faye sobbed, the couple were able to fund a lifestyle modest only by the standards of a Renaissance pope. 'Where in the Bible does it say a church has to be non-profit?' Jim asked when accused of double standards. Certainly, there was nothing in the Old Testament to stop Tammy Faye marketing her own brand of nylon tights. Praise the Lord and buy my tights.

The PTL television network attracted 2.6 million viewers on 161 stations across America. Bakker was paid $1.6 million a year, topped up with $200,000 bonuses (or 'love offerings') and royalties on his religious Country & Western songs. The couple bought his-'n'-hers Mercedes, Rolls-Royce cars, fur coats, assorted luxury bolt-holes across America, rides in private jets and kitsch home furnishings.

Famously, they built an air-conditioned kennel for their pet dog (though they later claimed it was only heated). When the dog met next door's bitch, they dressed the pooches up in wedding togs and spent $3000 on a party. It is fair to point out that by this stage a minority, at least, of their US audiences was tuning in simply to witness a phenomenon – rather as some British viewers watch *Eurotrash*, as a cult. I suspect the Bakkers knew this.

In 1987 Tammy Faye appeared on television to announce she was buying a pair of giraffes for Jim's birthday. All this squandering strained PTL's resources. Their fundraising became ever-more blatant. 'PTL is on the brink of disaster' ran one message to donors. 'Stations are cancelling our programme. Need help now. SOS.' Attached were forms for cheques.

By the late 1980s, competition between big-shot TV evangelists was as hot as that between Coca-Cola and Pepsi. One of the Bakkers' biggest rivals was a slick Louisiana preacher, Jimmy Swaggart, who liked to portray himself as a pastor of modest means but actually headed a $120 million a year ministry and lived in grand style, complete with $80,000-worth of Oriental carpets and a $50,000 piano. As America's top-rating hellfire religious ranter he boasted a proven track-record of crushing competition. In 1987 he had a small-time cable TV sermoniser, Marvin Gorman, unfrocked and bankrupted for adultery. Jim and Tammy Faye Bakker were his next target.

In early 1987, the *Charlotte Observer*, a paper based near PTL's headquarters, broke the news that Jim Bakker had not been faithful to his wife. Seven years earlier, he had spent a night (the paper said) in a Florida hotel room with Jessica Hahn, a secretary for the Full Gospel Tabernacle, a Pentecostal church in Massapequa, New York State.

On 19 March, Jim Bakker appeared on television, admitted the report was accurate, and quit. However, he wasn't resigning over the affair at all, he insisted, but as a tactical move to prevent a covert take-over bid for his church by a rival – later named as Jimmy Swaggart. 'I was wickedly manipulated by treacherous former friends and then colleagues who victimised me with the aid of a female confederate,' he claimed. Critics pointed out that he had sinned nonetheless.

For her part, Hahn insisted that she was simply a devout follower of Bakker who had been spiritually and emotionally 'shattered' by her hero. She said she was a virgin before she met him.

The events which had led up to the story's breaking were bizarre. Long before, Hahn had reported what had gone on to her pastor, the Reverend Gene Profeta, who passed the information to a friend, Paul R. Roper, a self-appointed specialist in clerical misdemeanour. Roper confronted PTL and in 1985 the organisation agreed to pay $115,000 hush-money. Of this Hahn received $20,300. The rest went to Roper and a colleague for 'expenses'.

On top of that PTL established a $150,000 trust fund, with interest paid monthly. Under the deal, if Hahn filed no lawsuit and stayed silent on the matter for 20 years, she would receive the $150,000.

But the story did not stay concealed for long. In September 1996, rumours had reached Jimmy Swaggart, already a sworn foe of the Bakkers. His show had been struck from the PTL network; Jim Bakker said it was because of his anti-Catholicism, Swaggart claimed there had been a struggle over airtime. Swaggart was also a frequent critic of Heritage USA – motivated (said his enemies) largely by the fact that he didn't own it. Swaggart passed what he knew to Bakker's Assembly of God church. Bakker resigned and the *Charlotte Observer* printed everything.

As the revelations mounted *Penthouse* and *Playboy* battled for exclusive rights to Jessica Hahn's story. The magazines wanted to rub salt in Jim and Tammy's wounds (not least because the couple had successfully campaigned for a US Justice Department anti-porn investigation). *Playboy* won, with a $1 million offer for topless pictures of Hahn, but before it could publish, *Penthouse* retaliated with a spoiler claiming that far from being a sexual innocent, she was a former prostitute who had lied about details of her affair with Bakker.

This news did not help the Bakkers. Jim Bakker was swiftly unfrocked and PTL became known in wittier circles as 'Pay the Lady'. And the scandal moved from sex to money. Accusations of corruption swirled around Bakker. In December 1988, he was indicted on 24 counts of fraud over sales of 'Life Partnerships' at Heritage USA. Followers of his TV show had been invited to buy

$1000 dollar bonds, entitling them to three nights' luxury accommodation every year at the park. The scheme raised £100 million but, as Bakker knew, there was room at the inn for only a fraction of those who had invested. PTL's sobriquet was updated to 'Pass the Loot'.

Meanwhile Jimmy Swaggart joined the heavenly chorus of sinners. As a preacher he should have remembered the folly of casting the first stone, but he had earlier had no qualms about denouncing Marvin Gorman (the small-time cable tele-evangelist) and then Jim Bakker for adultery. Now Gorman fought back, discrediting his discreditor. He hired a private eye, who tracked Swaggart into a cheap New Orleans motel in the company of a prostitute. The establishment had a sign in the window: 'no refunds after 15 minutes'.

Swaggart's millions of followers would have been shocked to see him slip out of the motel into a seedy backstreet in a red light district. They would have been even more shocked to find *two* tele-evangelists there. Gorman, tipped off by his private detective, was waiting in the dark. The detective stripped the valves from the tyres of Swaggart's car to prevent him escaping and Gorman confronted him as he struggled to fit a spare wheel, something he apparently did not know how to do. Swaggart begged for mercy, offered Gorman and his family well-paid posts in his church, and when these inducements failed, finally agreed to confess his sin to the church authorities.

But he didn't. So a few months later Gorman provided church elders with a dossier of photographs. Not long after, Swaggart made a lachrymose confession before 10,000 faithful in his octagonal Family Worship Centre: he had been guilty of 'moral failure' – though he omitted to tell them which sin he had actually committed.

It was a body-blow to the evangelical movement. Many had been not altogether surprised when the Bakkers, America's most openly-conspicuous consumers, had fallen from grace. But Swaggart himself had never shared their raffish reputation. He was regarded by millions, wrote my fellow parliamentary sketch-writer Simon Hoggart, as a clean-living 'Savanarola of the South'. Swaggart had denounced Jim Bakker as 'a cancer on the body of Christ', the US Supreme Court and Congress as 'institutions damned by God', and Roman Catholicism as a 'false cult'.

His ranting sermons were awesome. 'Don't try to bargain with Jesus,' he once yelled at a congregation, 'he's a Jew.' No matter. His church, the Assemblies of God, banned him from preaching for two years and then unfrocked him. Four years later Swaggart was caught by police with two more prostitutes (he said he was 'looking for parishioners') and, to cap it all, Gorman filed a $90 million defamation suit against him.

Yet nothing could stop the Jim and Tammy Faye show. In January 1989, fighting off all the charges of misconduct, the couple turned their living room into a makeshift studio, hooked up a camera to the cable TV network and once again brought viewers their glitzy mix of showbiz and hardline religion. Tammy Faye wore her trademark heavy eyeshadow. 'It's nice to be back with you,' the couple declared unabashed. 'We're here to tell you that if Jim and Tammy Faye can survive the holocaust of the last two years, I know that God will help you survive.'

Their message played on the fundamentalist Christian's love of public redemption and persuaded a disturbing number of Americans that the charges of fraud and sexual misbehaviour were a satanic plot. 'You will have boils, tumours, scurvy, and itch, for none of which there will be remedy. You will have madness, blindness, fear and panic...It is the word of God', one supporter screamed at Charles Shephard, the reporter who brought Bakker down. NBC announced plans for a TV mini-series, *Fall From Grace*, and, in a staged 'surprise visit' to a trailer park in California, Jim Bakker returned to the pulpit. Tammy Faye wore white – the colour of humility. 'She was not so much chastened as toned down, in the sense that although the eyes were heavily sculptured, you could see the irises', wrote one reporter.

But though the Bakkers tried their best, the good times were over. Viewers kept their credit cards tucked away. Heritage USA went into receivership. PTL, by now in the hands of another long-time business rival to the Bakkers, the Reverend Jerry Falwell (founder of the Moral Majority movement and a pal of scores of Republican politicians) had debts of $130 million and rumours spread that its assets were to be sold – to an Orthodox Jewish billionaire! The Bakkers called on the faithful to dial 1-900-HOPE and select one of 40 recorded messages. But at $1.50 a minute, it was an expensive way of hearing Tammy's favourite recipe for 'sloppy joe' hamburgers and the couple's tips for avoiding divorce.

'I think the Lord is housecleaning a little bit. I'm glad to see it happen,' announced Pat Robertson, the millionaire founder of the Christian Broadcasting Network and a perennial challenger for the Republican Party's presidential nomination. His own fortunes were beginning to suffer thanks to his errant colleagues.

Luck seemed to be running out for other TV evangelists, too. In March 1988, Michael Angellon gathered 350 worshippers and, in tears, confessed that 'There's sin in this camp!', revealing an affair with Dolly-Parton-lookalike Rhonda Hissom.

And another second-divison preacher, the remarkably-named Reverend Oral Roberts, owner of a combined TV ministry, university and medical centre in Tulsa, Arizona, came under fire for broadcasting the news that unless followers stumped up $4.5 million, God would 'call him home'.

He climbed his Tulsa Prayer Tower – a 200-ft-tall glass-and-steel spire on the Oral Roberts University campus and prepared for the life-threatening deadline. Jerry Collins, a stumpy, gruff dog-track owner from Sarasota, Florida, responded with $1.3 million, and Oral was saved. ('It's very seldom I ever go to church,' said the greyhound-racing philanthropist.)

Meanwhile, Jerry Falwell, who took over PTL when the Bakkers stepped down and was subsequently sued by them, joined in the mayhem when he announced that he had evidence of many 'homosexual encounters' involving Jim Bakker. This was a new – and, on the evidence of Bakker's sexual adventures so far, surprising – twist. Other preachers leapt in to confirm it. He also announced that PTL needed a quick $7 million 'miracle' in order to survive – later upped to $10 million.

In October 1989 Jim Bakker's fraud trial began in Charlotte, North Carolina. Dubbed by the press the 'tele-felon', Bakker, the court heard, had swindled $158 million from his flock, a crime which brought with it a possible 120-year prison sentence. Bakker denounced the proceedings as part of a plot by the Devil to undo him, and prayed theatrically throughout the trial. But with Judge Robert Potter presiding, the omens were bad. Local lawyers knew him as 'Maximum Bob' because of his send 'em down habits.

For Bakker this was all too much. He broke down in court, and was seen by a psychiatrist – who found him lying in a corner with his head under his lawyer's sofa. Bakker said he was running from 'frightening wild animals bent on destroying him'. He was taken in a police car to a prison mental hospital, curled up on the back seat like a foetus. Tammy Faye Bakker tried to put the best of her many faces on the situation by singing a hymn and cooing, 'It's not over till it's over.'

If it was all a ruse to avoid conviction, 'Maximum Bob' wasn't fooled. Bakker was fined $350,000 and sentenced to 45 years imprisonment – reduced on appeal to 8 years. Several of his PTL colleagues were also convicted. Tammy Faye Bakker, reduced during the trial to broadcasting to a tiny audience from a down-market shopping centre in Orlando, visited him in gaol – then announced she was divorcing him. 'I still love Jim but he can only drag me down,' she told reporters.

In 1993 she remarried in what the supermarket tabloid *National Enquirer* called a 'wacky, tacky affair'. Her new husband was Roe Messner, a bankrupt builder under criminal investigation and once one of Jim Bakker's closest friends. Messner was later gaoled for bankruptcy fraud.

Jim Bakker remained in prison until July 1993 when he was transferred to a 'halfway house' detention centre prior to release on parole at the end of the year. After four and a half years inside, he was both thinner and greyer than in his TV heyday. Prospects of a comeback were remote. PTL had folded and Heritage USA had become a downmarket hotel complex. After this string of scandalous video preachers, ratings for the Bible-bashing TV shows which epitomised the Reagan era had plummeted. 'Christian broadcasters', as the new generation of tele-evangelists call themselves, are less overt: quiz shows, soap-operas and even religious rock-climbing competitions are now the order of the day.

Still, a country with thousands of television channels to fill has a wide range of vacancies for B-list celebrities and in the early 1990s Tammy Faye Bakker Messner – for whose sheer effrontery, energy, and balls, it is hard not to feel affection, even awe – carved out a new niche as a vamp caricature on cable channel talk-shows and sitcoms. She even tried fronting a chatshow with a gay co-host, whom she considerably out-camped. She founded a wig company.

And she published a book, *Tammy: Telling It My Way*: 'At age seventeen I learned something wonderful. What I lacked in breasts I more than made up for in eyelashes...I discovered mascara...Now I really had eyelashes – long, dark eyelashes! I was completely exhilarated – for the first time in my life I felt pretty.'

The book was not well reviewed. Promoting it, Tammy Faye was eager to redeem herself. 'We lived no differently than any of the other tele-evangelists – and our bathroom fixtures weren't gold-plated; they were brass,' she said. She moved to a condo in upstate California built on an artificial lake, where residents travelled to and fro in private motorboats, and spent her time boating to the upmarket American equivalent of Tupperware parties. Latterly she has announced that, as she no longer makes retail purchases (shopping only by catalogue and wholesale), she cannot be regarded as frivolous.

Jim Bakker, released after five years in jail, also signed up with a publisher. His book, *I Was Wrong: The Untold Story of the Shocking Journey From PTL Power to Prison and Beyond* assured readers that he was a new man. He apologised for the excesses of the 1980s. Jessica Hahn, the woman who helped bring Bakker down, was not convinced: 'What he'll do is ask for everyone's apology, say he was wrong, say the Devil made him do it, rebuild the mailing list, rebuild his church.'

Bakker did re-appear in the pulpit, addressing a congregation in Marvin Gorman's Temple of Praise, but soon abandoned religion for the hotel business, bidding for a disused holiday resort in Georgia. Gorman himself was back in business after settling his action against Jimmy Swaggart for $1.85 million – and then admitting that he had committed adultery, after all.

Swaggart, meanwhile, bounced back into tele-evangelism, despite being unfrocked. But in the mid-1990s his show reached only 39 small-town channels rather than the 287 across the nation to which he had enjoyed access before the scandals. Oral Roberts, talked down from his prayer tower, continued to appear on a weekly show, *Miracle Now!*, but handed most of his family ministry to his son. And Jerry Falwell, Bakker's successor at PTL, reopened in public view in the late 1990s, tormenting President Clinton over a string of alleged sex scandals. He also met John Redwood MP.

Journalists were left enjoying the last laugh. A clutch of titles was proposed for the scams. By the end the list included *Evangelust*, *Godsgate*, *Heavensgate*, *Salvationgate* and *Gospelgate*. But my own favourite is *Pearlygate*.

# TRAGEDY

## HAROLD DAVIDSON, RECTOR OF STIFFKEY

## 'I do not know what the buttock is'

The Reverend Harold Davidson was the last Christian to be killed by a lion. Unquestionably he was a martyr – but to what?

So much biblical imagery comes streaming at us as we consider the life of Davidson that it is almost possible to see him as he saw himself: as a figure of vast, portentous significance. Surrounded by more women (though possessing less wisdom) than Solomon, his story moved through crowds of Mary Magdalens and Judas Iscariots until it ended, like so many of the earlier Christians' stories, among lions. Sadly, the parallel with the Roman *stadia* – from which Christians rarely emerged alive – is closer than with the lion's den which Daniel survived. Harold Davidson was no Daniel.

The Rector of Stiffkey (pronounced *Stewkey*: villagers remain sensitive on the point) dedicated his life and his ministry to girls. For over a quarter of a century he would catch the first train on Monday morning from Norfolk to London and the last one back to his flock on Saturday night. In the intervening days he set about rescuing fallen women with a zeal (one writer has observed) which in other circumstances would have earned him a deanery.

By his own estimation 'Uncle Harold' had assisted a thousand young girls. 'I like to get them from 14 to 20.' They were always pretty. Ugly girls, he thought, were in no moral danger. 'I believe with all my soul,' he wrote, 'that if He were born again in London in the present day He would be found constantly walking in Piccadilly.' Shorter (Davidson stood 5'3") and by all accounts less imposing than any messiah, the Rector of Stiffkey determined to do likewise.

47

'As a clergyman one spends one's whole life in bedrooms,' he remarked in a less elevated vein. But what did he do in them? It was to take a consistory court in Westminster to establish beyond reasonable doubt that the self-styled 'Prostitutes' Padre' did what the cynics had always claimed (and he had always denied).

Born in 1875, Davidson began his working life as an actor, a vocation some would say he never entirely quit and which, when it came to the crunch, he embraced again with passion and some talent. After joining the Church of England – he became Rector of Stiffkey in 1906 – his charity work at first extended to the needy of both sexes, but he soon decided that 'girls were more in need of assistance than boys'.

It was a belief he carried overseas. When, with the outbreak of the First World War, Davidson enrolled as a naval chaplain and found himself docked in Egypt, he was caught in a police raid on a brothel in Cairo. He insisted that he was there on rescue work, and – who knows? – perhaps he was. But as a portent for the future course of his life that snapshot of Davidson – compromised completely but insisting that the world accept his innocence – prepares us for many such scenes.

Back in London, he continued to consort with fallen women. In September 1920 he met a 20-year-old prostitute in Leicester Square, Rose Ellis. 'She was rather my despair,' he remarked later. Davidson set out on a sustained course of rescue work with her that lasted, in all, more than a decade.

It was later alleged that Ellis became Davidson's mistress. Davidson had made the charge hard to refute. He had taken Rose with him to Paris in order, he said, to find her a job as an *au pair*. He often took girls to Paris, he insisted – indeed, there was a time when he went there once a fortnight. He found Rose accommodation and paid the rent, introducing her to landladies as his secretary, 'Mrs Malone'.

He does seem to have been genuinely kind to his girls. But in 1932, false names and trips to Paris were as indicative of guilt as bad wigs and stick-on moustaches. 'If you were to be judged by the standards by which ordinary men are judged would you agree you would be convicted?' the prosecution was later to ask at Davidson's trial – for, as with most martyrs, a trial was written in his stars.

'Not by decent-minded men,' Davidson replied. *Honi soit qui mal y pense.*

And there was another young Mary Magdalen who, though their acquaintance was brief, caused Davidson more grief. When he met her in 1930, Barbara Harris was sixteen and had already had a string of lovers. She was also very pretty. Davidson, who never wore his clerical collar on rescue work, had spotted her in Marble Arch. Aware that at this early stage mention of the gospel was likely to deter, his first words to her were: 'Excuse me, miss, but has anyone told you how much you look like Mary Brian, the film actress?' Or so Barbara later alleged.

Barbara, whose real name was Gwendoline, would allege many things. But until they met across a courtroom, Davidson had treated her with paternal affection, finding her jobs and lodging and cultivating her mind with such improving novels as *Damaged Goods*.

Sometimes he wrote her stern letters: 'your greatest defect is your lack of loyalty. Loyalty is one of the greatest virtues. Do cultivate it.' Barbara had a habit of simply vanishing from Davidson's life for months at a time. Always, though, when her lovers (who included a street-performing Strong Man and an Indian police officer) abandoned her, she ran back to 'Uncle Harold' for help and money.

After Jesus Christ, Harold Davidson's principal role-model seems to have been the Victorian Prime Minister William Ewart Gladstone, who brought prostitutes back to 10 Downing Street in the sincere hope of reforming them. 'Old Glad-eyes' and 'Daddy do-nothing' were two of the Liberal leader's nicknames among the street women of London. Gladstone insisted (and, on the whole, historians believe) that he never abused his position as mentor. But there does seem for some men to be a thrill in the very company and conversation of fallen women.

Gladstone stuck to prostitutes who genuinely needed help, and thereby avoided scandal (just). Davidson's great mistake was to take his unusual method of evangelism off the streets and into the tea-shops. Men throughout the ages have been banned from inns and public houses. Davidson is almost unique in having been banned from tea-shops.

Oxford Street became his great field of missionary activity. Waitresses there soon learned to recognise him. Few cared for being 'pestered' (as one put it) by the diminutive, grey-haired clergyman they called 'the Mormon'. Instead of leaving tips,

Davidson left theatre tickets. He told the waitresses they had nice eyes and a pretty smile, showed them pictures of actresses who had come to him for confession and even followed them to their homes at midnight to invite them out for coffee. Some grew so wary of the Rector they would dart behind pillars or retreat into the ladies' cloakroom when he appeared.

Eventually managers had to ban him. 'But suppose the bishop asks me to come and have a cup of coffee?' he protested to one.

'If the bishop comes he will be served but you will not.'

In none of his gestures, so far as the Rector was concerned, was there the smallest hint of impropriety. 'Uncle Harold' was a tactile man who bestowed his kisses freely and an enthusiastic layer-on of hands. Those few who, like a certain Mrs Walton, remained convinced of the purity of his motives later bore witness to this in court. She was one of nine landladies who testified in his trial. 'Did he ever kiss you?' Mrs Walton was asked in cross-examination.

'Often,' she answered. 'On the cheek or forehead.'

'What did Mr Walton say to that?'

'He would kiss him too.'

'He kissed your husband?'

'He kissed the milkman too.'

While all this kissing was going on in London, back in Stiffkey there were those who, after a quarter of a century, began to feel neglected by their Rector. One of his churchwardens, Major Hammond, a Boer War veteran, had for some time been suspicious of the numbers of young girls making their way down to the rectory in Stiffkey. He snapped when Davidson failed to return from London in time for an Armistice Day service and Hammond wrote to the Bishop of Norwich citing the Clergy Discipline Act of 1892, demanding action.

The Bishop could not ignore Hammond. He set a company of private detectives on Davidson. Although they had difficulty keeping up with the Rector during his sleepless weeks in London they did pin down Rose Ellis. In a Charing Cross hotel, over eight glasses of port, Ellis spoke at length to a detective about her relationship with the Rector of Stiffkey. Her remarks, which were never used in court and have been lost, were typed up and signed by her on the following day as an authentic 'Statement of the Facts'.

Rather too late she realised that she had compromised her mentor and guardian. 'Foolishly I made a mistake under considerable temptation which has placed a friend of ours in a terrible position, and most unjustly so,' she wrote to another friend. The 'temptation' was the 40 shillings she had received from the detective. 'You are ten up on Judas – he only got thirty pieces of silver,' said Davidson to her, sadly. Davidson was moving nicely towards martyrdom.

The Rector wrote at inordinate length to the Bishop of Norwich, protesting his innocence and accusing the detective of having 'bribed her with money and drugged her with alcohol'. 'I have been actively engaged in rescue work for 38 years. This is the first time I have ever experienced anything even approaching the suggestion of blackmail.'

Credit and credibility, however, were ebbing away. In November 1931 he wrote a letter to the Duchess of Devonshire, in purple ink, declaring that his wife and children barely had food or coals, that there was no one in the world but her to whom he could turn, and asked for money – anything between £300 and £500 would do.

In an acrimonious correspondence with the Bishop of Norwich, Davidson accused the Bishop of double-dealing, treachery and hypocrisy, and sounded a ringing defence of his life and ministry:

For years I have been known as the 'Prostitutes' Padre', to me the proudest title that a true priest of Christ could hold.

The Bishop's solicitor complained that even at hour-and-a-half meetings Davidson would not stop talking. In January Davidson gathered his family together for a 'crisis meeting'. He asked his wife, and each of his children, what course of action he should take and wrote down their answers, which they signed. Unanimously they declared that he should resign – but only if he could do so without losing face. 'Tender your resignation,' his wife counselled. 'If you have any further trouble with his Lordship [the Bishop] or his agents, hand the whole proceedings to the Press in all its unappetising nakedness.'

So the Rector of Stiffkey contacted the newspapers, styled himself a 'second Wakeford' (see p86) and took to the front page. The *Herald* and *Empire News* paid £750 for his life story. After two instalments the Bishop of Norwich brought an action against the newspaper for contempt of court. The serialisation was stopped, but in Stiffkey Davidson's carnival continued. Rose Ellis now sold her story to the *Daily Herald*, accusing the detectives of having bribed her to say things against Davidson, and insisting that he was innocent.

The Rector had become famous. Sightseers in specially chartered charabancs came from as far away as Bournemouth to see the Reverend H. F. Davidson, war medals pinned to his cassock, proclaim his innocence from the pulpit. 'No character in the world's history suffered from misunderstanding and vituperation more than Jesus Christ,' he would declare to the cheering congregations who crammed into the church. But like Jesus he had been cruelly misunderstood.

And was not Jesus betrayed by a disciple? Such was the fate of the Reverend Davidson. On 9 February, his publicity campaign at a peak, Barbara Harris – 'little Miss Judas' he called her – sat down and wrote to the Bishop of Norwich (sending the letter to 'The Palace, Norwich'). The letter was transcribed for the court case and is preserved in the Norfolk Record Office. We have edited the letter, but kept Barbara's spelling and grammar. The underlinings, originally in red crayon, are the trial judge's.

16 Providence Place,
Shepherds Bush
Dear Sir,

I am writing about the Rev: H.F. Davidson, I have been waiting to do this for a long time and mentioned it to the Rev: Davidson and he told me it would not be believed, <u>my word would not stand against his</u>.

I am thinking that if he is let off he will do just the same and I am sorry for the girls in future.

You will have noticed that Davidson only helps girls, never boys, and also the girls are generaly about 16 or 17 years old.

I am <u>17</u> years old and He has known me for 18 months.

Davidson pretends he knew nothing about the charges made

against him, until a few days ago but <u>he often used to say I should keep my voice low when talking to him</u>, as detective were following, and sometimes only one man was behind.

A lot of people will stick up for Davidson, because they are afraid of their past, others might stand up for him because they believe him to be an eccentric old man (as I did when I first met him).

I know lots of things about him that may help you.

<u>I was accused by him,</u> and first came to know him about <u>18 months</u> ago.

I came from Marble Arch tube and he followed me. He spoke to Me when I got to Edgeware Road. he  said:

'Excuse me but arn't you Miss-so-and-so, <u>the film star.</u>'

He had <u>no clerical collar</u> on at the time and he never told me he was a Rector (I never knew for 4 months).

<u>I let him come to see me because he promised me each day that he would get me a job.</u>

<u>Davidson asked my land lady for a key</u> for the front door as he often wanted to see me late at night <u>on business,</u> I told her not to give him the key and she told me she had not thought of doing so.

He kept some preventatives in a trunk at his room at Wood-Lane . . .

<u>At first he kept to the chair but after the first few nights he did not</u>. He never got me a job for a long time, <u>I think it was three months I stayed at his room.</u>

He said he would divorce his wife and marry me.

I was almost frighted to go out in the evening when I had finished  because he used to wait on the corner.

Whilst I was taking these things I thought of his wife at Stiffkey Rectory, he had told me she was starveing and had no coals, and also he owed a lot of money in the village.

You see I had been to the Rectory before.

Davidson sent me down with a girl named Rosalie [Ellis], he sent me for a rest and said I could go to the sea every day (it so happened I never again saw the sea).

I went down as a conpanion to the girl, as she refused to go alone. When I got there we were made to do the work, and we had hardly enough food . . .

At last we got tired of waiting and Rosalie said as he was comeing that day, we should take our things to the station at Wells and wait for him. we did so. I had some money on me that Rosalie knew nothing about (I had not told her about it as she would have wanted to borrow it for drink and would not have paid back).

We waited two days and then decided to walk, and Rosalie remembered someone at a garage who might give us a lift to London.

I think we walked to Cromer or some such place, to this Garage, and we were starveing and cold and tired.

The people at the Garage were nice to us and gave us some dinner and we came to London in a car with a man and his wife.

We had slept in the fields for two days and had no food after my money was spent.

We had left because we knew Davidson wanted us to stay and work at the Vicarage and if he did not pay our fare, we should have no alternative but to stay . . .

All this can be proved if people are conserned to speak the truth.

And all this can stand being looked into and inquired about.

He has almost driven me potty by keep asking me to speak well of him if any detective asked me about him. [In the margin next to this point, in green ink is written, 'Potty'.]

He told me that I would not have a chance as he had made the Landlady (of his place) and the daughter, swear that I did not have his room . . .

I think it will be found out in the end, that half the people who are going to praise him are frightened of him . . .

Please do not let my name or address be put in the paper as I think of my Landlady and my people.

I will answer any quetions willingly.

I know all about Davidson cashing cheques when he has no money in the bank . . .

He says he helps women of the streets, (do you call girls of 15 years old, women.

Davidson did not even attempt to help me even when I was 15 although I would gladly have taken any help that was offered me.

I could not help being in difficulties at that age.

It is very hard to be good when once you have been bad.

Enquiries can be made at Wells station, (about us waiting for two days) for Davidson. Also enquiries can be made for the Garage at (I think) Fackenham or some name like that.

I think my word can be believed.

All this is in Sincerity.

BARBARA HARRIS.

I know.

He had the keys of a lot of girls flats, and front doors.

The letter is a minor masterpiece of vituperation. Barbara Harris was to prove the most dangerous of all the prosecution witnesses for she later alleged that Davidson had tried to rape her.

After various delays to give the defence time to collect evidence (Davidson was hoping to call more than 400 witnesses) Davidson was put on trial by the church, which planned to unfrock him. He was charged with adultery with Rose Ellis; of making an improper suggestion to waitresses in a London café; and of 'habitually associating himself with women of a loose character for immoral purposes'. The rector denied everything.

The consistory court was presided over by F. Keppel North, Chancellor of the Diocese of Norwich. Hearings are normally held in the defendant's diocese but Davidson's trial, which began on 31 March 1932, was held in Church House, Westminster. Given the witness-lists and the press interest, the proceedings would otherwise have involved most of Fleet Street and many of London's prostitutes (not to say tea-shop staff) decamping to Norwich.

Probably not until Mandy Rice-Davies appeared in the trial of Stephen Ward during the Profumo affair was an English court of law to see a beautiful female witness as cool as Barbara Harris, or have so much fun. For three days, incongruously sitting next to the Lord Chancellor and under intense questioning, Harris furnished the court and the newspapers with a stream of astounding revelations, beginning with the details of her own love life.

'I do not wish to put it insultingly,' said Richard Levy for the defence, 'but – to get the atmosphere – you have had relations with many men?'

'Yes.'

'White men?'

'Yes.'

'Black men?'

'Yes.'

'Indians?'

'Yes.'

'And men of other kinds?'

'No.'

Frank about herself, she was franker about Harold Davidson. 'Davidson is rather a different person from many people?' suggested Levy.

'Yes.'

'Kind-hearted spasmodically. To total strangers he would give things if they were in need?'

'Yes.'

'People who are quite strangers to him he will greet by putting his arms on their shoulders?'

'Girls,' she stated, brutally. Davidson, for his part, described putting his arms around women as 'an absolutely uniform automatic action'.

According to Harris – and in the end the case was her word against his – Davidson had repeatedly said he would divorce his wife and marry her. He had told her that God did not mind sins of the body, only of the soul and he reminisced about the Cairo brothel, telling her she 'would do very well' in such a place.

She recalled an argument between them which had ended in her giving the rector a black eye. She remembered a time she and her Indian lover entertained Davidson to tea while they were in bed, wearing pyjamas. She described an appendectomy scar on the rector's stomach. Reciting a joke Davidson then told her about such scars she prompted the Chancellor to remark that he had 'never heard a joke with less joke in it'.

She said Davidson was always kissing her, and once asked her to give herself to him 'body and soul'. On occasion, she said, he undressed.

'Did he do anything? You said something about his clothes being in a mess.'

'He relieved himself.'

'Did that happen once, or more than once?'

'More than once; it happened two or three times.'

Mr Levy protested. 'Do you usually like to keep friendly with people who try to rape you?'

'If they come in useful.'

The newspapers followed every word, agog. When unable to print the more lurid allegations they told their readers so. There was much amusement in court. Often the rector seemed to share it. He was admonished for bursting into laughter while Barbara was giving her evidence.

After Barbara Harris came a succession of waitresses and landladies, all of whom – hostile or friendly – bore out the dotty picture of Davidson. Dorothy Burn, a waitress, said of the rector that 'he kept on molesting me'. He invited her to the cinema, pursued her into the girls' dressing room, and asked her to come and stay at Stiffkey.

Again, Levy protested. 'There could be no harm in going to a clergyman's house where his wife and children were living, could there?'

'I don't know. I would not like to chance it.' The court erupted in laughter.

Next the formidable Flora Osborne stepped into the witness stand. Mrs Osborne was a landlady who had on six occasions tried to evict Davidson for failing to pay his rent; once she had climbed through a bathroom window when Davidson was getting undressed, to demand that he pay her. She had three summonses for assault to her name. She so terrified her husband that he had tried to escape abroad. She was not a woman to trifle with.

Mrs Osborne recalled a time when she and her husband had driven up to Stiffkey with Davidson, who had sat in the back of the car with his arm round an actress. At Stiffkey a photograph had been taken of the group, which had been joined by Davidson's wife holding a shrub in front of her face. This baffled the Chancellor. Who was in the picture? he asked. Flora Osborne explained that the group included *Mrs* Davidson.

'But is that a boy?'

'No, sir, it is the Reverend Harold Davidson's wife.'

'Does she always go about like that?'

'She refused to be taken, and put those leaves over her face.'

'Where was this taken?'

'In the grounds of Stiffkey Rectory.'

At least the actress in the photograph could not be said to have suffered any moral damage. She had since become a nun.

In the witness-stand himself, Davidson lived up to all the expectations the preceding evidence had aroused. At one point he started tap-dancing. Of brothels, he declared, 'I am a great authority on the subject.'

Court records suggest that the Chancellor spent the trial in a state of ostentatious bewilderment. His transcript of the trial is covered with question marks, underlinings, exclamation marks in red, green and purple crayon signifying varying degrees of astonishment. When Davidson started to explain why he had patted a waitress under the chin and complimented her on her teeth ('I have often done it if I wanted to look at [girls'] teeth, to see if they were even') Lord North interrupted him: 'Just attend, because I want you to do justice to yourself. Do you really say that you would pull her lips down and look at her teeth?'

'If a girl was asking me whether she was suitable for film work, supposing her teeth were all completely uneven, I should say, "no, you had better go to a dentist".'

'Would you open her lips and look at her teeth, just as you would a horse?'

'Yes, in many cases they would be asses for wishing to go on the stage.'

'Would you do it without her leave?'

'Certainly not. That is the whole point.'

Later Lord North wondered aloud whether Davidson was mad, and concluded that he probably was – 'about girls, certainly'.

But it was on the matter of buttocks that the trial reached its apogee of absurdity. Roland Oliver, for the prosecution, mentioned an occasion when Rose Ellis had treated Davidson for boils.

'Is it your view of decency to go to a flat and to get this pretty girl to dress your naked body?'

'You are making the most outrageous suggestion. I never said that.'

'Was the boil on the buttock of your body?' Davidson did not answer. 'Have you to think?'

'Yes.' He thought. 'I do not know what the buttock is.'

(In North's copy of the transcript, this answer is underlined in thick red crayon.)

'Do you not know?'

'Honestly, I do not.'

'Mr Davidson!'

'It is a phrase honestly I have never heard. So far as I remember, it is a little below the waist.'

'Are you serious?'

'Honestly I have never heard it. When it was mentioned the other day I had to ask what it was.'

Then there were photographs. Photographs were to Davidson what audio tapes are to American politicians. One showed him with a married actress: he looked absurd, grinning madly. 'It is the most horrible expression I have ever seen,' admitted Davidson.

But worse was in store. 'Mr Davidson,' started Mr Oliver: 'You told me this morning that for stage purposes you have very frequently been photographed with young women. Do you remember that?'

'Oh, yes, very often,' replied the rector, airily.

And did he, asked Oliver, remember having his picture taken with a young woman the day before his trial commenced? Davidson thought that he did remember this. The prosecuting lawyer whipped out a photograph showing Davidson dressed in black and wearing a clerical collar, with one arm on a girl's shoulder and the other resting on her waist. Save for a shawl hanging on either side, the girl, who in the picture is viewed from the rear, was naked. The rector could now be in no doubt what the buttock was.

The Chancellor peered at the picture through a magnifying glass. He was visibly taken aback. 'I am trying to be as much like a machine as I can, but I am only human,' he said.

'I hope you will not only be human, but you will also be judicial,' responded an alarmed Mr Levy.

Davidson recovered his composure. This was a set-up, he protested. Indeed he had been warned about it, but ignored the warnings. 'I was given particular warning that I should be trapped, about three weeks before.' He went on to rehearse a fantastically tangled conspiracy theory. 'One point was that I should be telephoned by a poor lady of title and asked to go to her house. When I got there I would find that I should be received by her. She would have removed all her clothes except her dress, and when I got into the house she would remove that and stand before me naked, and then two detectives would step out into the room and so discover me in that position . . .'

But the girl in the photograph, 15-year-old Estelle Douglas, was the daughter of one of the rector's friends, and hoped to start a career modelling swimsuits. Davidson called himself a 'poor fool of a parson', who had been duped.

After six weeks considering judgement, the Chancellor found him guilty on all counts of immoral conduct, declared Davidson's evidence 'a tissue of falsehoods', and sentenced him to deprivation from his holy orders. Costs were awarded against the rector who, as soon as proceedings ended, grabbed his silk hat, ran out of the door, down the staircase and into the lobby of Church House where he found Mr Levy, shook his hand and thanked him for all he had done.

The next Sunday in Stiffkey, Davidson, yet to be formally unfrocked, preached a sermon before a vast congregation, calling for an overhaul of the consistory court system and admonishing people not to forget that Christ, too, had lived among the poor and lowly. In the afternoon he went to Morston, the other church in his care, where Major Philip Hammond was warden. The doors had been bolted. Davidson went to visit Hammond at his home. The major swore at him, turned the rector round and booted him from his doorstep. Hammond was fined 40 shillings for assault.

The rector appealed twice to the Privy Council against the consistory court's verdict, first on grounds of evidence and then on points of law. In between the appeals, which both failed, he protested his innocence...

...from a barrel, in Blackpool.

With no money and huge costs to find he became – in the most literal sense – an exhibitionist. In fact, he became an exhibit. Davidson sat in a barrel on Blackpool Promenade, charging 2*d* for a viewing, from 10 o'clock each morning until midnight, with breaks for lunch and tea. 'While I am in the barrel I shall be occupied in preparing my case,' he told the press. 'Desperate ills require desperate remedies.'

'The bishop,' he went on, 'has pilloried me before the world as a most objectionable character and a menace to decent young people, so much so that I have become reconciled to allow people to look at me and see me for what I am.' Davidson's behaviour even provoked editorial comment from *The Times*, which noted that he appeared alongside an exhibition of performing fleas.

But the crowds who came to see the rector soon swelled to 6,000. The Blackpool authorities prosecuted him in the Magistrates' court for obstruction. Davidson then resumed his career in showbusiness (he had funded his way through Oxford by acting), by now clearly the greater of his talents. Obtaining a licence from Birmingham magistrates, Davidson performed a variety act in music-halls and cinemas. In July 1932 he took five curtain calls at the Prince's Cinema in Wimbledon. The following month he was barred from the nudist Harrogate Sun-bathing society. 'I am considering establishing a similar sort of thing among my parishioners at Stiffkey,' Davidson told reporters.

But for sheer drama, the ceremony at Norwich Cathedral – where, after the failure of his appeals, sentence was to be executed on Friday 22 October 1932 – could not be beaten. At 11.45 the rector was due to appear in the Beauchamp Chapel of the Cathedral to learn his fate. Minutes before, the Registrar appeared with a telegram. It was from Davidson.

HAVE MOTORED THROUGH NIGHT TO BE PRESENT CATHEDRAL TODAY ELEVEN FORTY FIVE STOP HAVE BEEN SLIGHTLY DELAYED STOP IF LATE PLEASE ALLOW FEW MINUTES GRACE STOP HOPE SEE YOU AND ARCHDEACON ABOUT BUSINESS MATTERS AFTERWARDS STOP HAROLD DAVIDSON RECTOR OF STIFFKEY

Suddenly Davidson's small, battered car drew up beside the Cathedral. He was accompanied by his sister, and a girl. Greeted by cheering onlookers he took off his silk top hat, thanked the crowds and darted into the chapel. He sat at a table opposite the Bishop's Throne. There was silence.

Preceded by robed officials bearing wands of office, the bishop entered with a gold and silver pastoral staff, and sat on his throne. Davidson's name was called three times. He answered, 'Here.' The bishop led prayers (which pointedly warned of 'false apostles' in the church) and then picked up the manuscript on which the sentence was written.

Before the bishop could begin to read, Davidson jumped up. 'May I be allowed to say anything before sentence is passed?' There was an uneasy pause, in which the bishop conferred with his solicitor.

'Yes, if you please, briefly.'

'I wish before you pass sentence to say that I am entirely innocent in the sight of God of any of the grave charges against me. It is the Church authorities which are put on trial and not myself, and whatever my sentence may be I shall work the rest of my life, if God gives me strength and health to do so, towards the reform of the procedure under which these Courts are conducted.'

Davidson then launched into a justification of his work, insisted that he did not regret anything he had done – though mentioning that next time he'd do it 'a little more discreetly'. Finally, and ominously, he warned: 'I hope that every clergyman in the Church of England will support me in the campaign I intend to lead.' He sat down.

The bishop stood up, deprived him of his ecclesiastical promotions, signed the necessary documents, and announced: 'I shall now move to the High Altar.'

Davidson leapt up again. 'May I give notice before the Court that if there is any mode of appeal which the law allows against this sentence I shall make inquiries and prosecute it.' And without waiting for the bishop he rushed into the cathedral itself and sat down in the front pew. Eventually the bishop and his minions caught up, and knelt for some time before the altar in prayer.

So far Davidson had merely been deprived of his offices in the Church; he was still a priest and seemed to imagine he would remain one. But then the bishop turned to Davidson and told him in a low voice that he had brought great scandal upon the Church, and that he would be unfrocked. 'Now, therefore, we, Bertram, by Divine permission, Bishop of Norwich . . .' he began pronouncing the sentence of deposition from Holy Orders.

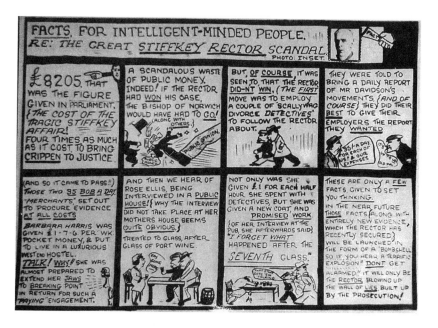

Davidson distributed copies of this cartoon in Stiffkey
when trying to raise funds for his appeal.

When he had finished a stunned Davidson once more sprang up and cried out in a high-pitched voice that he would appeal to the Archbishop of Canterbury. As he continued, ranting hysterically, the bishop and his assembled officials processed sombrely out of the church, ignoring the wailing former Rector of Stiffkey.

Perhaps at this point in the story I may enter a hesitant plea for Mr Davidson, who was plainly unhinged. It is hard to argue that this sex-maniac should have continued as a priest, but the picture – of all the robed and gilded authority of the Church, in trappings of office and circumstances of ludicrous piety and with the whole fatuous company of British journalism slavering on the sidelines, coming down like some divine sledgehammer to crack this obvious nut – is easier to view as farce than as tragedy, or even justice.

Davidson did of course appeal to the archbishop and of course the appeal was dismissed. Having exhausted every legal process, in the words of the affair's best historian, Ronald Blythe, Harold Davidson now 'joined the great company of buffoons'.

In 1936 he gatecrashed a meeting of the Church Assembly in Westminster, at which the Archbishop of Canterbury, Dr Cosmo Gordon Lang, was present. He jumped up and insisted that he be heard in the name of justice. After being rebuked by the archbishop, Davidson threw a bundle of pamphlets, with the headline 'I accuse!' onto the assembly below. He was chased out of the building by attendants.

He returned to his Blackpool barrel and lasted ten days of a proposed thirty-five day fast designed 'to bring the Archbishop of Canterbury and the Church authorities to their senses' – before being arrested, tried and acquitted of starving himself with intent to commit suicide. Moving south, he exhibited himself on Easter Monday on Hampstead Heath, next to a dead whale. Elsewhere, he entered a glass oven and was slowly warmed while an automated demon prodded him in the behind with a three-pronged fork.

The former rector was haunted, too, by some of the ghosts of his trial. Mrs Flora Osborne, the terrifying landlady, pursued him through the courts to recover £43 he owed her. Davidson was sentenced to nine days in a Liverpool gaol. When he returned to Blackpool it was in an open carriage, flanked by two young negresses who threw flowers into a jubilant crowd.

And then, in July 1937, Davidson was hounded into a lion's den.

He was not thrown to the lions; he chose them. In Skegness Amusement Park, in a lion-cage measuring 14ft by 8ft, the former Rector of Stiffkey began a series of performances in which he denounced the Archbishop of Canterbury, the Bishop of Norwich and the entire leadership of the Church of England. With him in the cage was a lion named Freddie, normally a docile beast fed by an eight-year-old child.

One hungry evening, Freddie, perhaps in despair at Davidson's loquacity or perhaps unable to resist precedent from the ancient world, turned on the deposed priest and fatally mauled him. The lion (and his lioness) were in the care of a 16-year-old female lion-tamer, Irene Violet Somner. 'When Mr Davidson went in, the lion Freddie was in his way and he tried to slip in between him and the back of the cage,' she told the inquest. 'When Mr Davidson tried to get out of the way, Freddie reared up on his haunches to get him with his front paws. I got into the cage and tried to beat the lion off, but it dragged Mr Davidson into a corner and we could not move him until Freddie dropped him.'

Captain Rye, the proprietor of the booth in which the ex-rector performed, was not a man to pass up a money-making opportunity. If the public would pay to see a rector and a lion, why not a lion that had eaten a rector? But he was finally forced to close when Freddie's victim died of his wounds a few days after the attack. 'We regretfully inform the public that the rector has passed away,' said a notice pasted outside.

Thus, protesting innocence to his last gasp, was Harold Davidson martyred.

He has not been forgotten by his former parish. 'Here in the village he was respected and above all loved by the villagers who relished his sermons, recognised his humanity and forgave him his transgressions. May he rest in peace,' writes a parishioner in the guide to St John the Baptist Church, Stiffkey. I second that.

# DR WILLIAM DODD

## 'I am now a spectacle to men and soon shall be a spectacle to angels'

The Reverend Dr William Dodd, in the words of Horace Walpole had 'all the qualities of an ambitious man but judgement'. He might have added 'luck', for Dodd's demise on the scaffold at Tyburn was less a result of villainy than the unlucky coincidence of crass deceit, political expediency and a savage penal system. This extraordinary man, a wretched poet, sentimental preacher, third-rate novelist, occasional journalist, timid radical, fop, dandy and macaroni, who wore a diamond ring, powdered his face and reeked of perfume, managed by his own self-pity and self-regard to move the metropolis to a state of hysterical mourning on the day of his execution. One of Samuel Johnson's best remembered aphorisms – that the prospect of death 'concentrates the mind wonderfully' – is a slight misquotation of a remark meant as a comment on Dr Dodd.

Although few can have confronted death with less courage (reminded of his impending doom, he tended to faint), tens of thousands of Londoners lined the streets to watch in silence as the pale-visaged parson made his way from Newgate to the gallows. After his death his prison cell was left untouched, and became a kind of shrine for tearful young women.

Famous and intermittently fashionable, Dr Dodd was viewed with feelings ranging from the ecstatic to the excoriating. For some he was the finest preacher in England, a tireless patron of charities, and deserved to be made a bishop. For others he was the 'Macaroni Parson' – a reference to his sartorial extravagance – whose charitable work merely sought to offer help in circumstances he himself came to share, such as debt, licentiousness and unnatural death. Brought down by attempting to defraud his friend, patron and former pupil, the fifth Earl of Chesterfield, of £4,000, he had committed a crime which would today warrant at

Dr Dodd in his heyday. His hand rests on his Bible,
whose production was a further drain on his resources.

worst a spell in Ford Open Prison. In the eighteenth century the law required his head.

The son of a Lincolnshire clergyman, Dr Dodd's original plans after leaving Cambridge were to pursue a literary career. Prospects seemed promising: he wrote a comedy, *Sir Roger de Coverley*, and sold it to a theatre manager for £100. In a theatre he met, and soon after secretly married, a beautiful but low-born girl named Mary Perkins.

Some have seen this as a selfless act of true love. Walpole writes curtly that Dodd 'stooped to rise': Perkins was a former mistress of the Earl of Sandwich and according to one report had been generously provided for. But Dodd's father was sufficiently alarmed at the course his son's life was taking to hurry down to London to retrieve *Sir Roger* from the manager and persuade his son to take up the cloth. He was appointed the curate of West Ham, then in Essex.

He wrote a novel, *The Sisters*, packed with accounts of taverns, tarts and rakes. This clammy mixture of moralising and sexual titillation ('Leicart stuck close to Miss Lucy and ventured at length...to thrust his glowing hands into her snowy panting bosom...'), draws a little too much from what sounds like personal experience. One of the more alarming scenes in the book involves two young bucks, a prostitute and a red hot poker. Dodd assures his readers this is based on a true incident.

*The Sisters* was written two years after his ordination. He had already produced an anthology of Shakespeare; he soon embarked on a commentary of the entire Bible. While no one could accuse him of lacking energy (or literary flexibility) it is small wonder that few viewed him as a man of consistency or conviction. A satirist once remarked that Dr Dodd wholly believed in the 39 articles. 'And so he would if there were nine times as many.'

Dr Dodd came to prominence in 1758, preaching for a newly-formed charity. The Magdalen Hospital, a 'Publick Place of Reception for Penitent Prostitutes', needed someone to publicise its work. Dodd, already making his mark locally as a fine preacher, proved an inspired choice.

The Magdalen was an extraordinary institution. Its objectives were commendable and progressive – to take women off the streets and rehabilitate them. Its style, however, was sensationalist, melodramatic and prurient, a kind of holy cabaret. It was a phenomenal success. Walpole, in a letter which records his first encounter with Dodd, gives an account of an expedition he made to the Magdalen chapel with Prince Edward in 1760 – such a society phenomenon had the place become. He describes how the 'Magdalens', some 130 in number, were arrayed at the west end of the chapel, and broke into song ('you cannot imagine how well') as soon as the royal party entered. Walpole commented on the attractiveness of some of them. This, it seems, was what lured many to the chapel, including the lecherous Earl of Sandwich.

As for Dodd, so powerful was his preaching (one woman wrote to describe his 'harmonious voice, a heart of passion and the power of showing that he felt his subject deeply') that most of the Magdalens and many of the women in the congregation were reliably moved to tears.

His weekly sermons attracted enormous crowds and huge donations. Through the patronage of Bishop Squire of St David's, Dodd was appointed a royal chaplain to George III, as well as a prebend at Brecon. For a number of years he edited the *Christian Magazine* and contributed articles to the *Public Ledger*. A lottery windfall enabled him to build a chapel in Pimlico, which – with characteristic eye to patronage – he named the Charlotte Chapel, after the King's consort. It attracted one of London's most popular and fashionable congregations.

But his expensive taste in clothes and love of glittering company ensured he was almost always hard up. One magazine reported his imprisonment for debt.

And the rumour-mongers were never far off. He appeared in the *Town and Country* magazine's '*tête à tête*' column, which every month exposed secret dalliances. Dodd was linked to a 'Mrs R-----n', one of his Charlotte Chapel congregation. It was rumoured that he encouraged his wife's drinking so that she would be incapacitated, leaving him free for other attachments.

In 1765 he took as his pupil Philip Stanhope, godson and heir to the fourth Lord Chesterfield. The relationship was close and affectionate. Chesterfield often expressed pleasure with his choice of tutor whom he called 'the best and most eloquent preacher in England, and perhaps the most learned'.

By any standards Dr Dodd's career was a success. He was well connected at court and (through Chesterfield) with the aristocracy. Although not rich compared with many who filled his chapel every Sunday, he worked hard and could reasonably hope for advancement in the Church.

Dr Dodd was notorious for the shamelessness with which he would ingratiate himself with the powerful in the hope of gaining preferment. William Cowper, eight years after Dodd's death, summed up this image of Dodd's character:

> ... loose in morals, and in manners vain,
> In conversation frivolous, in dress
> Extreme, at once rapacious and profane,
> Frequent in park with lady at his side,
> Ambling and prattling scandal as he goes:
> But rare at home, and never at his books,
> Or with his pen, save when he scrawls a card,
> Constant in routs, familiar with a round
> Of ladyships, a stranger to the poor,
> Ambitious of preferment for its gold.

It is a harsh portrait. There were many who were loyal, even devoted to Dodd, and who described his enemies as merely jealous, but the poem captures sentiments which were widely held, and would prove damaging when his fate came to depend upon the mercy of the King.

His first stumble arose from a crude attempt to enrich himself. In 1774, the lucrative living of St George, Hanover Square became available after the elevation of its incumbent. The living was in the hands of the Lord Chancellor, to whose wife, Lady Apsley, Dodd sent a letter offering her £3,000 if she succeeded in persuading her husband to grant him the living. Lord Apsley traced this letter back to Dodd's clerk.

In fact there is evidence that it was *Mrs* Dodd who had dictated the letter, her husband then chivalrously refusing to shuffle off the blame onto her. Whatever the truth, the disgrace was immediate. Apsley informed the King, who struck Dodd off the list of his chaplains. And he was ridiculed in the theatre by Samuel Foote who incorporated a 'Doctor and Mrs Simony' into one of his comedies. Mrs Dodd is cruelly lampooned too – Dodd seems genuinely to have been hurt by the portrayal of his wife as a voluble gossip. But the descriptions of Dodd which the

Der
**unglückliche Prädicant
zu London/**
in grabschriftlichen Gedanken lebhaft abgeschildert.

Welcher
Alldorten auf seine mit eigener Hande ausgefertigten Erz-
falschen, und sehr viel betragenden Wechselbriefen also schändlich
ist ausbezahlet worden/ nemlich am 27sten Junii 1777.

London/
Aus dem Englischen in das Hochdeutsche übersetzt per A. S, d. M. P.

Dr Dodd's death excited interest as far afield as Germany. Hanging with him is
15-year-old Joseph Harris, executed for stealing £2 10s 6d.

playwright puts into her mouth are close to the mark:

> Even the dowager-duchess of Dropsy was never known to nod
> at my Doctor; and then he doesn't pore, with his eyes close to
> the book, like a clerk that reads the first lesson; not he! but all
> extempo're, madam; with a cambrick handkerchief in one
> hand, and a diamond ring on the other; and then he waves
> this way, and that way; and he curtsies, and he bows, and he
> bounces...But then his wig, madam! I am sure you must
> admire his dear wig; not with the bushy, brown buckles,
> dangling and dropping like a Newfoundland spaniel; but
> short, rounded off at the ear, to show his plump cherry
> cheeks; white as a curd, feather-topped, and the curls as close
> as cauliflower.

Dodd would not forget this. Writing his best-selling *Thoughts in
Prison* from his cell in Newgate, three years later, he was still
smarting at the 'coward mimic' Foote's attack.

The disgraced cleric fled to Switzerland, penning before he left
a letter to newspaper editors protesting his innocence. He stayed
with his former pupil Philip Stanhope, now Lord Chesterfield,
who retained affection for Dodd, entertaining him lavishly.
Chesterfield offered to arrange another living, this time in
Buckinghamshire.

Dodd was away for several months. On the journey back to
England he stopped off at Paris. A startled Englishman reported
seeing him at the races, dressed in the full outfit of a seventeenth-
century musketeer, blind drunk, betting (and losing) heavily on
the horses.

Back home, Dodd struggled to rehabilitate himself: his
reputation was tarnished, and he was an easy target for scurrilous
paragraphs in the newspapers, which invariably referred to him as
'Dr Simony'. Moreover his finances were in a hopeless state and
he was forced to sell the Charlotte Chapel ('the concern', he
called it) and even his diamond ring. One contemporary
biographer remarked with understandable horror that at this time
Dodd 'descended so low as to become editor of a newspaper'.

This was the *New Morning Post* set up at the end of 1776 in
opposition to Henry Bate's *Morning Post* (see p235). Bate
frequently printed stories hostile to Dodd, accusing him of

attempting to debauch a 16-year-old girl, the orphan of a baronet, entrusted to his care.

But Dodd continued to keep up an extravagant lifestyle. He held large dinner parties, lived in fashionable areas and borrowed heavily. Tradesmen would pound at his door day and night for repayment. He used his furniture as a security for repayment. Unwilling to compromise his lifestyle, but unable to raise enough money through preaching and writing Dodd settled on his ultimately fatal course of action. He was at his wits' end.

On 1 February 1777 he forged a bond for £4,200 (well over £250,000 at today's prices) in the name of Lord Chesterfield. In the eighteenth century forgery was one of more than 350 capital offences on the statute books. England's 'Bloody Code' ensured that even the most trivial of crimes could be punished with death.

Dodd, more than most, knew the risk he was taking. Not only had he preached against the brutality of indiscriminate capital punishment, he had once prosecuted a highwayman who had stolen his purse from him. To the clergyman's dismay his evidence proved sufficient to send the culprit to the gallows at Tyburn.

In forging the bond, Dodd depended on common knowledge of his intimacy with Chesterfield. He explained to a stockbroker named Robertson that he was acting on behalf of the peer who, to save face, had asked him to carry out the transaction on his behalf. Robertson agreed to be discreet and set about looking for a willing banker.

Two days later Dodd met Robertson again, and was told that the bankers Messrs Fletcher and Peach were prepared to provide the money, albeit at exorbitant rates of interest. But doubt remained; although Chesterfield had apparently filled in the bond, and Dodd had signed as a witness, another witness was needed. Robertson hesitated and Dodd played a daring game of brinkmanship.

A servant was summoned for despatch to Chesterfield, to confirm that he had indeed authorised the bond. Dodd wrote the letter for him to convey.

As the servant was about to leave, Dodd suggested that the deal would probably be cancelled, once his lordship thought that anyone else knew about it. Robertson's commission was on the line. He called back the servant and signed.

All might have been well had it not been for the suspicions of the bankers' solicitor, Mr Manly. Manly noticed there was a peculiar marking on the bond: a letter 'e' on the number seven was clumsily blotched. He knew that such a defect could have been used to claim the invalidity of the bond and so jeopardise repayment. He was right: during his trial, Dodd's solicitors tried precisely this tack in an effort to prove that the bond was an invalid document. But by that point the money had been repaid and they were trying only to save Dodd's life.

Manly decided to check with Chesterfield. He went to his house and, apologising for the delicacy of the situation, explained he 'had come about the bond'. Chesterfield was confused; he knew nothing of any bonds. The only bond he had ever taken out he had repaid and destroyed a few years previously. When Manly produced the bond Chesterfield denied ever having seen it in his life.

Fearing that Dodd might be planning to flee the country, Manly hurried to the Lord Mayor of London, Sir Thomas Halifax, and a warrant was issued for the arrest of Dodd and Robertson. Dodd – who according to one rather unlikely newspaper report was sitting down with his friends for a farewell dinner before heading for Dover – answered the door to Manly. In terror he admitted the forgery, insisting he had intended it as only a temporary measure, and repeated as much when Fletcher, Peach, Robertson and the constables arrived. Robertson appealed to Dodd to confirm the stockbroker's innocence in the affair. Dodd cried 'I do! I do! I do!'

It seemed as though the problem might be sorted out without recourse to law. Dodd repaid as much of the money as he could and gave security for the rest. This, said Manly, was the only way to avoid a trial. Much was later made of the fact that for a few moments Dodd was left alone in the room with the bond sitting on a table and a fire burning in the grate. It would have been a simple matter to arrange for the evidence to go up in smoke.

Dodd expected to be forgiven. Manly assured him that, having restored the money, he had escaped. Although taken with Robertson to the York Coffee House in St James's Street under the supervision of constables, he was confident that he could now walk free. He was quite unprepared when early the next morning, Saturday 8 February, he was arrested for forgery and taken to the Lord Mayor. Halifax, a city man who took a dim view of forgery, rejected Dodd's appeal for the hearing to be held in private.

It was a pitiful sight. Covering his tears with a handkerchief growing wetter by the minute, and surrounded by a large and hostile crowd, Dodd protested he had never intended to defraud Chesterfield, that he would have repaid the money within six months anyway, and that no one had been harmed. He begged that the matter be left to rest.

But despite the bankers and Chesterfield's reluctance to prosecute, Halifax insisted that Fletcher and Peach be bound over to prosecute. Dodd was taken into custody and the story reached the newspapers.

On the Tuesday an angry Lord Chesterfield, alarmed lest his erstwhile tutor had forged bonds in his name all over London, placed a newspaper advertisement urging any further creditors to make themselves known to him at once. None did. Dodd's behaviour had not been that of a professional con-man, but a panicking profligate.

Wild rumours circulated: that Chesterfield had fled the country to avoid having to give evidence against his former friend; that Dodd had made repeated attempts to flee gaol. The *Morning Post* (the rival to his own *New Morning Post*) reported that the University of Cambridge had decided to convene a special synod to strip Dodd of his doctorate. Mrs Dodd was said to be suffering from a hysterical disorder, and doubts were expressed that she would live much longer. One correspondent reported that 'forgery is at present the general topic in all companies'. Another wrote to the *Morning Chronicle* condemning the 'cruel licentious-ness of ballad-singers, who are permitted to roar, at the corner of every street, songs upon an unfortunate divine': the letter was sent from the Percy Coffee House where the correspondent could hear 'a dozen mendicants bawling under the windows'.

Dodd's trial was set for Saturday 22 February. Proceedings were due to begin at ten o'clock; by dawn the crowd was already immense.

A vignette on this scene is provided by the tale of a group of law students promised a specially reserved gallery, but unable to get into the court for three hours. When they did finally force their way through they were shown into a 'tiny hen-coop' which was then locked from the outside. Disappointed, they forced their way out, found the gallery which was rightfully theirs and discovered that the sword-bearer's servant was charging two guineas for

admission. The students battered down the door, booted out the
'greasy porter' who was looking after the places, and finally took
their seats.

And the man at the eye of this storm was in a wretched state.
At ten o'clock Dr Dodd was escorted into the court on the arm
of a friend. He burst into tears as he sat down. After arguments
about whether Robertson's evidence was admissible – and there
was a strong legal argument that having originally been charged
as a conspirator with Dodd, he should not be able to appear as a
witness against him – the judge, Mr Justice Willes, allowed the
trial to proceed. Dodd pleaded not guilty to all the charges.

Dodd's solicitor defended him with gusto but in the absence of
any legal technicality to overturn the proceedings there was little
he could do. Lord Chesterfield testified that the handwriting on
the bond was that of his old tutor.

Before the judge's summing up Dodd was given the chance to
present his own defence. The thespian manqué rose to the
occasion. His legal arguments were specious, amounting to the
assertion that he had not intended to defraud Lord Chesterfield
as he would have paid everything back. But Dodd had always
been best at the emotional plea and summoning all his oratorical
powers he threw himself on the pity of the jury. He had, he said,
been 'persecuted with a cruelty scarcely to be paralleled' after
express assurances from Mr Manly that he would not be
prosecuted. He bewailed the suffering of his 'dear wife'. He
showed a sudden concern for tradesmen. If he were to die, he
said, his creditors – 'honest men who will lose much by my death'
– would be left out of pocket.

It was a brilliant performance: there was hardly a dry eye in the
house. But within ten minutes the foreman of the jury, choking
back his tears, delivered a unanimous 'guilty' verdict, while
recommending Dr Dodd to mercy. One man clapped his hands
and whooped with delight. The rest of the courtroom was
stunned into silence. Dr Dodd groaned and collapsed.

His miseries were compounded by fresh public humiliation. Mr
Manly organised a sale of Dodd's possessions. Dodd only found
out about the auction – held in his own house, off Oxford Street
– when he saw it advertised in the newspapers. I have been able
to track down the auctioneer's catalogue, unpublished since the
sale. No document could give a more revealing picture of Dodd's

lifestyle. No fewer than 546 lots, from a scrubbing brush to Dr Dodd's vast book collection, were put up for sale. Among the more esoteric of Dr Dodd's possessions were four bird cages, two silver-mounted pistols, a double-keyed harpsichord, a brass-barrelled coach gun, a mahogany shaving stand, a collection of moths, a 'doom teaster for a bedstead', and a guitar. He and Mrs Dodd slept on a goose-feather mattress in a four-poster bed with carved mahogany pillars, covered by a crimson damask quilt.

Dodd's gallery rivalled London's best. He owned pictures by Titian, Holbein, Poussin and Van Dyke, some landscapes by Barret, portraits of George III and his wife, busts of Shakespeare and Milton, and a half-length portrait of a lady reclining on an urn. Dr Dodd's largesse as a host is attested to by the set of thirty-six knives and forks and the same number of wine glasses, fourteen decanters and five dining tables. No wonder Dr Dodd had recourse to fraud.

Among the hundreds of finely-bound volumes in his library were works by Shakespeare, Dryden, Milton, Homer, Virgil, Cicero, Pope, Swift, Voltaire, Addison, Augustine, Spencer, Rousseau, Locke and Bacon – and of course William Dodd. Although there were a good number of religious works – copies of Wesley's sermons, Pope Clement XIV's letters, Luther's *Discourses*, a translation of the Koran and manuscript copies of Latimer's sermons dating from 1562 – many books are altogether more risqué: Venette on conjugal love and Lignac on the *Casus de l'Homme et de la Femme dans l'état du marriage*. Poignantly there is a copy of the *Life of the Earl of Chesterfield*, a man who held Dodd in high esteem and never lived to see his protégé's attempt to defraud his son.

In his cell, Dodd might have wished for the *Afflicted Man's Companion*, *The Art of Dying Well* and *Dialogues of the Dead*. No doubt he was happier to leave behind his copy of *The Nature and Plan of Hell*.

From being highly hostile, the public mood soon became extravagantly sympathetic. I find a curious echo here of this abrupt swinging round of public sentiment in the immediate aftermath of the death of Diana, Princess of Wales. Suddenly, all the good was remembered. Critics slunk away. The same happened for Dodd.

Newspapers were bombarded with letters supporting him.

Suddenly his good deeds seemed to outweigh the bad. Correspondents pointed to his charity work, to his popularity as a preacher and to the fact that no one had been materially damaged by the forgery. It was remarked that Dodd's confession had been obtained under assurances that it would not be used. Some people tried to argue that it would set a terrible example to see a clergyman hanged publicly. Others retorted that the clergy set a pretty terrible example anyway.

The most notable intervention was Samuel Johnson's. He assumed the role of chief script-writer for Dodd. Dodd and Johnson had met a few years previously. Now confined to a cell in Newgate Dodd asked a mutual friend to persuade Johnson to help him. According to Boswell, Johnson read the letter 'walking up and down his chamber and seemed much agitated, after which he said "I will do what I can"; and certainly he did make extraordinary exertions.' Few pens commanded the force of Dr Johnson's and scholars view the compositions he produced for Dodd as among his best.

All in all, as we shall see, Johnson was to write Dodd's speech after the verdict and before sentence; his 'Convict's Address to His Unhappy Brethren' – a sermon delivered in the prisoners' chapel at Newgate; numerous letters appealing for clemency; Dodd's petition to the King and Mrs Dodd's petition to the Queen; and his 'Last Solemn Declaration' left with the Sheriff at his place of execution. Extracts from many of these found their way, as was intended, into the newspapers. Boswell says that Dodd hardly wrote a word of any of them.

Boswell quotes only one occasion when the clergyman rejected Dr Johnson's phrasing. One of Johnson's drafts for him included the confession of 'hypocrisy'. Dodd struck the word out. 'With this,' Johnson noted grimly in the margin, 'he said he could not charge himself.'

On 16 May, after the rejection of an appeal to have the verdict overturned on the grounds that Robertson's evidence was inadmissable, Dodd went to receive sentence at the Sessions of the City Recorder who asked him if he had anything to say in mitigation.

He did, for Johnson had written him a speech. In it he cried for mercy. He called himself 'a dreadful example of human infirmity' and reiterated the (now familiar) argument, that he had intended to defraud no one and that no one had been harmed. 'I have fallen from a reputation, which ought to have made me cautious, and from a fortune which ought to have made me content. I am sunk at once into poverty and scorn: my name and my crime fill the ballads in the streets; the sport of the thoughtless, and the triumph of the wicked!'

It is said even the stony-hearted Lord Mayor, Halifax, wept. But in vain. Dr Dodd was told he must hang. He left the courtroom groaning 'Lord Jesus receive my soul!'

The campaign to save Dodd became desperate. The last hope for clemency lay with the King. Newspapers offered almost daily reports of Dr and Mrs Dodd's health and published ever more frantic letters in support.

Johnson now composed a sermon for the prisoner, delivered in the chapel of Newgate prison on 6 June. 'I will labour to do justice from the pulpit,' wrote a grateful Dodd to Johnson. Its real audience lay outside the prison walls. 'Many excellent things hast thou uttered, most unhappy of men! but this appears to me to have exceeded them all!' enthused the *Morning Chronicle*.

Johnson concealed his involvement but praised Dodd's new fluency. 'Depend upon it, Sir, when a man knows he is to be hanged in a fortnight, it concentrates his mind wonderfully.'

On Friday 13 June the King and his Privy Council met to decide Dodd's fate. George III was sympathetic; others hard-hearted. Lord Mansfield's view was decisive. Walpole tells us that he 'hated the popular party as much as he loved severity'. It had become necessary to show the masses that property would be protected by law.

The King bowed to his Privy Council and Dodd was ordered to be hanged at Tyburn on 27 June. On hearing the dreadful news Mrs Dodd clasped her hands together. 'O God! enable me to bear this!' Following her husband's example, she fainted.

A desperate Dodd now wrote a note to Dr Johnson begging for help with a letter he wished to write from himself to the King. The note, says Boswell, was brought to Dr Johnson when in church. He stooped down and read it, and wrote, when he went home, the following...

May it not offend your Majesty, that the most miserable of men applies himself to your clemency, as his last hope and his last refuge; that your mercy is most earnestly and humbly implored by a clergyman, whom your Laws and Judges have condemned to the horrour and ignominy of a publick execution.

I confess the crime, and own the enormity of its consequences, and the danger of its example. Nor have I the confidence to petition for impunity; but humbly hope, that publick security may be established, without the spectacle of a clergyman dragged through the streets, to a death of infamy, amidst the derision of the profligate and profane; and that justice may be satisfied with irrevocable exile, perpetual disgrace, and hopeless penury.

My life, Sir, has not been useless to mankind. I have benefited many. But my offences against GOD are numberless, and I have had little time for repentance. Preserve me, Sir, by your prerogative of mercy, from the necessity of appearing unprepared at that tribunal before which Kings and Subjects must stand at last together. Permit me to hide my guilt in some obscure corner of a foreign country, where, if I can ever attain confidence to hope that my prayers will be heard, they shall be poured with all the fervour of gratitude for the life and happiness of your Majesty. I am, Sir,

Your Majesty's, &c.

A sort of delirium seized British public opinion. Looking back at Dodd's case forty years later, Henry Angelo remarked how sorrow became a 'national epidemic'. 'My prayers are accompanied by those of thousands,' concluded one correspondent begging the King for mercy. Far from accepting the inevitable Dodd's supporters went into overdrive. A petition, signed by 23,000 householders and headed by the foreman of the jury which had convicted him, was presented to the King by the popular hero of the American war, Earl Percy, on 25 June.

As all this was going on around him, Dodd drifted back to earlier days. He summoned the editor of the *Morning Chronicle*, William Woodfall, to his cell in Newgate and asked a favour: could he find a manager for the play his father had snatched from the stage almost thirty years before: *Sir Roger de Coverley*? Far from being concentrated, Dodd's mind appears to have wandered.

By 26 June, the eve of his execution, there was nothing Dodd's supporters could do but bawl for mercy. The *Gazetteer* published an enormous letter (by Johnson, but unsigned) to the King, stating that the *vox populi* – 'oh! may it be the *vox Dei*!' – did not believe justice would be served by the death of Dr Dodd, and listing twelve reasons why he should be reprieved. One man wrote to the King offering to be publicly whipped and spend a year in prison in return for Dodd's freedom. Even Queen Charlotte, who was too upset to eat, could not sway her husband.

Dodd finally resigned himself to execution. He was not, in his last days, careless of the help of friends. 'With a warmth of gratitude,' says Boswell, he wrote to Dr Johnson as follows:

June 25.

Accept, thou *great* and *good* heart, my earnest and fervent thanks and prayers for all thy benevolent and kind efforts on my behalf. – Oh! Dr Johnson! as I sought your knowledge at an early hour in life, would to heaven I had cultivated the love and acquaintance of so excellent a man! – I pray GOD most sincerely to bless you with the highest transports – the infelt satisfaction of *humane* and benevolent exertions! – And admitted, as I trust I shall be, to the realms of bliss before you, I shall hail *your* arrival there with transport, and rejoice to acknowledge that you was my Comforter, my Advocate, and my *friend*! GOD *be ever* with *you*!

'Dr Johnson,' says Boswell, then wrote Dr Dodd a 'solemn and soothing letter.' It is also (and it was not meant for publication) sensitive and kind and somewhat belies Johnson's terrier-barking reputation. It has also the virtue of containing truth...

*To the Reverend Dr Dodd*

Dear SIR,

That which is appointed to all men is now coming upon you...

Be comforted; your crime, morally or religiously considered, has no very deep dye of turpitude. It corrupted no man's principles; it attacked no man's life. It involved only a temporary and reparable injury. Of this, and of all other sins, you are earnestly to repent; and may GOD, who knoweth our frailty and desireth not our death, accept your repentance...

...Your affectionate servant,

### SAM. JOHNSON.

Dodd's friends showed no end of ingenuity in their efforts to have him freed. A man was employed to lurk around the prison gates, his pockets stuffed with cash to bribe the turnkey. The celebrated waxwork modeller Mrs Wright made a likeness of Dodd's head, and smuggled it into the prison under her petticoats. The plan was to leave the waxwork in the cell while Dodd was smuggled out in the crowd.

Another scheme involved 'a certain woman in the lower class of life whose features happened to be extremely like Dodd's'.

'On a day agreed, the Doctor's irons having been previously filed, she would exchange dresses...Dr Dodd was to have put a bonnet upon his head, to have taken a bundle under his arm and to have walked quietly out of the prison.' The plan failed.

On the morning of 27 June, after praying in the prison's chapel, Dodd was led from Newgate. 'I am now a spectacle to men and soon shall be a spectacle to angels,' he declared on the way – oddly enough the same words Bishop Atherton (see p157) had used on the way to the scaffold in 1640.

It is possible to confirm the accuracy of his first prediction. It is three miles from Newgate to Tyburn and Londoners lined the streets to watch the journey. 'Never,' Angelo wrote, 'did so general a sympathy prevail as on this occasion, throughout the country.'

> In London every visage expressed sadness; it appeared, indeed, a day of universal calamity; yet, strange to say, people of all conditions flocked to town to see the melancholy procession, or rather mournful cavalcade, move onward...The streets were thronged at an early hour with groups of both sexes hurrying to their different stations; all the windows of every house, for the whole distance, were crowded to see the passing spectacle. The most unfeeling shuddered, as the mourning-coach which contained the malefactor approached; thousands sobbed

aloud, and many women swooned at the sight...Dodd's corpse-like appearance produced an awful picture of human woe. Tens of thousands of hats, which formed a black mass, as the coach advanced, were taken off simultaneously, and so many tragic faces exhibited a spectacle, the effect of which is beyond the power of words to describe. Thus the procession travelled onwards, through the multitude, whose silence added to the awfulness of the scene.

The violence of public sympathy became a serious worry to the authorities. Two thousand men were placed on standby in Hyde Park, in case of disturbances.

But at Tyburn there was something of a jamboree. Bandstand seats had been sold in advance at exorbitant prices, while trees 'were literally loaded with human beings'. Angelo himself had secured a plumb view from the window of a nearby distillers. Many of Dodd's friends and acquaintances were there to witness his execution. Dr Dodd was brought onto the scaffold, and spent some time in prayer during which his hat was blown off by a gust of wind. He continued to pray – to the annoyance of the crowd which, wrote one spectator, 'rather wished for some more interesting part of the tragedy'.

Waiting to be executed next to Dodd was a 15-year-old boy, Joseph Harris. He had robbed a coachman of £2 10s 6d, compared with Dodd's £4000. Yet Dodd drew all the sympathy.

One would hardly have expected that, on the scaffold and before a vast crowd which had turned up specially to see him die, a man of Dr Dodd's predilection for public performance would have resigned himself to taking a final bow. Anything but. Dodd intended to survive his execution. The prisoner's friends had equipped him with a contraption designed to take the pressure of the rope from his neck and the hangman had been bribed not to pull down on his legs after the cart moved off. At an undertaker's nearby a surgeon was waiting with a hot bath which it was hoped would help revive him.

At length Dodd finished his prayers and surrendered himself to the hangman. His last moments were not without comedy. As the halter was being put round his neck his wig was knocked off, revealing a shaved scalp.

Then he was hanged. If the ruse to help him survive the

execution did succeed then Dodd must be counted the victim of
the public interest he had generated, for the crowd was so great
that the hearse could make only slow progress to the undertaker's.
After two hours spent trying to revive him – using the methods of
the Humane Society for the Recovery of Persons Apparently
Drowned, a charity which Dodd had himself successfully
promoted – Dodd was pronounced dead, and taken for burial in
Cowley, Middlesex.

'Poor Dr Dodd was put to death yesterday,' wrote Dr Johnson
to James Boswell, 'surely the voice of the publick, when it calls so
loudly, and calls only for mercy, ought to be heard.

'...I wrote many of his petitions, and some of his letters. He
applied to me very often. He was, I am afraid, long flattered with
hopes of life; but I had no part in that dreadful delusion.

'...His moral character is very bad: I hope all is not true that is
charged upon him.'

What, on reflection, was Samuel Johnson but Dr Dodd's
eighteenth-century spin doctor? Though Dodd made himself
famous by his own efforts, it is unlikely that the final and
astonishing orchestration of public sympathy for him could have
been achieved without Johnson's eloquent and canny public
relations exercise on his behalf. If you study the prose he crafted
for Dodd, and note Boswell's observation – that Johnson urged
upon Dodd a self-humiliation the clergyman found hard to accept
– you will see that Johnson was acting as more than a ghost-
writer: he was a professional publicist.

I am afforded a wry smile by the striking similarity between
Johnson's advice to Dodd (grovel; confess; don't wriggle) and the
advice our modern publicist, Max Clifford, says he always gives
those in trouble: if found out, be honest and look for mercy rather
than a retrial.

For a few years after Dr Dodd's death there were reports that he
had been sighted on the Continent or elsewhere – in particular in
Lincolnshire. One newspaper published a letter from Provence
stating that Dodd was living there 'beyond the reach of his enemies'.

Those who knew Dodd were ambivalent after his death.
Despite the very public lengths Johnson went to on Dodd's behalf
he was only lukewarm about him in private, and later even
admitted that he probably deserved to hang.

The Bishop of Bristol expressed sorrow on hearing of Dodd's

death sentence. Asked why, he replied that 'he is to be hanged for the least offence he ever committed'; the sentiment was not unusual. The Church kept an embarrassed silence throughout. The only response I have been able to find was a sermon arguing that the evidence of Christianity was not diminished by the frailty of one of its ministers. It was a mean-spirited performance.

But Dodd's case did have one lasting and important effect. Dodd's execution was the first case 'to stir the public conscience, and to force it to question whether the absolute capital punishment was socially and morally justifiable for all the offences for which it was then appointed', according to legal historian Radzinowicz.

This was of course too late for Dr Dodd and of no consolation for Mary Dodd, who retired to Ilford traumatised and broke, and died insane seven years after her husband's execution.

Surveying Dodd's story one is torn between amused contempt for his hollow showmanship and self-regard, and affection for an essentially harmless and perhaps beguiling man. Whatever he lacked it was not the power to move people in large numbers, and he used this power for no bad purpose and some good ones. 'A person should be allowed as preaching well,' wrote Dr Johnson of Dodd, 'whose sermons strike his audience with forcible conviction...He was at first what he endeavoured to make others; but the world broke down his resolution, and he in time chose to exemplify his own instructions.'

# MYSTERY

## JOHN WAKEFORD

## A Period Drama

In the golden age of the whodunnit the case of Archdeacon John Wakeford was bound to be a sensation. The archdeacon, a senior churchman and a renowned orator, was convicted of adultery first by a church court and then on appeal by the Privy Council, in a case where no woman was ever produced or even named. At the time this was compared with a conviction for murder without the identification of a corpse. Wakeford was deposed from his living, evicted from his home, and eventually left to die in a lunatic asylum, driven mad by efforts to prove his innocence.

The nation was for a while struck by the idea that Wakeford might be the victim of a massive Anglican conspiracy. Books appeared detailing elaborate impersonation theories. A film was made in which Wakeford starred as himself. A popular newspaper launched a massive campaign to have his conviction overturned. Sixty thousand people signed a petition, presented to the King, demanding an exercise of the royal prerogative to pardon Wakeford.

Guilty or innocent – and there are still those who defend him – it was a pointless end to what should have been a luminous career.

From today's perspective the saga of John Wakeford seems deliciously quaint. The archdeacon was accused of spending three nights in the Bull Hotel, Peterborough with a woman who was not his wife. Like the Agatha Christie novel the case resembles, hotel maids, private detectives, policemen, bishops and lesser curates were all to feature as witnesses.

A policeman's son, Wakeford was born in 1859 and ordained

86

in 1884. In the early years of his ministry he displayed (like so many of the subjects of this book) a manic, evangelising energy. As a young Devon curate he trudged the Dartmoor hills, spreading the Gospel on foot. He hoped to set up a monastic order whose members would 'wear a simple habit of cassock and belt and go afoot from place to place preaching'. The Bishop of Chichester wrote to him that 'I really do not know of any Diocese where one man, untitled, has effected so much in so brief a time.'

Such zeal caught the attention of William Ewart Gladstone – an Anglican evangelical himself. He referred to Wakeford as 'a clergyman as to whose qualities and services I possessed unequivocal testimony' and in August 1893 appointed him vicar of St Margaret's, Anfield, Liverpool. Here Wakeford achieved celebrity, his emphasis on the confessional giving rise to the nickname 'Pope John'.

We find him in October 1907 delivering a sermon against the private ownership of the railways. In May 1910, on the death of Edward VII, he preached to an enthusiastic congregation of 20,000. He became a socialist. Those who know the Church of England will have discerned a figure courting the hostility of a section of his peers.

In June 1912 Wakeford moved to Lincoln Cathedral, first as prebendary and then as precentor. The bishop had appointed him as a reformer but in the small world of a cathedral close Wakeford found, instead of the noisy public controversy in which he revelled, a quieter malice. Yeats's remark, of Irish politics, 'Big hatred, little room' is true of cathedral politics, too.

Particularly at Lincoln. There does seem to be something in the air there. Readers will discover in a later chapter (see p116) that until very recently a dean and sub-dean of Lincoln have been engaged in a deeply unchristian feud. Archdeacon Wakeford seemed cursed from the moment of his arrival. Much of the rancour emanated from the dean, Dr Fry, who refused to talk to the cathedral organist (they would only communicate by notes) and who had fallen out with the rest of the chapter over his dismissal of a senior verger.

Wakeford and the dean engaged in a lengthy dispute over whether the cathedral doors should be locked during the services, and soon the dean started paying Wakeford's chauffeur to keep tabs on his movements.

Wakeford's relations with neighbouring clergy were equally bizarre. The Reverend Charles Moore, Vicar of Kirkstead was a fogeyish cleric who, in eighteenth-century fashion, used to take his Sunday services in hunting pink. He grew to loathe the archdeacon. They had quarrelled over the reopening of a dilapidated church on Moore's land, an argument which assumed national proportions in the letters page of *The Times*. Wakeford won – the church was reopened – only to find it barricaded with barbed wire when he tried to conduct a service there.

These enemies proved Wakeford's undoing. He had (according to rumour) stayed overnight three times at the Bull Hotel in Peterborough accompanied by a woman who was not Mrs Wakeford. Moore heard the rumours and engaged a retired policeman, Inspector Agar, to investigate. The story Agar unearthed was puzzling. As related to the Privy Council, it reads like one of those complex (and for non-aficionados, pointless) tuppenny whodunnits. Non-aficionados can skip a page or two here.

Wakeford made his first visit to the Bull Hotel in March, in order (he said) to prepare sermons. A policeman, Sergeant King, had seen him. The archdeacon had not been alone. The manager testified that Wakeford had been accompanied by a woman and that the couple had stayed in a room containing one double bed: Room 15. Wakeford signed the register 'J.Wakeford, Precincts, Lincoln' (his correct address was 'The Precentory, Lincoln'). Later, the manager added the words 'and wife'.

A chambermaid, Cissie Young, recalled finding a pair of pyjamas and a nightie when cleaning the room. (Mrs Wakeford indignantly denied her husband wore pyjamas.) The following day he was spotted in Peterborough Cathedral, with 'a girl'.

Wakeford agreed he had been accompanied. It was further alleged that he had visited a preparatory school accompanied by 'a girl'. This he denied. Finally it was alleged he had visited a church two miles outside Peterborough with – as its vicar testified – 'a girl'.

Some hotel guests recalled seeing a 'gaitered clergyman' dining with a woman; some insisted he had dined alone. Hotel records showed that Wakeford had been charged for two people: his hotel bill came to £4 2s 6d, a remarkable sum for a single man.

The next visit to the Bull was in April. Wakeford was in Peterborough, *en route* to Lincoln. He had to get back (he said) in time for a meeting of archdeacons. The Bishop of Lincoln said there was no such meeting.

Mr Pugh, the Bull's manager, makes a second appearance in this bedroom farce. He had received a card from Wakeford requesting in advance a double-bedded room. Wakeford arrived with (it was said) the same woman. In the register he signed his name as before; again this was followed by the words 'and wife' – which Mr Pugh denied adding. This time the woman signed her name too: 'M. Wakeford'.

Inspector Agar's evidence was passed to the bishop by the spiteful Herbert Worthington. He was Wakeford's brother-in-law! His letter, from Nether Seale Rectory, ended:

> My sister, Mrs Wakeford, for years – 17 or 18 anyhow – has told me the disgraceful way her husband has behaved, and my dear father, now gone from us, often discussed the matter with me. I leave the evidence in your Lordship's hands to deal with.
>
> I am always yours very faithfully,
>
> Herbert E. Worthington,
> Rector of Seale and Rural Dean
>
> NB – I hold my sister's letter, dated July 6th, to say she has not slept in Peterborough these three years.

Or so Worthington claimed. When it came to trial Mrs Wakeford denied that there had been differences between herself and her husband, but on the basis of Worthington's letter the bishop decided to prosecute. On Wakeford's insistence the charges were heard before a consistory court, presided over by the Chancellor of the Diocese of Lincoln and judged by five assessors who had been picked by the dean – hardly a disinterested party. In February 1921 Wakeford was convicted of adultery. He declared at once that he would appeal.

Already the case had established itself as a famous mystery. A certain 'Evelyn Porter', cited by Worthington in his letter to the Bishop of Norwich, was discounted as a possible 'other woman'. This left a gaping hole in the prosecution's case: no woman could

be produced or even identified whose name was linked to
Wakeford's. Into this evidential gap swam a vapid figure: the
notorious 'Girl in the Cathedral'.

Wakeford had been seen by the Dean of Peterborough in the
cathedral with a girl described as being about 17 and 'in a pitiable
condition'. Wakeford did not deny this. He had met her only that
day, he said, and seeing she was having trouble reading an
inscription, deciphered it for her. The encounter was innocent: he
had met the girl for the first and last time that day. He had no idea
who she was.

However, as far as the prosecution was concerned she was the
adulteress who had shared Wakeford's bed at the Bull Hotel.

Before the appeal both prosecution and defence lawyers
searched frantically for her. But when the Privy Council convened
on 7 April 1921, in 9 Downing Street, where huge crowds had
gathered in the hope of getting a seat in the public gallery and
where reporters from every paper had converged, the girl was as
elusive as ever. The case proceeded without her.

The hearing proved more Cluedo than strip-poker or a bodice-
ripper. There was, it is true, lengthy discussion on whether
Wakeford wore pyjamas or a night-shirt, but that was about as
sensational as it got. Since there was no woman, the audience was
denied much in the way of kiss-and-tell.

Cross-examined, Wakeford blamed everything on a conspiracy.
'If you ask me who arranged it, I say, with great regret, my
brother-in-law and Moore.' At his initial trial Wakeford had
spoken Delphically of 'the crowd against me'. 'There is another
instrument, but he is a foolish person. He is used by them,' he
said. The effect was to make him sound unhinged.

In his judgement Lord Birkenhead (better known as F.E.
Smith, the Lord Chancellor and leading Conservative politician)
considered the question of conspiracy too absurd to be plausible.
He articulated persuasively the best objection to Wakeford's line
of defence. 'By what amazing coincidence did it come about that
the appellant should have selected on this occasion the one hotel
in Peterborough whose landlord was ready to be corrupted, able
to carry with him into this maze of slander and perjury his wife
and servants, and zealous to commence a systematic course of
perjury in support of the plan?'

Birkenhead had spent time with his magnifying glass. 'It is

John Bull knocking on the doors of the Hall of Justice.

interesting to compare the "f" in "Wife" with the "f" in "Wakeford" of 14 March,' he said, comparing the Bull's register with Wakeford's handwriting. 'The most distinctive feature, however, which appears in all those specimens of the appellant's handwriting is the shape and position of the dot upon the "i" ...'

Birkenhead decided the handwriting was not forged. On such pinheads did the archdeacon's fate dance.

But it was the Girl in the Cathedral who really caught the public imagination. Though Birkenhead thought it understandable that the 'woman in the hotel' should remain in the shadows, he fretted that there was nothing to stop the girl seen with Wakeford in the Cathedral stepping forward.

It was inconceivable that she should not have heard about the case – unless she were dead. 'Surely it is also inconceivable that any woman or girl who had been with the appellant in the Cathedral in the circumstances described by him, should be so callous that, when a word from her would clear an innocent man, she should so obstinately hold her peace.'

Birkenhead dismissed Wakeford's appeal. The Bishop of Lincoln's order of deprivation, suspended until the result of the Privy Council hearing was known, was enforced: 'that the archdeacon be deprived of all his ecclesiastical promotion within the diocese of Lincoln, and especially the archdeaconry of Stowe and of the canonry and the precentorship of Lincoln Cathedral,

## THE VITAL SIGNATURES.

*March 14th, 1920.*

*April 2nd, 1920.*

Lord Birkenhead concluded that the handwriting in the Bull Hotel register was
Wakeford's, sealing the Archdeacon's fate.

of the vicarage of Kirkstead, and of all the profits and benefits
appertaining thereto, and of any other ecclesiastical promotions in
the diocese of Lincoln.'

But many people were unconvinced by an improbable drama in
which Wakeford, a 58-year-old cleric sporting gaiters, shacked up
with a young floozy in the full view of a hotel teeming with horse
farmers. *The Times* expressed misgivings. An archdeacon had lost
his reputation, not to say his income, and was about to be evicted
from his home.

And now Horatio Bottomley entered the scene. The former
Liberal MP, millionaire tycoon and 'swindler of the century'
emerged as the improbable agent of Wakeford's attempted
redemption. Bottomley was editor of the mass-circulation *John Bull*
newspaper, a shady pre-war version of the *Sun*. Bottomley's own
disgrace and imprisonment (for defrauding his readers) was still to
come; for the moment he scented that church, sex and a mysterious
*femme fatale* provided a scandal his readers would enjoy.

Given that the Girl in the Cathedral was the only woman upon
whose existence both defence and prosecution could agree, there
seemed a good chance she might be found. In the twin causes of
justice and newspaper sales, Bottomley resolved to find her.

And so on 7 May 1921, *John Bull* announced that there would
be a £1000 reward 'for finding the lady'. Bottomley's editorial,
*Cherchez La Femme*, shows a knack for catchy hyperbole. 'It is safe

to say that no lawsuit of modern times has aroused wider public interest or stirred deeper human feelings than that which upon a million tongues has briefly been referred to as the "Wakeford Case".'

Wakeford was 'a clergyman of lofty eloquence, deep spiritual fervour, and, hitherto, unblemished reputation'. Bottomley wrote of the 'breathless improbability that a man in the archdeacon's position, not known to suffer from mental aberration, or to be addicted to any habit that might temporarily unbalance the judgement, should, in broad daylight, consort with a woman not his wife in the public streets of a Cathedral city, and afterwards spend the night with her at one of its hotels.

'Let us assume that there is one woman alive in Great Britain who can remove one way or other these last lingering doubts as to the guilt or innocence of Archdeacon Wakeford. If humanely possible, she must be found... [We] cannot fail to be impressed with the fact that a large and influential section of the public is still convinced of Archdeacon Wakeford's innocence... With some confidence we await the result.'

It was a good ruse. After a week there was no news, so Bottomley upped the reward to £2000. 'The mind of the British public will never be thoroughly satisfied that justice has been done until the case is robbed of this element of mystery.' The 21 May edition announced in a headline that it was 'On The Track Of The Wakeford Woman'. But no one stepped forward.

And then on 28 May there came the cautious announcement: 'Important Wakeford Witness Found'. Inside was an unsigned statement.

I have special reasons for remembering Monday March 20th. It was a wet day, and I went out for a walk after breakfast. My husband had left for business some time before, and I had arranged with him to meet him in the Cathedral Yard at about half-past ten. I went to the Cathedral and waited about – as I was rather early for the appointment.

While waiting...a clergyman came up to me from the direction of the sundial, and spoke to me. He said: 'You seem to be interested in the Cathedral,' and I replied that I was, and had thought of trying to sketch the windows. The clergyman said that it was a very fine building and that there

*John Bull* keeps the story going, announcing their 'monster petition'.

was a lot of beautiful work inside. After some minutes friendly conversation, the clergyman walked away.

I attached no particular importance to the incident at the time, although when I saw the newspaper photographs of Archdeacon Wakeford I remembered the face as that of someone I had spoken to previously. I have now been shown several photographs of Archdeacon Wakeford, and I identify him as the clergyman I talked with at the Cathedral.

The encounter could hardly have been more proper. Or less interesting. A young wife waiting to meet her husband outside a cathedral, passing the time talking to a clergyman about water-colours. The following week *John Bull* was confident, 'Wakeford Girl Found!' The former archdeacon and the Girl in the Cathedral had been introduced, with witnesses to the occasion, and they had immediately recognised each other. At last – proof!

Where had she been? Why had she held her tongue? Freda Hansen had heard of the case, she said, but it had not occurred to her she could have been of any use to Wakeford. She had a point. It is one thing to spend a few minutes chatting to a clergyman one morning before Easter, another to discover two years later that one is the sought-for key to a sensational adultery trial in Downing Street. Mrs Hansen was a rather timid, nineteen-year-old primary school teacher.

For *John Bull* it was time to take a stance. 'If there is any justice left in England, means must be found either to reopen the proceedings and submit Mrs Hansen's statements to judicial scrutiny, or alternatively, to invoke the Royal Prerogative for the purpose of setting aside a judgement which the public conscience can no longer approve.'

The Royal Prerogative had been mentioned – and *John Bull* now started gathering signatures for a 'monster petition' to the King. Wakeford toured the country, giving lectures, accompanied by Mrs Hansen.

Next came the movie! This – *The Wakeford Mystery* – also starred both Wakeford and Hansen. At one point a mysterious hand is seen inserting 'and wife' in the Bull Hotel's register. The film played to packed houses all over the country, though in some towns vicars denounced it from their pulpits.

Next *John Bull* published a pamphlet, *The Mystery of the*

*Wakeford Case*, written by the editor, Charles Pilley. (Bottomley was under arrest for fraud.) 'It is vital that the sinister air of mystery which surrounds this case should be dissipated, and that the puppets who have hitherto figured as prosecutors should be replaced by the architects of a design which has too successfully imposed upon the courts,' declared Mr Pilley in language that suggests he had less keen an eye than his predecessor for the tabloid wordbite. More of a wordchew.

An authoress writing under the cryptic letters 'M.L.T', developed the theme further in her pamphlet *Was Archdeacon Wakeford Impersonated?*

'Was there the Big Thing behind this, that looms so darkly behind other of these persecutions of the Clergy of the Church of England? For Archdeacon Wakeford's case is, after all, only one of many; and in their main features and plan of campaign, they are strikingly alike.'

The book imagines the nitty-gritty details of impersonating Wakeford. 'The impersonator carries a small suitcase for his theatrical properties. He has previously studied his victim; his dress, his demeanour, his walk. He can don or discard, at need, the apron, gaiters, hat. He can be, at one moment, unobserved: at the next, very conspicuous. His properties may even include some facial disguise ... (blue glasses ... a moustache and beard)'. This, declared M.L.T., was the 'only sane solution' to the Wakeford mystery.

The conspiracy theory sparked off by a little local difficulty in Lincoln had escalated into a plot involving the full-scale persecution of Church of England clergymen by deadly agents: strange chameleon figures, possessed of blue glasses, false beards and a supernatural ability to appear or disappear at will. Seldom has Anglicanism been accused of being so effective. It was a measure of Wakeford's desperation that he thought there might be something in the idea.

*John Bull* continued to plug the petition, describing the 'wonderful enthusiasm at every meeting' at which Wakeford and Hansen spoke. 'Each week now seems to be marked by some fresh development in the Wakeford case,' it reported in November. 'Public interest in the Wakeford case shows no sign of abatement,' declared the edition in January 1922. 'Wakeford is winning!' roared *John Bull* on 4 February, and, the following week, 'All for Wakeford!', and then the next, 'Rally round Wakeford!' In the *Manchester Guardian* Wakeford himself sounded ebullient.

> I am aware that I have the confidence and sympathy of the great majority of thinking people. The judgement of professional men and of business men is with me. The working-classes as a whole entertain no doubt on this subject; on every side I am assured of their trust and respect.

On 8 April *John Bull* announced confidently, 'It is our firm conviction that this stern and uphill fight is nearly won.' Sixty thousand signatures had been gathered, and had by now been presented to the King. The papers waited, breathless, for His Majesty's decision.

But in the next issue – nothing. One searches in vain for mention of the deprived archdeacon. There is a prominent article on 'Moral Lepers from the East' which growls that 'it is high time that the public conscience was roused to a sense of the peril and scandal of Chinatown in London' – but no more mention of the paper's hero, John Wakeford. Nor did *John Bull* ever mention him again.

One has to turn to *The Times* to find out what happened. After all the hullabaloo it was a dreadful anticlimax. In a brief paragraph we learn that Wakeford had presented the petition to the Home Office, and received the following reply: 'The Secretary of State is advised that the petition does not disclose any grounds upon which his Majesty should be advised to comply with the prayer thereof.' John Wakeford, for whom a modern spin-doctor would no doubt coin the phrase 'People's Precentor', had left the monarch unmoved. And that was that.

Wakeford retired to Biggin Hill with his wife. On 6 March 1928 he was admitted to Barming Heath Lunatic Asylum. On 13 February 1930 he died. Mrs Wakeford followed him to the grave soon afterwards, having spent her last few years in poor health and penury. There is no indication that *John Bull*, ardent for the Wakefords when circulation depended upon it, came to her aid.

Was Archdeacon Wakeford guilty? John Treherne, who discusses the question in his book on the affair, *Dangerous Precincts*, concludes that on balance he was not. Reading the whole of Lord Birkenhead's long judgement I conclude that probably he was. But, guilty or innocent, he was placed in the impossible situation of proving a negative – that he was not with a woman, whose name no one knew. He was driven mad in the attempt. Whatever his culpability, Wakeford's was a peculiarly pointless way to fall.

Before his trials began Wakeford wrote 'It is nothing to the world if one man goes up or down.' He was right. The Wakeford Sensation rapidly vanished. But the Bull Hotel in Peterborough, which still stands, has paid its own tribute to the man who briefly made the establishment famous. Room 15 – the scene of his supposed adultery – was named 'The Wakeford Suite' – and still is. A quick call to the hotel recently revealed that no one working there has a clue why.

# CHARLES VAUGHAN

## 'What I have just written may perhaps surprise'

Scandals are not always the less destructive for being concealed; merely the threat of public disgrace can end a career. Thus it was with the Reverend Dr Vaughan, one of the most devout and inspirational Head Masters Harrow School has ever known, who, on 16 September 1859, suddenly and bafflingly announced his resignation. Aged just 43 and on the brink of a brilliant career in the Church, he would for the rest of his life refuse every significant offer of ecclesiastical preferment. Here was a man who would have become a bishop, perhaps even Archbishop, a man of transparent religious devotion with a high gift for communication and teaching in an age and a church not noted for piety, who turned away all offers and ended his life in a minor clerical post in Wales.

It was a century before a collection of posthumously published memoirs revealed the truth: that for the rest of his life Vaughan was being blackmailed, threatened with the exposure of a homosexual love affair with one of his pupils.

By 1859 Vaughan had been the Head Master for fifteen years, and in that time transformed the school from a rabble of 69 drunk, stone-throwing pupils to an institution of vast prestige. A former pupil and protégé of the great Dr Arnold at Rugby, Vaughan was appointed at the age of 28, and set about a comprehensive moral, spiritual and financial regeneration of the school.

At its core was the pulpit, from which Vaughan exercised his immense moral authority. 'No preacher has ever so definitely regarded his pulpit as a place from which he could carry out a prolonged and closely articulated course of teaching,' wrote Canon R. R. Williams, fifty years after Vaughan's death. 'His utterances to his boys were marvellously tender, and showed that he understood their weaknesses and temptations,' wrote Frederick How in *Six Great Schoolmasters*. Perhaps this last remark was truer than even its author realised.

When Vaughan quit, numbers at Harrow had increased fivefold, the school was viewed as among the finest in England, and Vaughan's own position as one of the century's great and (in the best sense) pious headmasters was secure. But there was another side to Harrow and another side to Vaughan.

No document better captures the extraordinary, primitive depravity of Victorian public schools than the memoirs of John Addington Symonds. Unpublished in his lifetime – and locked away in the London Library and embargoed for fifty years after his death – they were written, in part, to describe in himself 'the evolution of a somewhat abnormally constituted individual'.

A homosexual man, that is. Symonds was one of the first gay men to recognise himself as such in the modern way: he viewed his homosexuality not as one of those unaccountable things some people sometimes *do*, but as a central description of his own interior self, whether or not accompanied by outward behaviour. 'The unconquerable instinct,' he called it. Our own age often overlooks the relative modernity of the categorising of sexual orientation, as distinguished from practice.

Symonds wrote his memoirs for posterity alone. To have published them in his lifetime would have destroyed his reputation, shamed his family, humiliated his wife and probably led to his arrest – this was 1889, just six years before Wilde's trial and imprisonment for indecency and sodomy. He viewed his book as 'unique, in the disclosure of a type of man who has not yet been classified'. To understand, as Symonds plainly did, not only what he was, but how revolutionary was the way in which he was seeing himself, is evidence of a man of depth and subtlety.

'I am anxious therefore that this document should not perish,' he wrote to his first biographer, who drew on the memoirs without once mentioning their powerful underlying theme.

What Symonds records is the slow development of a homosexual consciousness. From his early childhood fantasies of grappling with naked sailors in Bristol, to a passionate but chaste affair with a chorister during school holidays, through to an altogether more physical relationship at 41 with a 24-year-old Venetian gondolier named Angelo, Symonds charts with candour his progress towards homosexual love.

He had married at the age of 24 and fathered four daughters. It was not until he was 30 that he experienced physical intercourse with another man. Meanwhile although unable fully to desire women he longed to be 'normal'. This conflict – and the mingled terror, fascination and jealousy with which he recognised homosexuality in others – caused the downfall of Dr Vaughan.

At Harrow, where he was a pupil for four years from 1854, Symonds was revolted by the sheer bestiality of the homosexual activity of the boys around him. 'They filled me with disgust and loathing. My school-fellows realised what I had read in Swift about the Yahoos.'

For Symonds, homosexual love was described in Plato's *Symposium* and *Phaedras*: spiritual, idealised, nothing to do with what he witnessed at school. 'The talk in the dormitories was incredibly obscene,' he wrote. 'Here and there one could not avoid seeing acts of onanism, mutual masturbation, the sports of naked boys in bed together.' He recalled some of his contemporaries, such as one Barber: 'He was like a good-natured longimanous ape, gibbering on his perch and playing ostentatiously with a prodigiously developed phallus'; or Cookson, 'a red-faced strumpet, with flabby cheeks and sensual

Reverend Dr Charles Vaughan depicted in *Vanity Fair.*

mouth – the *notissima fossa* of our house'; or the much sought-
after Ainslie, 'whom we dubbed Bum Bathsheba because of his
opulent posterior parts'.

Symonds steered clear of all this. He did develop crushes on
fellow-pupils but was too timid to pursue them. He allowed
himself to talk only of 'the superb athletic beings round me,
whose lives were completely joyous to themselves and satisfying to
aesthetic contemplation'.

Then something happened which brought what had been
concealed out of the shadows and into a harsh light. A note was
intercepted by a form master. It was from one boy to another,
named O'Brien: a handsome youth 'who went by the name of
Leila'.The note informed 'Leila' that a good bed had been made
ready and that he was to meet him later that afternoon.

The master handed over the note to Dr Vaughan, who
summoned all the boys together and condemned the use of
female names. He reprimanded the two boys concerned – with
what young Symonds viewed at the time as a 'very inadequate
form of punishment'. Symonds concluded that Vaughan cannot
have realised the significance of the note, 'and how widespread
was the evil in the school'. But Vaughan realised it all too well.

In Symonds's narrative the 'Leila' affair emerges as a traumatic
episode which 'added to my mental and moral confusion'.
Confusion turned to chaos when in January 1858 Symonds
discovered that his friend Alfred Pretor was having an affair with
their headmaster. Symonds thought Alfred 'a fair scholar, but a
vain and corrupt lad, without intellectual or moral foundation'.
Pretor showed him a series of passionate letters Vaughan had
written him. Symonds read them incredulously.

The effect on him was overwhelming. The disgust he describes
at the revelation was accompanied by a strange, almost
exhilarating – but deeply confusing – recognition that here, in his
own headmaster, was some intimation of something lurking in
Symonds's own mind. 'I was disgusted to find it in a man holding
the highest position of responsibility, consecrated by the Church,
entrusted with the welfare of six hundred youths – a man who had
recently prepared me for confirmation, from whose hands,
kneeling by the side of Alfred Pretor, I received the sacrament,
and whom I had been accustomed to regard as the pattern of my
conduct.'

And yet disgust 'was mitigated by a dumb persistent sympathy. My own inclinations, the form which my erotic idealism had assumed, prevented me from utterly condemning Vaughan.' There was another emotion: Symonds was jealous. He viewed Pretor as 'a physically and emotionally inferior being'. He did not just condemn his head's morals; he condemned 'Vaughan's taste'.

The 'love drama' he saw unfold daily as Pretor showed him the letters Vaughan continued to write him excited his imagination as much as his indignation. From the mass of contradictory emotions this triggered, one prevailed: 'I desired to overcome the malady of my own nature.' Having recognised in Vaughan what he did not wish to acknowledge in himself, Symonds hoped (we may guess) to exorcise it by exposing his headmaster.

Though he may not have known this, the syndrome is common. Almost every gay man has observed how it is often in those whom we suspect to be repressed homosexuals themselves that the most angry or distressed response to homosexuality in others is triggered. Typically, such people are unable to leave the subject alone.

Symonds could not. For the present, however, he did nothing but watch Vaughan. He began to notice behaviour which previously would have signified little to him. Once, when being taught Greek iambics in his study – 'the scene of his clandestine pleasures' – Vaughan 'began softly to stroke my right leg from the knee to the thigh'. Before the year was out Symonds's father had removed him from Harrow, a place he viewed as bad for his son's health, and started him at Oxford. But Symonds kept the letters, some of which he had obtained from Pretor.

At Oxford what he knew continued to disturb and obsess him. His reluctance to expose Vaughan was strong: after all, he 'felt a deep rooted sympathy with Vaughan. If he had sinned, it had been yielding to passions which already mastered me.' By now, Symonds had fallen for the angelic chorister from Bristol Cathedral. And to expose Vaughan would be to betray Pretor's confidence. When in the end he did so, Pretor had not sanctioned this and never forgave him.

But Symonds persuaded himself he had never liked Vaughan, 'a man for whom I felt no love, and who had shown me no special kindness' – sentiments which are belied by letters that Symonds himself wrote home from school, suggesting that Vaughan had indeed been kind to him and that Symonds had at the time been grateful. Now however he worked himself into an indignant fury. He records the anger in his memoirs but it sounds more like self-justification than real rage. 'My blood boiled and my nerves stiffened when I thought what mischief life at Harrow was doing daily to young lads under the autocracy of a hypocrite...The evidence was plain and irrefragable.'

Accordingly – and, as Symonds describes it, virtually unwittingly – he blurted out the story to the Balliol Professor of Classics, John Conington. Apparently shocked, the professor – himself a closet homosexual – advised Symonds to tell his father. From now on Symonds persuaded himself the matter was out of his hands. He returned home to Clifton twice in the summer of 1859 and showed the letters to his father.

Dr Symonds, an eminent surgeon, wrote to Vaughan saying he had proof of his relationship with Pretor but promising not to publicise the scandal if he resigned and never accepted any further preferment in the Church.

Vaughan came to Clifton, inspected the letters and agreed to Dr Symonds's conditions. A few days later Vaughan's wife came to Clifton and literally threw herself at Dr Symonds's feet. 'Would Dr Symonds not withhold the execution of his sentence? Her husband was subject to this weakness, but it had not interfered with his usefulness in the direction of the school at Harrow.'

Though moved Dr Symonds refused to back down. Accordingly in September 1859 Dr Vaughan announced his resignation.

Vaughan offered no hint of the real reason. In a circular to the parents and boys of Harrow he wrote that he had 'resolved, after much deliberation, to take the opportunity of relieving myself from the long pressure of those heavy duties and anxious responsibilities which are inseparable from such an office, even under the most favourable circumstances. With how much reluctance I form and announce such a resolution, it is needless for me to say...'

An inquisitive mind might have noted that his reluctance was expressed with more passion than was his wish to overcome it and retire. Dr Vaughan could not hide his regret. 'How can I sever myself, even in imagination, from this place?' he asked at the last sermon he preached as Head Master. 'How am I to say those last words, Finally, brethren, farewell? I know not ... Three months ago it seemed to be possible: the clearest and most decisive judgement dictated it: but today it is hard to execute ...' Few, if any, in the congregation can have known that the clear and decisive judgement was not his own, but another's.

Symonds had been painfully aware of the moral ambiguities of his treatment of Vaughan.

'Conscience, it is true, supported me. I felt that the course that I followed was right. But I could not shake off the sense that I appeared disloyal to my friends ... I ought to have informed them of the step I meant to take. I suffered deeply in both spirit and in health ... my brain and moral consciousness – the one worn with worrying thought, the other wracked by casuistical doubts – never quite recovered from the weariness of those weeks.'

Strangely but not, for Vaughan, inappropriately, it was from the pulpit that he came closest to an open expression of mental anguish over his homosexuality. Some of his sermons seem to offer the same relief as others seek by writing a private diary. In one, on 'Loneliness', Vaughan talks of 'the sense of sin unconfessed and unforsaken, only felt as a weight, a burden, and a danger!'

Other sermons suggest he was experiencing a very similar struggle to Symonds. 'We must not look in this world for freedom from temptation ... even victory, the victory of years, does not exterminate the foe' – how like Symonds' 'unconquerable instinct' this sounds. And in one poignantly prescient moment, he remarks: 'One man, by a plausible manner eludes for many years the discovery of his wickedness; perhaps he dies with it still hidden.'

The tenderness of such utterances was born not merely of Vaughan's empathy with boys, but from lonely experience. Reading them today one wonders how much of this was a sort of coded message – to nobody, really, or to God alone, for Vaughan would have been mortified if anyone had cracked the code; how much was composed as a poet sometimes composes, in private dialogue with himself, but via the pulpit or printed page; how much might have been intended specially for that minority of boys who were themselves struggling with their homosexuality; and how much was an honest attempt, drawing on his private struggles, to offer useful lessons to a wider audience. Probably his sermons were shaped by each of these purposes. They must at least have given him some relief.

It is worth wondering whether he could have been the tireless, knowing, understanding and loving teacher he was, without that great internal conflict provoked by fear and guilt. How many lives of devoted public service have been fuelled by private frustrations?

Soon after Vaughan's resignation Symonds broke off his relationship with his beloved chorister (Willie). 'I recognised that in my own affection for Willie there was something similar to the passion which had ruined Vaughan.' A cynic might remark that, having destroyed Vaughan he needed to ensure that no similar scandal enveloped himself; but it may also be that Symonds felt he had, in his sacrifice of his old mentor, exorcised something in himself.

John Addington Symonds went on to become one of the most celebrated men of letters of his day. In Vaughan's obituary he was cited as among the distinguished old boys who owed their eminence to Vaughan's brilliance as a headmaster.

It was at first widely assumed that Vaughan's stated reasons for resigning were disingenuous and that the move was designed to pave the way for a luminous ecclesiastical career. If so, his timing – so young and with a formidable reputation already – would have been astute. Almost immediately the Prime Minister, Lord Palmerston, offered him the bishopric of Rochester (later held by Michael Turnbull, p170). Vaughan indicated that he would accept it. On the news the boys of Harrow were granted a half-holiday. But when Dr Symonds heard of Vaughan's intentions he sent him a warning telegraph ordering him to withdraw his acceptance. He did so. The half-holiday was cancelled.

Not long after, Vaughan was offered the bishopric of Worcester, but this time he refused immediately and thereafter turned down every significant offer of preferment. The author of Vaughan's entry in the *Dictionary of National Biography* written not long after his death (and based partly on private information), remarks that Vaughan never discussed his reasons for such self-denial with even his closest friends. 'I was afraid of ambition,' he told them. The truth indeed – if not the whole truth.

Such unworldliness seemed to shape Vaughan as a model of Christian humility. A leading article in *The Times* written to mark his death described him as the 'salt of the church'. 'Few divines of equal gifts and reputation have thought less of self-advancement.' In a church stuffed with factious and ambitious clerics more interested in party than piety, Vaughan was a welcome and outstanding exception. With more Vaughans, suggested *The Times*, the Church of England would have nothing to fear from Roman Catholic attempts to subvert England.

Now it was clear that Vaughan's resignation was not a careerist ploy, many drew similar conclusions. But cynics remained. Symonds records an incident when the Bishop of Oxford, Samuel Wilberforce, approached his friend Hugh Pearson: 'I am certain that Vaughan had some grave reason for leaving Harrow and refusing two mitres. An ugly story must lie behind. If I discover the truth I shall be an enemy.' Pearson denied knowing anything.

A while later the bishop met Pearson again and said he had learned 'the whole dark secret' from a lady he was sitting next to at a dinner party. And what have you done? Pearson asked. 'Oh, I've told the Archbishop of Canterbury and the Prime Minister.'

Although he never accepted a bishopric, Vaughan still exerted enormous influence over the Church. He was appointed Master of the Temple, where he trained scores of priests including a future Archbishop of Canterbury, Edward Benson. He set out his precepts to his ordinands: 'Dwelling among you week by week, living wholly for you, seeking not great things for himself, may he but serve you and eat the bread of quietness in an office which he looks upon as the most delightful and the most honourable in the world!'

Only some years after Dr Symonds's death did Vaughan finally permit himself to accept a relatively minor appointment, as Dean of Llandaff. *The Times* noticed that this was 'to a very slight extent a departure from the ideal which he set out for himself' at the Temple – but only the churlish could begrudge. In 1882 he was appointed to the court position of Deputy Clerk of the Closet. It would be half a century before that term took on the second meaning so apt in poor Dr Vaughan's case. He died in 1897 at the age of 82, outliving Symonds by five years.

On his deathbed Vaughan gave strict instructions that no biography of him should ever be sanctioned; he also instructed (albeit forty years too late) that all his correspondence should be destroyed – and at the time this seemed to the world just another example of his humility and self-effacement. He could not have known that the autobiography of the man who destroyed him would rise to the surface, when its author's embargo was finally lifted in 1977.

Phyllis Grosskurth, Symonds's biographer, edited what Symonds described as 'this sterile piece of self-delineation'. Symonds thought it would never be printed. Or did he? And, if he really wanted to erase the record, why did he write – or why, having written, did he not himself destroy – this account? The memoirs were published by Hutchinson in 1984.

Symonds seemed to want somebody outside himself to understand. Whether he had much thought for Dr Vaughan in this, or whether it was himself he wanted to explain, is hard to know. But the consequence of publication was a new understanding of Dr Vaughan.

The trail of events which brought these truths to the surface was an inherently unlikely one. They emerged somewhat by chance. One wonders how many thousands of comparable cases through history lie unknown and now unknowable: suppressed chapters in a book of which this sad episode forms the isolated fragment which sees the light.

To find Dr Vaughan's story is like surveying the ashes after a time of book-burning – to catch a single charred but half-legible page, blowing in the wind. Of what great library might this be a part?

# WRANGLING PARSONS

## EDWARD DRAX FREE

## A Shoot-out at the Rectory?

Parish priests, like drains, are most likely to be noticed when they go wrong. They hardly attract attention so long as they turn up as required to take Sunday services, bury, baptise and betroth, refrain from molesting or assaulting parishioners and in old age depart the ministry with good grace to make way for a young man to continue the cycle.

The Reverend Dr Edward Drax Free was incapable of any of these. In consequence he attracted a good deal of attention.

Few clergymen can have had such bizarre and difficult relations with their parishioners as the rector of Sutton. Dr Free slept with, physically assaulted, robbed and insulted the people supposedly under his care. He did not baptise or bury them – except for an inordinate fee. For months at a time he did not take church services. He reared cattle in the church yard and sheltered them in the church porch. With the assistance of a succession of housekeepers he fathered at least five illegitimate children. He so subverted, upturned and inverted the entire function of a country rector that – as the Bishop of Lincoln put it to his peers in the Upper House at the height of the crisis – Sutton was returned to a state of primitive heathenism.

Of course the fates eventually caught up with Dr Free, plucked him from his throne, reduced him to beggary and despatched him to the hereafter with the rogue wheel of a careering chariot. But not before he had raised hell on earth. Pursued through the courts by his own churchwarden (who dedicated much of his life and capital to ridding Sutton of its rector), Dr Free was denounced by *The Times* as 'likely to be celebrated in history' for

the sheer, bloody-minded resilience he displayed in holding onto
office. So determined was he to stay put that – uniquely for a rural
village in late Georgian Bedfordshire – his ministry all but ended
in a shoot-out at the rectory.

The scale of Dr Free's villainy is captured in a document at
Lambeth Palace: a list of charges including fornication,
drunkenness, lewdness, profligacy and a fair proportion of the
remaining misdemeanours it is possible for a clergyman to
commit. The sheet is five foot high, and two feet wide – ten
square feet filled, in impeccable copperplate hand, with the
crimes of one man. To provide the reader with a sense of its
magnitude Lambeth Palace were kind enough to allow me to be
photographed standing next to it. The effect can be judged in the
picture section.

Edward Drax Free arrived in Sutton in 1808 aged 43 to the
delight of the Fellows of St John's College, Oxford which he had
left. For years they had despaired of the man, a college fellow and
former Dean of Arts.

At Oxford Dr Free had made his presence unbearable by
innumerable little acts of belligerence: college records show, for
example, that he had been 'guilty of violence towards the bursar'.
A short stint as the vicar of St Giles, Oxford, just up the road from
St John's, had provided temporary relief, but he was soon kicked
out after the churchwardens clamoured for his removal, and Free
was returned to college. The living of Sutton, rather further from
the Bodleian Library, offered a solution. Confined in a mediaeval
quad there is only so much damage a man can do. Dr Free
realised his full destructive potential once released in – and upon
– an English village.

It is impossible to retell Dr Free's shambolic career in Sutton as
a narrative. But the trail of human devastation he created is amply
recorded in another remarkable document in Lambeth – a book
of depositions made in preparation for Free's trial. Here we hear
the laments of the people who suffered: his parishioners.

It seems from these that what struck even the most casual visitor
to Sutton was the squalor around All Saints church. Free turned the
churchyard into a farmyard, as one deponent, William Hale,
recorded. 'It was quite a common thing to see the horses running
about and the pigs rooting up the graves.' Hale describes the horses,
pigs and cows which were unwelcome mourners at his father's

funeral. Free kept sheep in the church porch – penning them in with a hurdle – which was often strewn with dung and straw.

Free viewed the whole of Sutton – humans, animals, buildings and land – as potential sources of revenue. He cut down 300 oak trees on glebe land and sold the wood. He stripped lead off the roof of the chancel and sold it. He collected tithes due to him with a zeal which bordered on the inhuman: the octogenarian Robert Oake had 'a little bit of garden where he grows a few potatoes and turnips' and Free claimed part of these.

One of his parishioners, Phoebe Smith, was a poor, illiterate widow (in the book of depositions she signs her name with a cross), but her statement is typical. She often saw Dr Free's cow in the churchyard, as well as his sow, 'and she cried to see that sow nuzzling about the graves, because she had two children buried there . . . she cannot at all say where one of them lies as the mound is gone and all about there the ground is as flat as if there had never been a grave there at all.' Once she saw a hole in a grave – dug by pigs – 'such as that she could just see the coffin that lay in it'. She had seen dung in the church porch.

When Mrs Smith arrived at the funeral to bury her child she was greeted by the clerk, who demanded four shillings. Free insisted that the money be paid before the service could be carried out but Smith did not have the money. Though Dr Free relented and performed the burial his clerk followed the Smiths home to collect the debt.

And this was as nothing to the experiences of John and Mary Saville, who lost a child on a Saturday 'after a sharp illness'. On Monday (by which time the child was already starting to 'smell strong') they sent a woman to ask Dr Free to bury it the following day. He refused, apparently because the person sent 'was an impertinent woman for speaking to him in the street'. By Tuesday the corpse was 'in such a state that it was not fit to be kept any longer', and the dead child's grandfather pleaded with Free to bury the corpse that afternoon. 'Not till tomorrow at two o'clock,' said Free. The same day the coffin burst. Thereafter, 'it became and continued so offensive that they hardly knew how to bear it, or what to do, pinched for room as they were'. Finally, the funeral was performed on Wednesday.

'He has a swaggering way with him that is not like any other clergyman,' recalled Saville. 'He damned people continually

speaking to them and of them,' said another villager in his
deposition. 'The same also he used to his cattle when driving
them, especially if he was a little tipsy, then he damnes them as of
course.'

Not surprisingly, parishioners began to shun church services.
Robert Oake said that he only went to church in Sutton because
he was too infirm to walk to a nearby village. 'A few Sundays back
there was no one there but [Oake] and the Clerk, and after
waiting a little while Doctor Free said as there was no
congregation he should go.' When people did turn up they found
he galloped through the service. The speed with which Free could
despatch Evensongs was perhaps his only redeeming virtue as a
vicar.

There was certainly no danger of having to endure an
interminable sermon – or sometimes, indeed, any sermon. Dr
Free would stay away from Sutton for months at a time avoiding
his creditors. These absences did not prevent him locking his
churchwardens out of their church. During one feud they had to
hold meetings in the porch.

Though an unattractive man, notorious for excessive swearing
and drinking, he had remarkable success with women. This may
have had less to do with hidden personal charms than a rather
forward manner. Dr Free was not afraid of rejection. A succession
of housekeepers turned up to the Sutton rectory, and soon found
that part of the job description was to act as the rector's
concubine. The point was made forcibly by the location of their
bedroom: next door to the rector's, with an unlockable
interconnecting door. It was reinforced by his habit of walking
around in a dressing gown, which – as one girl stated – 'he used
to throw open so as to show his bosom, which was disgusting'.
She saw that he had a nasty skin disease. When another housekeeper, Marie Mackenzie, answered Free's bell, she found him
'stripped naked below the waist'. 'He would then ask her to lie
with him: he did so continuously.'

Of six housekeepers employed, four were for a while his
mistress, producing five children, most of whom died young, or
were stillborn. Only one child was alive for certain at the time of
his trial. When Marie Mackenzie miscarried it was 'occasioned by
the virulence of Dr Free who smacked her down on the stairs in
the passage of his house'. This led to an indictment at the Bedford

assizes, although after interminable legal wrangling (one of Free's specialities) he escaped prosecution. Another relationship ended with the 25-year-old Maria Crook smashing the windows of the rectory before leaving to give birth to Free's child in a parish workhouse in Hanover Square.

It says something about the social hierarchy of early nineteenth-century rural England that in spite of this flagrant and persistent offence to the sensibilities of the ordinary people of Sutton it was not his debauchery, his neglect of his parishioners, his assault of tradesmen, his threatening of churchwardens with a horsewhip and farmers with a hammer, or his unorthodox farming techniques which proved Dr Free's undoing, but his decision to pick a fight with the local squire. As Dr Outhwaite suggests in his splendid monograph on Dr Free, there was something admirably egalitarian in his rudery. Free did not recognise class: he treated everyone with contempt. That included the eighth baronet, Sir Montagu Roger Burgoyne whom Dr Free attempted to prosecute for failing to attend his church services.

Edward Drax Free infused this small battle with something of the drama of the Holy Roman Empire.

It was merely the portrayal on a parochial canvas of the great battle between church and state which forms one of the magnificent enduring themes of history: the Emperor Henry abasing himself in the snow before Pope Gregory at Canossa, the papal exile in Avignon, Henry VIII snatching monastic property for himself, popes excommunicating not just kings, but entire kingdoms.

In this case it was clear (though no one knew quite why) that Dr Free wanted nothing less than the total humiliation of the principal landowner of Sutton. In March 1817 Dr Free brought a prosecution against Burgoyne at the Bedfordshire Lent Assizes, citing an Elizabethan statute which made non-attendance at divine services illegal. He accused Burgoyne of failing to attend church in the preceding nineteen months, thereby 'spreading contagion' around the country.

Under this law, introduced to force Catholics to attend Church of England services and a dead letter for more than a century, individuals found guilty were fined £20 for each month they had avoided services. Dr Free was therefore demanding that Burgoyne pay him £380. He produced one witness who insisted that she had never seen Burgoyne in church. On closer investigation it transpired that she was one of Free's mistresses. In his defence Burgoyne insisted that the reason he did not attend Dr Free's services was that there were rarely any services to attend. When they had taken place, and when there had been a sermon, it had consisted of a tirade of personal invective against himself.

Burgoyne was found not guilty. He died shortly after the trial, but in his place Free had to contend with the squire's uncle, also Montagu Burgoyne, who was of a more vigorous constitution. He became the animating spirit behind huge and strenuous legal attempts to oust Free.

It was a very personal campaign. In 1818, when Montagu Burgoyne's eldest daughter died, he had decided to have her interred in a new family vault in Sutton church. As ever, Free treated death as a potential gold mine, and charged 100 guineas for the vault. The experience seems to have helped Burgoyne bond with the villagers. Although at first not even a resident of Sutton, he managed to get himself elected as churchwarden, in order to fight the rector. He gathered much of the evidence against Free – even advertising in London papers to track down the various women he had debauched.

But Free proved a wily adversary. Each time he was brought to court (charged on various counts of immorality and lewdness) he insisted that the court had no jurisdiction in his case. It was not until June 1829, a full five years after Burgoyne commenced proceedings, that a trial actually took place, in the Court of Arches. Defending himself (by now no one would act for him) Dr Free heaped abuse on Burgoyne. In a final flourish he announced that he intended to publish a pamphlet which he would call *Burgoyniana, or Anecdotes of the Burgoyne Family.* It never appeared.

'Slight deviations in morality from the infirmity of human nature might be punished by admonition,' lamented Sir John Nicholl, the judge at Free's trial, 'but after this history has gone forth no hope must be entertained that the respect can be restored which ought to exist betwixt parishioners and their clergyman.' Dr Free was sentenced to deprivation from the living of Sutton, and ordered to pay costs.

No one expected Dr Free to go quietly: he succeeded in postponing the execution of his sentence of deprivation until it was finally confirmed by the Court of Delegates in February 1830.

Free decided not to recognise the verdict, and barricaded himself into his rectory with his housekeeper and a gun. The Archdeacon of Bedford (admitted as a sort of peace emissary) saw that the house had been stripped bare, its contents sold. But nobody could persuade the deprived rector to go.

Dr Free started shooting from the rectory. The Sequestrator considered storming the place but 'dreading the commission of murder' concluded that the only way to get rid of him was to blockade the rectory and starve him out. 'This they endured for ten days, when this unhappy man was compelled by hunger to quit the house,' wrote a triumphant Montagu Burgoyne. Free went to a nearby village, and then walked to London, because no one would take him there.

Thereafter Free's fate was obscure and wretched. Hoping that he could live off his old Oxford college, he petitioned to be reinstated as a Fellow claiming that the college had a duty to provide for him. In November 1838, Free complained that he had no food, no bed, and was 'in a condition of utter destitution and starvation'. 'I have no bed to lie on, and have been for three days without food,' *The Times* reported him as saying in January 1839.

And then on Friday 16 February 1843 a wheel flew off the carriage of Mr Edward Rolls, of Rolls and Co., varnishing manufacturers. Mr Rolls was thrown clear but still holding the reins was dragged along by the horse. Somehow the Reverend Dr Edward Drax Free found himself in the middle of all this. He was run over. Taken to the Royal Free Hospital he lived until two o'clock the following morning. A nurse sat with him, and observed that 'sometimes he appeared to be speaking, but she could not make out what he said'. An inquest was held but the mishap was judged 'perfectly accidental'.

Many will have felt that the cartwheel came 40 years too late.

# THE CURSE OF LINCOLN

## Britain's Unhappiest Cathedral

When Dr Edward King was appointed Bishop of Lincoln in 1885 he was told the clergy in his diocese could be divided into three categories: those who were about to go out of their minds; those who had already gone out of their minds; and those who had no minds to go out of. The remark showed both prescience and a firm grasp of history, for Lincoln has a troubled past. Perhaps it is the fault of the Cathedral's patron saint and founder, St Hugh. He set a peculiar precedent when, on a visit to Fécamp abbey in France, he gnawed two fingers from the mummified hand of Mary Magdalene, seized them as relics and galloped back to Lincoln.

The first cathedral to be built in Lincoln was destroyed by an earthquake and some might say it would have been better to have left the rubble undisturbed. The present Cathedral, built in the thirteenth century, was almost immediately ransacked by soldiers of King John; it has since been nearly destroyed by fire three times and in the last century its spires collapsed. Foolishly, they have recently been restored.

The second cleric to occupy the bishop's throne, Bishop Bloet, was described as 'a most profligate, indolent and licentious man'. A fifteenth-century cleric, Dean Mackworth, had a habit of attending chapter meetings backed by armed men to stop rivals challenging his behaviour. In 1780 the bishop, Dr Thurlow, was pursued by an angry mob and forced to flee dressed as a woman.

According to local tradition, Lincoln's ill-fortune springs from an imp, sent by Satan to wreak havoc and turned to stone by angels for trying to trip up the bishop and assault the dean. The malignant imp, now hidden among carvings in the Cathedral's masonry, has been blamed for many of the Cathedral's subsequent woes. He has certainly been active in the twentieth century.

In the 1920s, the odd affair of Archdeacon John Wakeford filled first Lincoln's church consistory court and then the front pages of the popular press (see p86), destroying Wakeford's career and consigning him to insanity. And in the 1990s, Brandon Jackson, Dean of Lincoln, and his adversary the sub-dean, Canon Rex Davis, stumbled down a similar path, to the dismay of the Archbishop of Canterbury, the growls of *Daily Telegraph* leader writers and the secret pleasure of seasoned watchers of clerical misdemeanour.

In the late 1980s and early 1990s Lincoln became a sort of cathedral-equivalent of a road-accident black spot. Or, in the words of the Archbishop of Canterbury, who tried, and very conspicuously failed, to find a solution, 'a scandal dishonouring the name of the Lord'. The Cathedral staff became almost entirely dysfunctional. The Bishop of Lincoln threatened to resign and at Christmas 1996 refused to preach in his own cathedral. He lived next door to the dean, but the two spoke only rarely. The dean and the sub-dean spoke not at all and communicated only by written notes. A verger, said to have had a failed affair with the dean, became involved in a consistory court hearing, lost, and left first Lincoln and then the Church of England.

The local police and a set of counsellors brought in to clear the air got nowhere.

The dean, Brandon Jackson, without actually pointing a finger at the imp (though he supported a campaign which called for the figure to be hacked from the Cathedral's stonework) has spoken darkly of 'currents of conflict, hate and evil that have been swirling around [the] cathedral for centuries'. He suggested on national radio that the Cathedral be closed for six months, for exorcism.

This dispute began in 1988 when the Cathedral Chapter, in an attempt to raise funds for restoration work, took its copy of the *Magna Carta* to Australia. The document was set up in a stall in Brisbane at the World Expo88 and, in all, 900,000 people queued to see it. But when, at the end of three months, the donation box was opened and the money counted, it contained £938, or just over one-tenth of a penny per visitor. Had the imp flown to the antipodes? Lincoln Cathedral lost £56,000; the Australian government absorbed further losses of about £579,000.

In 1989, to sort out the muddle arising from this disaster, the Prime Minister Margaret Thatcher appointed Brandon Jackson as

Dean. Jackson recalled that 'Margaret Thatcher told him to "go and sort it out, get rid of those dreadful Canons."' 'I don't know the man, but I know of him. There will be blood on the carpet at Lincoln before he's finished,' she said of her appointment at the time.

She was right. A low-church evangelical Christian, Jackson had built a reputation as a godly trouble-shooter at Bradford Cathedral and on Yorkshire TV – where he once had his own religious chat show. From the start he was out of place in Lincoln, a cathedral where High Anglicanism was part of the natural order.

The sub-dean, Canon Rex Davis, took particular umbrage at the new arrival. It was he who had organised the trip to Australia, and travelled there with his family. When Jackson provided material for an explosive article in the *Church Times* about the Magna Carta exhibition, the split between the two men became both public and irreparable. The bishop, the Right Reverend Robert Hardy, held an inquiry – or 'visitation' – into the trip, which censured Canon Davis and three other canons. Brandon Jackson promptly called in the police, a move which can only have been intended to inflame the situation.

'I have found it virtually impossible to work with you. Let's face it, we have both found a match for one another; you are not going to give way to me and I am no pushover for you', Jackson wrote in a memo to Davis (which was later leaked). 'You are now in a very difficult position . . . You may think that if you keep your head down for long enough it may all pass over. It will not. The matter has got to be resolved.'

It was not resolved. The police found no grounds for prosecution, and, in the vain hope that the Cathedral Chapter might be pacified, Bishop Hardy sent Dr Jackson and his four fellow canons to group-therapy sessions. The counsellors, led by a local university professor, tried their best. Jackson's enemies forced themselves to smile.

'Normally the Chapter insists on referring to me as "Mr Dean". But in the group it was "Oh, Brandon" this, and "Oh, Brandon" that. They were so nice and friendly. Absolute bosh!' Jackson said later. The therapists' report pointed to 'massive unconscious forces' and suggested that the rival groups were in mental and physical danger. Science had no more success than religion.

Cathedral services conducted by the squabbling clerics soon came to resemble political hustings. When Jackson took offence to the presence of a life-sized golden statue of a man, believing it to border on the profane, the statue was moved to precisely the spot where he liked to pray before a service. This ensured that every time he raised his eyes he would be confronted with a set of gilded male genitalia.

So unbearable did the tension become that the bishop took the extraordinary step of urging the entire Chapter to resign. No one did, of course. This exposed one of the idiosyncrasies of English cathedrals: a bishop, or even an archbishop, cannot dismiss a cathedral dean, provost, canon, rector or vicar unless convicted by a church court of 'conduct unbecoming a clerk in holy orders' or by a secular court of a criminal offence.

Perhaps it was more than coincidence, then, that in 1994 Brandon Jackson learned that he was to be investigated after allegations of an affair with a verger named Verity Freestone. Jackson was not surprised to learn that the bishop had ruled there was enough evidence for the case to go before a consistory court.

Described in the *Daily Mail* as 'a large, lumpy woman', Miss Freestone had confided in the Precentor of Lincoln (the post once held by Wakeford) that in 1993 she and Jackson had conducted a brief and sexually disappointing affair. The allegations became public in March 1995. Dr Jackson went before his congregation to deny them. An indication of the level of solidarity he could expect from fellow members of the Chapter was that Canon Brian Hebblethwaite chose the moment to preach a sermon on selfishness, lust, and 'base desires'.

The trial was held in a former lunatic asylum. There were some who considered that such a setting, chosen by Bishop Hardy, lacked solemnity. Others found it peculiarly fitting.

In court Verity Freestone claimed the alleged affair had begun soon after she had resigned as a verger because she found the job too difficult. Depressed, she had turned to Jackson for help. On one occasion, she said, 'we hugged and he put his hands under my chin and gave me a full kiss and I felt very shaken. He said: "Don't forget I love you".' The dean – an avid marathon runner – had turned up at her house in running shorts and clutching a bottle of wine, while his wife was away.

He had told her (she claimed) that she had 'come-to-bed' eyes;

and to bed was where they went. But according to Freestone, attempts at intercourse failed.

Jackson denied that there was truth in anything Freestone had said. The only thing he would admit to was that he may have blown on the back of Freestone's neck during a procession in the Cathedral. There was nothing sexual in this, just a form of 'rebellion' against the stuffiness of such occasions. 'I did the same to the chief verger.'

The defence had indicated a history of counselling and anti-depressants on Freestone's part, and the court accepted Anne Rafferty QC's defence that Freestone's allegations were 'pathetic fantasies'. The Very Reverend Brandon Jackson was acquitted. Freestone later announced that she would never step through the doors of Lincoln Cathedral again, and that she had lost her faith.

Matters in the Close deteriorated. On the night of his acquittal Jackson appeared on television. 'It seems that they want to have a public execution of the dean. Next they'll be selling ice cream and popcorn and tickets for the show.'

For the next two years the dispute clattered on. Lincoln, dubbed 'Britain's unhappiest cathedral', was now a regular feature in the broadsheet papers. In December 1995, cathedral staff signed a statement calling for the squabble to cease, complaining that the church had become 'a place of ridicule'. At Christmas, the city's mayor pleaded with the clergy to make up. In 1996, the Archbishop of Canterbury, Dr Carey, called for the resignation of both Brandon Jackson and Rex Davis. They ignored him.

'Wherever I have gone, people have spoken about the scandal. I have felt it very deeply. We just cannot allow this to carry on being a cancer in the body of Lincoln,' said an exasperated Dr Carey.

Another year passed. Then Brandon Jackson surrendered, announcing, in July 1997, that he had decided to resign from the Cathedral 'specifically at the request of the Archbishop of Canterbury and at quite some personal cost'. The news broke on the day Verity Freestone was ordered by a judge at Lincoln County Court to pay, at £4 a month, Jackson's £5,125.71 legal bill, an order with which it will take her 107 years to comply.

Jackson departed Lincoln. 'It has become increasingly clear to me that I have been at the wicket too long. There is no chance at all of a result, and, therefore, the only sensible thing to do is to declare the innings closed. There are other grounds to play on with more favourable wickets, with runs to be scored and games to be won. Future prospects are exciting,' Jackson told the press. Why he chose to draw his metaphor from cricket is unclear. Kick-boxing or trench warfare might have served his subject better.

Jackson's enemies at Lincoln suggested that he had been induced to leave by the offer of a six-figure retirement package. This was untrue. He was awarded the purely formal title of Dean Emeritus and a six-month sabbatical. Accepting Jackson's resignation the Archbishop of Canterbury made it clear that the affair was not settled. 'My request to the sub-dean to consider his position stands, and I ask him to search his conscience, ' he wrote pointedly, of Rex Davis.

'I have searched my conscience with some vigour,' responded Davis. The search, apparently, yielded no reason to depart. As I write, he remains in his post. So does the imp.

# MESSIAHS

## ABIEZER COPPE

## 'Hills! Mountains! Cedars! Mighty men! Your breath is in your nostrils!'

Every so often another claimed Messiah visits us. The Reverend Prince in these pages (see p127) is one. David Icke, the former television sports presenter and green activist, another. England in 1649 – a year of general anarchy, when Charles I was beheaded and Cromwell's puritanical new order inaugurated – was host to one of the strangest: Abiezer Coppe, who ruined it all by eventually changing his mind and turning mortal.

Coppe started promisingly. After leaving Oxford University without a degree (his studies were interrupted by the Civil War) he became first a Presbyterian and then an Anabaptist minister, during which time he claimed to have baptised seven thousand people. But in 1649, in his native Warwickshire, he appears to have gone mad. He started to preach stark naked in the daytime, sleeping with members of his congregation by night. 'I so strangely spake and acted I knew not what,' he would later remark of these days, from the calm of Newgate prison. 'For I was (really, in very deed) besides myself.'

Coppe was at the forefront of a strange, short-lived religious group which others called the Ranters. One historian has described the Ranters as the 'extreme left wing' of the revolutionary movement. They emerged after Cromwell had crushed the Leveller movement, which advocated an ultra-radical republicanism. Stripped of this political platform the Ranters were pushed to an even more extreme position, from which they urged that revolution be taken to its logical conclusion, rejecting all law and morality.

From the title page of a contemporary pamphlet denouncing the Ranters.
'I have concubines without number,' Coppe had declared. 'I can if it be my will,
kiss and hug Ladies, and love my neighbours wife as my selfe, without sin.'

A key Ranter belief was that there was no sin. They also believed in total sexual liberty. Coppe happily subscribed to these views. What distinguished him from other Ranters, however, was his belief that he had been chosen by God to announce to the 'Great Ones of the World' that they had better change their ways – or else. 'Go up to London, to London, that great City, write, write, write,' God had, it was claimed, told Coppe. The result was a book called *The Fiery Flying Roll*, subtitled *A word from the Lord to all the Great Ones of the Earth: Being the last WARNING PIECE at the Dreadfull day of JUDGEMENT*. This was published on 1 January 1650, in London.

Inspiration had come after a vision in which a naked Coppe was taken on a four-day trip to hell and back. In his preface Coppe describes what was an unusual and clearly very painful process of literary production. 'And behold I writ, and lo a hand was sent to me, and a roll of a book was therein, which this fleshly hand would have put wings to, before the time. Whereupon it was snatched out of my hand, & the Roll thrust into my mouth; and I eat it up, and filled my bowels with it, where it was as bitter as worm-wood; and it lay broiling, and burning in my stomack, till I brought it forth in this forme. And now I sent it flying to thee, with my heart, and all.' Heaven be praised that one is, oneself, less driven as a writer.

Much of the ensuing work is pure gibberish. 'Hills! Mountains! Cedars! Mighty men! Your breath is in your nostrils!' declares Coppe at one baffling moment. But there also runs through the book the authentic voice of religious and political radicalism, directed particularly to the clergy ('the ministers, fat parsons, Vicars, Lecturers &c.' who serve Christ only 'to maintaine their pride, paunches, and purses'). Coppe also calls for the 'Great Ones' to abase themselves before thieves, beggars, harlots and publicans. Occasionally God (speaking through Coppe: it is often hard to tell who is supposed to be talking) will single out one of the lowly as in particular need of help – 'such as poor despised Maul of Dedington in Oxonshire'.

What really excited the indignation (and imagination) of those opposed to Ranters in general and Coppe in particular was their disregard for morality and authority. This was at the centre of Coppe's theology: that as part of God's divine reconstruction of the world, to be achieved through the continuation of the revolution, he demanded the subversion of all 'honourable' things. Honourable things were in fact corrupt and hypocritical. 'Elderships, Pastorships, Fellowships, Churches, Ordinances, Prayers &c. Holiness, Righteousness, Religions of all sorts...' were part of the conspiracy of Honour. Therefore, believed Coppe, they had to be 'confounded' by things considered 'base' by traditional authority. The thesis is not without interest.

Indeed it proved too interesting. Honour included sexual honour. 'I have chosen, and cannot be without BASE things, to confound some in mercy, some in judgement, though also I have concubines without number, which I cannot be without,' he declares. 'I can if it be my will, kisse and hug Ladies, and love my neighbours wife as my selfe, without sin.'

Upon the publication of *A Fiery Flying Roll* Coppe was arrested and imprisoned. A month later Parliament ordered all copies to be seized and burned by the hangman, and in August passed an Act against the Ranters. According to the official *Die Veneris* for 1 February 1649:

Several Passages in a Book printed, entitled *A Fiery Flying Roll*, composed by one *Coppe* were this day read.

*Resolved by Parliament* That the book entitled *A Fiery Flying Roll* composed by one *Coppe* and all printed copies thereof, be burnt by the hand of the Hangman in the New Palace Yard at Westminster, the Exchange, in Cheapside and at the market-place in Southwark.

*Ordered by the Parliament* That the Sargeant at Arms do forthwith cause diligent search to be made in all places, where any of the said Blasphemous Books entitled *A Fiery Flying Roll* composed by one Coppe, are or may be suspected to be, and to seize them, and cause the same to be burnt at the places appointed. And that all persons who have any of the said Books in their custody, do cause the same to be burnt at the places aforesaid.

The order was flouted. The British Library has *three* copies of *A Fiery Flying Roll*.

At first Coppe clung to his views. When brought before

Parliament's Committee of Examinations in October the *Weekly Intelligencer* reported that he 'disguised himself into a madnesse, flinging apples and pears about the roome'. After languishing in prison for a few more months he published *A Remonstrance of the sincere and zealous protestation of Abiezer Coppe* in January 1651, appealing to Parliament to free him and partially retracting his views. He also denied rumours that he had ever gone to bed with two women in Coventry. Parliament was unmoved and Coppe remained locked up.

In May, thoroughly fed up with prison life, he published *Coppe's Return to the Wayes of Truth*, in which he declares 'mine UNDERSTANDING is returned unto me'. At great length he refutes all the errors attributed to him. He also takes the trouble to deny (what in fact seems entirely probable, given his earlier remarks on concubines) that he had anything to do with the numerous children whose mothers were claiming him as the father. 'Some of them (indeed) look somewhat like my children,' he concedes, 'but I will not be so full of foolish pity, as to spare them.' And just to make sure the message has been taken, he adds: 'I will turn them out of doors, and starve them to death.' Parliament seems to have been most impressed by such robust language and Coppe was released.

Soon after, Coppe changed his name to Dr Higham and moved to Barnelms in Surrey, where he would occasionally preach. Not everyone was convinced that Coppe had reformed. When he preached a recantation sermon the Reverend Tickell subjected it to close analysis, and published an 80-page critique expressing doubts that Coppe's essential views were not still those of a Ranter. But the last published writing from Coppe is a poem on virtue entitled *A character of a true Christian*. It is dull enough to suggest that the author had returned to Christian orthodoxy.

Coppe died in August 1672 and was buried in Surrey under the name of Dr Higham. His time in the limelight was brief, spectacular but ultimately ineffectual. Still, to come back from Divinity and live to tell the tale is unusual. Abiezer Coppe founded a career, fame and an income on asserting a set of claims, and then a second career on retracting them. In our own day only Germaine Greer has achieved this.

# HENRY JAMES PRINCE AND
# JOHN HUGH SMYTH-PIGOTT

## 'The Lord hath need of £50.
## The Spirit would have this made
## known to you. Amen.'

One consequence of believing yourself to be the Messiah is a failure of irony; and a consequence of believing yourself to be in the presence of the Messiah seems to be a failure of the ordinary critical faculties. The Reverend Henry James Prince was far too absurd to sense his own absurdity, his supporters too infatuated to raise even an eyebrow. Even among critics, absolutism seemed to kill levity, for critics hated him as passionately as followers adored him.

Was there nobody to laugh? The man was the Son of God – or the work of Satan. That he might just be a colossal joke occurred at first to few.

Having declared himself to be the Messiah on New Year's Day 1846, Mr Prince, an ordained Anglican priest who in spite of everything was never unfrocked, cocooned himself from the world in a large house in a small Somerset village surrounded by devoted worshippers. Most of them failed to see the joke even after Prince – who had declared himself immortal – died. They buried him standing up in order to facilitate his resurrection.

He was succeeded by the Reverend John Hugh Smyth-Pigott who was also absurd. He, too, claimed to be the Messiah; he, too, died. In all, the joke lasted over a hundred years without many getting it. Even after Smyth-Pigott's death in 1927, his followers lingered (for they had been told that they, too, were immortal) waiting as they grew old for something to happen until the last died in 1958.

The Agapemone, the mansion which Prince built for himself and his followers in the village of Spaxton in Somerset, was a considerable folly and a great Victorian scandal as well as a joke.

Today the phenomenon would be described as a religious cult. Under the mesmeric influence of Prince's personality many were persuaded to part with their money, sever themselves from their families and withdraw from the world into the splendour of the Agapemone – the Greek word which translates as 'Abode of Love' – where they awaited the Day of Judgement. As with so many cults the problem facing outraged relatives and campaigners was that adherents appeared to be lucid and there by choice; they could not be shown to be imprisoned or insane.

But from behind the forbidding walls of the Agapemone stories of sexual abandon crept out, many unprovable and some, no doubt, fanciful. One had it that Prince would place his female followers on a revolving stage which the menfolk would spin and, like some human wheel of fortune, whichever lady landed opposite Prince when the wheel stopped turning would for that week be 'the Bride', or 'Mrs Prince'. This was sexual roulette on an impressive scale. There were darker rumours of the ceremonial deflowering of virgins in the chapel.

The public were entertained by press stories of dramatic escape attempts, kidnappings and even full-scale assaults launched by disgruntled former inmates. It was ludicrous stuff made doubly so by the high seriousness with which the Agapemonites took themselves. Moralists were appalled that in England a man could make blasphemous claims and live like an oriental despot with impunity and – worse – with so many pretty girls.

Prince was either completely self-deluded or a splendid fraud. The luxury and self-indulgence which characterised his life suggest the latter. Local tradesmen did well out of Spaxton's Second Coming and humoured him by addressing their bills to 'My Lord, the Agapemone'. Using the modern arguments with which we deck our defence of the monarchy, he could have been defended as a substantial bringer-in of tourist revenue for the local economy. Prince travelled through Spaxton and surrounding villages in a carriage attended by outriders, protected by bloodhounds and preceded by a man dressed in liveried purple who announced his arrival by calling out, 'Blessed is he who cometh in the name of the Lord!' At the Great Exhibition of 1851 he turned up in a carriage purchased from the dowager Queen Adelaide, wearing scarlet robes lined with white ermine, topped with a crown.

The house he built in Spaxton was surrounded by high walls designed both to keep strangers from coming in and (it was said, but never proved) the inmates from getting out. He lived with his female followers; male devotees were relegated to cottages on the estate.

Prince insisted on being addressed as 'Beloved'. Over the years he produced a succession of unreadable tracts and pamphlets with titles such as *The Shutters Taken down from the Windows of Heaven, or, A Hook in the Nose of Leviathan*. His fantasies were internally consistent. When he made one of his followers pregnant he blamed the Devil.

To read history cold is to gain no sense of how compelling Prince must have seemed to his followers. Why did anybody *believe* him? Yet many did. Perfectly sensible men and women, people quite capable of inspecting a yard of cloth for imperfections or bargaining realistically over the price of a horse, people who before the cult swept them up had ordered their own and their families' lives in small aspects and large without evidence of undue credulity or emotional instability, suddenly seemed to lose all their judgement.

What a pity it is that so few ever try to describe how it felt to be swept up in such mass hysteria! A judge (as we shall see later) found it strange that any rational mind could be 'so weak and degraded' as to believe another's claim to divinity. But the judge was a Christian.

It all started in Wales, where Prince was a theological student in the late 1830s and gathered around himself a group of fanatical evangelists, some of whom later formed the nucleus of the Church of the Agapemone. As a curate in the the small village of Charlinch in Somerset, just down the track from Spaxton, he came quickly into conflict with the church authorities after causing havoc by dividing his congregation into the saved and the damned. 'Husbands threatened to murder their wives, and wives threatened to forsake their husbands,' Prince wrote, apparently with pride, in his pamphlet, *The Charlinch Revival*.

Barred from preaching by the Bishop of Bath and Wells and dismissed from Charlinch, Prince, and the Reverend Samuel Starky (his rector in Charlinch, won over to Prince's ministry) toured the towns of the south of England with the message that the Day of the Lord was nigh. Just how nigh, Prince showed on 1

January 1846. At a tea meeting in a Weymouth inn he announced his own divinity to a small crowd of followers. Some reports have it that his entrance was heralded by trumpets.

From the earliest days of Prince's strange ministry there were rumours of odd activity. In July 1846 the Dorset County Magistrate, Colonel Howarth, wrote to the Home Secretary reporting that Prince was impersonating the Almighty and that he received his worshippers 'naked in body, but veiled'. He had, he said, already sent three young women to the County Lunatic Asylum 'driven mad by the doctrines they hold'. Each night Weymouth was in a state of near-anarchy as the population attacked Prince's followers with stones. Such public vilification was a recurring feature of the Agapemonites. It was not for mere display that Prince purchased his bloodhounds. For although he inspired loyalty in his followers, this did not extend to their relatives.

Least impressed of all were the Nottidge family. Their wealth was swallowed up by Prince and his church through a series of arranged marriages between five impressionable sisters – Agnes, Clara, Harriet, Louisa and Cornelia – all unmarried, and devotees of the Devon messiah. Prince met the girls soon after his dismissal from Charlinch. Each stood to inherit on the death of their aged, rich and ill father £6,000, £30,000 in all. This was a great deal of money in 1840. Prince set about winning them over to the faith – and to the fold.

Soon all five were living with him. Sometimes they would find notes under their plates at dinner: 'The Lord hath need of £50, to be used for a special purpose unto His glory. The spirit would have this made known to you. Amen.'

Old Mr Nottidge died in 1844. The rest of the family was adamant that his daughters could not just hand over their wealth to Prince. Prince therefore summoned Harriet and told her that it was her duty to marry one of the evangelical Lampeter Brethren. She consented. Next, Agnes – at 28, the youngest – was told that 'God was about to confer on her a special blessing which the spirit directed them to make known to her but that before they should tell her what it was she must make a solemn promise that she should do what was required of her.' Poor Agnes apparently complied, only to discover that the special blessing was none other than the ageing Reverend George Robinson Thomas. He was to be her husband.

More spirited than the rest, Agnes resisted, briefly. Two days later Clara, 36, was told that she was to marry another of Prince's followers, William Cobbe. All three couples were married a few weeks later. In one afternoon, Prince netted £18,000 for the Church of the Agapemone, more than enough to set about constructing the Abode of Love. There was nothing the Nottidge family could do.

Agnes was of a rebellious turn of mind. Discovered writing a letter to Louisa warning her not to come to join Prince, she was banished to live in an attic, put to work in the scullery, and told that she could never see her husband again. Soon it emerged that she was pregnant. Procreation, like death, was considered an unmentionable in the Agapemone and Agnes was expelled, taking her child but leaving behind her £6,000. She went home to mother: hardly the first disappointed bride to do so but among the most strangely disappointed.

None of these events deterred Louisa Nottidge, at 43 the oldest spinster, from joining Prince in the Abode of Love in the summer of 1846. The main building as yet unfinished, Louisa was lodged in an out-house, under the guardianship of Prince's wife (being the Messiah had not prevented Prince from marrying, any more than being married seemed to prevent this Messiah from philandering).

In November Louisa's brother, the Reverend Edmund Pepys Nottidge (a rather more sane clergyman), her brother-in-law, Frederick Ripley, and a policeman friend, turned up in Spaxton and at first tried to reason with Louisa. This failing they kidnapped her, bundling her into a carriage and driving her to the Moorcroft House Lunatic Asylum in Middlesex. She was not released until May 1848 when the Commissioners of Lunacy decided that she was not mad, merely deluded. On her release she promptly handed over £6,000 to Prince's bankers and returned to the Abode of Love where she lived for the few remaining years of her life.

In 1849 she successfully prosecuted her family for wrongful imprisonment. The following year the Reverend George Thomas (Louisa's husband) was discovered lurking in a shrubbery at the Nottidge family home, intending to abduct his four-year-old daughter. Meanwhile the Agapemonites came under attack in their village. Five inmates were forced to protect themselves with riding whips and hockey sticks.

This all culminated in a court case which followed Louisa's death in 1858. In *Nottidge v. Prince*, the Nottidge family contended that Prince had obtained Louisa's £6,000 under false pretences by claiming to be God Almighty. Prince did not demur. In court, he elaborated his personal theology, that he stood in a direct line which began with Adam and continued through Noah, Abraham and Jesus Christ. In his judgement Vice-Chancellor Stuart declared that Prince had 'falsely and blasphemously exercised a powerful and undue domination over the mind of Miss Nottidge by assuming a false character'.

It was a rather tricky legal judgement by a judge intent on finding for the plaintiff one way or another. Whether to maintain your true identity, but to claim the added characteristic of being inhabited by the Divine, really amounts to 'assuming a false character' is a moot point.

The judge offered a tortured argument. He did not rest his judgement on any finding that Prince knew he was not the Messiah and was only pretending. Allowing that Prince *might* be deluded but sincere, the Judge suggested (rather questionably) that claiming to be a messiah amounted to 'assuming a false character'. A moment's reflection shows the difficulties with such an argument. Many leaders from the Inca to the Dalai Lama and the Emperor of Japan have claimed to be a god on Earth.

Aware that this was tricky ground, the vice-chancellor added a second bias for his judgement: that it amounted to undue 'influence over the mind' for a religious figure to persuade his followers to give away so much, so lightly. The argument casts into doubt two millenia of religious giving.

It was (this author would submit) a pretty wretched judgement, knocked together to assist an obviously deserving plaintiff. Referring to the claim to be a messiah the vice-chancellor delivered himself of a remarkable *obiter dictum*:

> To rational minds it may seem surprising that any human being could be found with an understanding so weak and degraded as to submit to the influence and guidance of a person who thus speaks of himself.

So much for Matthew, Mark, Luke and John.

The judge ordered Prince to hand back the £6,000, with interest. A month later the Reverend Lewis Price (Harriet's husband), who had become disaffected with the Agapemonites and defected without her, led an assault party to Spaxton to recover his wife. Scaling the garden walls, they broke down the doors of the house and discovered the Agapemonites inside barricaded behind furniture, and armed with sticks and guns. But there was no sign of Harriet, who had been hiding in a disused water cistern. Price eventually discovered his wife in Salisbury, where he retrieved her, apparently against her will.

But the strangest episode in the history of the Agapemonites took place in 1856.

The Reverend Henry Prince produced a new twist in his theology, namely that it was his divine duty to deflower virgins. He made it known in the Agapemone that the Lord would require a virgin, the 'favoured one' for his divine purposes. On the appointed day, the women, dressed in white robes, lined up before the altar of the chapel (which also served as a billiard room). Sporting a scarlet robe and observed by the rest of the brethren, including his own wife, Prince picked out the prettiest and – to the accompaniment of the singing of hymns and organ music – deflowered her on a couch before the altar. Religious cere mony it may have been, but the act still produced a child. Prince denied any responsibility for it and blamed the Devil.

It was not until 1867 that the investigative journalist William Hepworth Dixon, in the course of writing a two-volume work about peculiar cults, *Spiritual Wives*, paid a visit to the Agapemone and gave an exotic account. Dixon was the only man ever to interview Prince. Unlike many contemporary witnesses he does appear to have been amused by the whole thing. Met at the gates by the Reverend George Thomas, Keeper of the Seven Stars and the Seven Golden Candlesticks, he was shown into the chapel, scene of 'that daring rite, the strangest mystery, perhaps the darkest iniquity of these latter days'. Dixon, it will be learned from his rousing defence of St George [see p190], was prone to hyperbole. Awaiting an audience with Prince, and seated on a grand red sofa, he had time to observe that in one corner of the room there was a harp and in the other a large, luxuriant palm tree. In the middle stood the billiard table. All the accoutrements for Paradise!

Prince's office, he writes, 'was like a lady's boudoir'. Prince sat in a semi-circle of his followers; on his right was the Reverend Samuel Starky, in a previous incarnation the Rector of Charlinch but now the Second of the Two Anointed Ones.

Dixon asked Prince about the beliefs of the Agapemonites. 'You accept the physical resurrection as the doctrine is laid down in the English Church?' he inquired.

'No,' replied Prince. 'We reject that doctrine. We are the resurrection; and in that we are the life.'

'Do you expect to die?' pressed Dixon.

'No, never. We have no such thought.' The dead, Prince added, were 'men who have not been wholly saved'.

But Dixon was less concerned with the doctrine of the Agapemonites than with the identity of the 'favoured one', 'Sister Zoe', a girl of quite astonishing good looks. Dixon believed her surname was Paterson. Sister Zoe was 'one of those rare feminine creatures who lash poets into song, who drive artists to despair, and cause common mortals to risk their souls for love'. Sitting next to Prince she was dressed in white, and had big blue eyes – 'those lustrous orbs!' Dixon was smitten.

Was she the girl who had been solemnly despoiled by Prince ten years previously?

Earlier Dixon had seen a child playing in the garden. 'She is a broken link in our line of life; a child of shame; a living witness of the last great triumph of the Devil in the heart of man,' said Prince, when Dixon mentioned the girl. George Thomas intervened, his voice trembling with emotion. 'She is Satan's offspring – Satan's doing in the flesh.'

Dixon tried to get more from Zoe. Was not 'Zoe' too familiar a name for a stranger like himself to use? 'Pray do so,' she replied. 'It is very nice.' But, he went on, would it not be easier for him to call her Miss...? 'Call me Zoe,' she answered with a patient smile. 'Zoe; nothing but Zoe.'

I said to Zoe, holding her hand in mine, 'May not I hear some word to know you by when I am far away?'

'Yes, Zoe,' she said and smiled.

'Zoe...what else?' Her thin lips parted, as if to speak. What was she about to say? Was the name that rose to her lips Paterson...a word unspoken for years in the Abode of Love?

Who knows? Instead of answering me, though her fingers were linked in mine, she turned to Prince, and whispered in her melting tones, 'Beloved!' Prince answered to me for her, in a voice of playful softness; 'She is Zoe; you must think of her as Zoe; nothing else.'

And Dixon departed, able only to muse how the 'brothers and sisters seem to have no sharp sense of that which appears to me so wild and strange'. In this, his least overblown observation, Dixon comes closest to expressing the bafflement of succeeding ages.

But as all are forced to admit who bring to the study of cults the yardstick of the anthropologist rather than the theologian, observations which, made of a cult we take to be phoney, and which excite incredulity, alarm or laughter, can be made equally of what is called true religion; and here they excite devotion. It is a defence ever available to the cult leader that Jesus made claims which were no less wild: and he, too, met persecution, disbelief and outrage.

In spite of Prince's edicts against death, one by one the Agapemonites began to pass away, though he himself held out longer than most. Prince eventually died in January 1899. His baffled followers, for whom it is impossible not to feel pity, delayed before burying him, hoping he would resurrect himself. But his corpse behaved distressingly like any other corpse, and they were compelled to bury him – in the garden, upright. No angels came to roll the stones away.

Still, that wasn't the end of the story. The world had waited over 1,800 years from the ascension of Jesus Christ to the revelation of Henry James Prince. This time a new Messiah emerged with remarkable speed. The Reverend John Hugh Smyth-Pigott, formerly a member of the Salvation Army, ex-curate of St Jude's Church, Mildmay Park, London, and a long-standing member of the Church of the Agapemone, now donned the mantle of Prince's messianism, and within three years the Agapemonites had a new leader.

They also had an astounding degree of success. Prince may have been deranged, but he had won followers far beyond Devon – first in Reading and Wales; then in Norway and Sweden and by the time of his death in Germany, the United States and India.

Indeed Smyth-Pigott had a rival – Mizra Ghulam Ahmad, chief of Qadian, Punjab, who issued a pamphlet declaring himself to be the Messiah and leader of the Agapemonites. The pamphlet argued that whoever lived longer was the true leader. Ahmad died in 1908, long before Smyth-Pigott who still insisted he was immortal anyway.

On 7 September 1902 Smyth-Pigott announced his elevation to the congregation of the Agapemonite church in Clapton, North London.

'Incredible as it may seem,' said the next day's *Morning Chronicle*, 'a man got up in the centre of the altar and declared that he was Jesus Christ.' In 1902, as now, the newspapers enjoyed a silly season in summer. It was not yet over. The next week the press were in a lather – whether over a 'blasphemy' or because they thought the Messiah really had returned it is unclear. Smyth-Pigott received phenomenal coverage.

The following Sunday Smyth-Pigott repeated the performance in front of the national press. This time he advertised in advance. Crowds had begun to converge around the church at six o'clock that morning. By the time Smyth-Pigott turned up at 9.30 there were an estimated 6,000 people present, by no means all of them sympathetic.

The Salvation Army marched past, singing: 'We shall know Him when he comes/By the nail-prints on his hands!' As Smyth-Pigott made his way into the church, the crowd attempted to storm the building. To ease the crush the police were compelled to let more people into the church, where they found Smyth-Pigott seated on a throne, above him the words: 'I am the resurrection and the life.'

To the accompaniment of jeers from outside the church, and heckles from within ('Where are the nail-prints on your hands?'), Smyth-Pigott repeated the announcement made before, and, rather ungraciously, relegated Henry James Prince to the position of John the Baptist to his Jesus Christ – 'Before the second coming there was a man sent from God, whose name was brother Prince.' He emerged from the Church escorted by mounted police and protected by a professional boxer.

'Had he been an unpopular Prime Minister no greater care could have been taken of his public appearances,' wrote the reporter from the *Daily Mail*. As his carriage sped away he was chased by hundreds throwing sticks and umbrellas. He stuck his head out of the window, 'and seemed to invite martyrdom', observed the *Mail*. As a publicity coup Smyth-Pigott could not have bettered the performance.

Back in Spaxton, Smyth-Pigott followed the example set by Prince and started producing children. Like Prince, Smyth-Pigott was married and like Prince the mother of his children was not his wife. Unlike Prince he neither blamed Satan for his own offspring, nor attempted to conceal their existence. In June 1905 Ruth Anne Preece gave birth to a boy, who was named Glory. Agapemonites from Norway, Sweden, India, Germany and France attended the christening. 'Our sainted leader breathed into Anna's nostrils and she bore a man child, the Glory of the world,' one Agapemonite told the *Bridgewater Mercury*. Glory was followed in 1908 by Power.

All of this was too much for the Bishop of Bath and Wells. He was moved to act against Smyth-Pigott in a way from which the church authorities had shrunk in Prince's case. Not only had Smyth-Pigott blasphemously declared himself to be the Messiah, he was producing illegitimate children. At a consistory court hearing to which he did not turn up, Smyth-Pigott was charged under the 1892 Clergy Discipline Act, and (under a seventeenth-century law) of 'adultery, whoredom and uncleanness and wickedness of life'.

Found guilty, he was sentenced to deposition from holy orders. In March 1909 at a ceremony at Wells cathedral, accompanied by portentous organ music, the bishop unfrocked Smyth-Pigott, again in his absence. 'I am God. It does not matter what they do,' Smyth-Pigott was reported as saying. The following year his third and last child was born, named Life.

Smyth-Pigott lived another seventeen years; his successor in the Agapemone did not declare himself to be the Messiah and as the years condemned the inhabitants of the Abode of Love, the sect came to serve more as an old people's home than a fanatical religious group. When a reporter from the *Daily Herald* visited in December 1955, he found a dozen old women aged between 70 and 94 preparing for a 9 o'clock bedtime.

The final inhabitant died in 1958. Smyth-Pigott's children, Glory, Power and Life, who, disappointingly, preferred to be known as Patrick, Lavita and David, sold the buildings. They were recently up for sale again.

And thus ended Britain's most recent Second Coming, and probably this millennium's last. We seem to have despatched our latest Messiah rather unceremoniously. I do hope it *was* a hoax.

# TREACHERY

## JUDAS ISCARIOT

## 'Woe unto that man by whom
## He is betrayed!'

There have been many villains in the history of Christianity. Judas was the first in a long line of those who abused their association with things spiritual to satisfy his worldly appetite. His villainy was definitive.

Sydney Smith once remarked that he had to believe in the Apostolic Succession, because there was no other way to account for the descent of the Bishop of Exeter from Judas Iscariot.

Yet for selling his Messiah for only thirty pieces of silver, Judas Iscariot deserves a measure of sympathy. He got a worse deal than countless successors who were to sell less for more.

We know surprisingly little about Judas. The general ignorance has licensed innumerable apologists for the Apostle, and to claim that Judas was the most misunderstood man in history has become a standard assignment for essayists. Upon the mere twelve hundred words written about Judas in the New Testament, every possible interpretation has been placed. Depictions of the man range from the most wicked human being in the history of the world, to the unappreciated architect of the Christian religion. A whole branch of religious studies has developed around defending or vilifying him. Poetry, novels, paintings, plays and films have all been based upon them.

Here is what we learn about Judas from the New Testament. One of the Twelve Apostles, Judas was surnamed Iscariot – though no one can agree why. Appointed to be treasurer of the group, he displayed his aptitude for the post when, at the house of Simon the Leper, he complained at Jesus's pouring an entire urn of expensive oil on the head of Mary Magdalen. Deciding to betray his Master for no better reason we know of than greed (the Bible says Satan 'entered him') he went to the Jewish High Priest, Caiaphas, and negotiated a sum of thirty pieces of silver.

At the Last Supper before his arrest, which Judas attended, Jesus indicated that he knew Judas was about to betray him. The disciples begged him to tell them whom he meant, but in vain.

Afterwards, while Jesus and the other disciples were in the Garden of Gethsemane, Judas arrived with the Roman authorities and identified Jesus by kissing him. Jesus was arrested and taken away to his trial and crucifixion. Overcome by remorse, Judas handed back the money he had received from Caiaphas, and hanged himself. The Book of Acts adds that his stomach burst open and his bowels poured out.

And that is almost all the Gospels say about Judas. There is nothing about his background, about his physical appearance, or about his personality. But he has become the archetype of traitors for all time, his name an immediately understood reference, in hundreds of languages, for betrayal. The tree on which he hanged himself was said thereafter to bear its purple-pink blossoms early, on still-leafless branches; and a variety of small tree which flowers in this way has been named the Judas tree.

From the very beginning, Judas has been the unhappy subject of a free-for-all. The rationale in the minds of his vilifiers has been that this is a man wholly without redeeming virtue – and a fit object, therefore, even for falsehood. The second-century Bishop of Hierapolis in Papias gave himself licence to expand upon the Gospels:

Judas was so swollen in his body that where a wagon could go through easily, he could not go through; nay, he could not even insert the mass of his head. His eyelids were so swollen, he could not see the light at all, nor could his eyes be seen even with an optical instrument; so deep did they lie from the surface.

His genitals were repellent and huge beyond all shameless-ness. From his whole body flowed blood mixed with worms, which exuded particularly during his natural needs. After many trials and sufferings, they say, he died in his own place, which, because of the stench, has remained deserted and uninhabitable to the present day. Until today no one can pass by that place without holding his nose. So great was the exudations from his body that it spread over the ground.

There is no doubt that the association between Judas and Jewishness – an association anti-Semites somehow neglect to extend to the Messiah himself – has been damaging to both sides of that equation. It has provided a 'Christian' excuse for anti-Semitism and a racist excuse for vilifying Judas.

Traditional tales – none with much basis in evidence – have arisen about Judas's early life: that he had been abandoned by his parents when a baby; rescued by a king whose son he murdered, and went on to murder his father and marry his mother before finally joining the Apostles and betraying Jesus. Dante places Judas in the fourth round of the ninth circle of hell, where he is gnawed by Lucifer, the skin repeatedly stripped off his back.

But apologists, too, abound, and they have been ingenious. 'Is there anyone in history who has been so hideously slandered as has Judas?' asks William Klassen, author of the most recent book defending Judas, *Judas: Betrayer or Friend of Jesus?* Klassen, a theology professor in Jerusalem, and a Christian, began to suspect that Judas may have been misunderstood when he started taking his classes actually dressed as Judas, sporting first-century attire. Astonished by 'the anger that so many people displayed towards me in the role', he was led by the experience, he says, to a detailed re-examination of the four Gospel accounts.

Through cunning linguistic science, Klassen is able to conclude that 'it is possible to depict the events of the Passion week with the best motives on the part of all people involved and still end with the tragedy of Jesus' crucifixion.' For those unconvinced by his textual analysis, Klassen concludes his book with a mock 'suicide note from Judas Iscariot', which 'throws some light on our much-maligned associate'.

Klassen is not alone. Hyam Maccoby's *Judas and the Myth of Jewish Evil* is a compelling survey of the growth of Judas-linked anti-semitism, somewhat spoiled by a tendentious reconstruction of the Gospels to make Judas not only the brother of Jesus but the author of parts of the New Testament.

A mass of novels, biographies, 'autobiographies', and 'gospels' of Judas have been published. These books commonly omit to mention that they are works of fiction: they have been discovered concealed in the Vatican archives, or have come into the hands of the 'translator' via a medieval monk and Nazi dissidents.

Judas is sometimes a shrewd mover who, anxious lest Christ fade into obscurity, arranges a spectacular 'event' – the crucifixion – to spearhead his message. Judas, the first spin-doctor.

In other accounts he is something of a dupe and sold Jesus for thirty pieces of silver never realising that his master would end up being executed. It was all a terrible mistake. Some works have Judas as a pious genius who realises that, to fulfil the prophecies of the Old Testament, someone has to betray him. In some Muslim writing, Judas is not a traitor but Jesus' rescuer, who lied to the Jews in order to confuse them as to Jesus' identity – Jesus being thus saved. The cosmographer ad-Dimashqi suggests that Judas assumed Jesus' likeness and was crucified in his place.

In the Orthodox churches Iscariot is listed among the saints: not as a mark of approval, but because he fulfilled prophecy. Jesus himself lends this very Judaic view some authority when he is reported as remarking during the Last Supper (Luke, Ch 22) 'I say unto you, that this that is written must yet be accomplished in me.' In St John's version (Ch 13) Jesus actually sends Judas out to arrange the betrayal, saying 'That thou doest, do quickly.' However, there is no authority for the thought that Jesus might have forgiven Judas. 'Truly,' he says in Luke's Gospel, 'the Son of man goeth, as it was determined: but woe unto that man by whom He is betrayed!'

Unauthorised interpretations suggest that Christ was himself to blame for failing to fulfil the Apostles' expectations of him. One blasphemous work, *The Lost Testament of Judas Iscariot*, has Jesus actually asking Judas to 'betray' him so that he will be freed by the populace, and become more famous still.

And so the theories proliferate, each more fantastic than the last, most – fictional or claimed as factual – arguing that Judas has, as one put it, 'been suffering under an exaggerated weight of censure'. Certainly the author of this book has yet to hear any convincing answer to the question which occurs to every child when first taught the story of Judas's betrayal: why did the Romans need anyone to tell them who Jesus was, anyway? If he was the famous teacher of whom they had heard so much complaint, had they really no means of identifying him for themselves? Besides, as the Gospels report, Jesus was happy to confirm to them that he was the man Judas said he was.

There is something rum about the tale of Judas. So sketchy is the original account that succeeding generations have been able to read what they wish into the events, projecting their own pet demonologies onto the villain and surrounding cast. As such, the story of Judas Iscariot – though he lived before unfrocking had been invented – is not untypical of other 'villains' in this book, whose real personality has long been buried beneath a mound of infamy and supposition.

# THE CRIME NOT TO BE NAMED

## PERCY JOCELYN

## The Arse Bishop

*The Devil to prove the Church was a farce*
*Went out to fish for a bugger.*
*He bated his hook on a soldier's arse –*
*And pulled up the Bishop of Clogher*

Anon.

'No event in the last century is more to be lamented both on private and public grounds – it will sap the very foundation of society, it will raise up the lower orders against the higher, and in the present temper of the public mind against the Church it will do more to injure the Establishment than all the united efforts of its enemies could have effected in a century.' Thus wrote George Dawson, private secretary to the Home Secretary, Robert Peel, the morning after Percy Jocelyn, Bishop of Clogher, was discovered *in flagrante delicto* with a Grenadier Guard in the back room of a London pub.

The scandal of the Bishop of Clogher was so great that, in the days afterwards (wrote the Archbishop of Canterbury) 'it was not safe for a bishop to shew himself in the streets of London', and so great that the Home Secretary was prepared to pervert the course of justice to prevent a trial taking place in this country. It was so great that for 178 years afterwards the Church of Ireland refused to let historians see their papers on the affair; and so great that, earlier this century, Archbishop D'Arcy of Armagh instructed that they be burnt – an instruction fortunately ignored. When at the beginning of 1998 I requested to see them, it required the personal decision of a more enlightened Primate of All Ireland, Archbishop Eames, finally to authorise their release.

What a palaver! The incident was certainly embarrassing, though it is hard to see why the Church should continue to find it so at this distance from the events. The papers, on which I have drawn heavily for this chapter, reflect worse upon the political establishment which covered the case up than upon the Church, which did at least push for a trial – even if it was in Ireland.

Meanwhile, the man at the centre of all this, Percy Jocelyn, reamins enigmatic. 'I never thought Percy would crawl out of the woodwork,' the present head of Clogher's family, Lord Roden, told me when I asked about the bishop. Percy was treated to none of the panegyrics a bishop might normally expect. The one known portrait of him, exhibited in the Royal Academy in 1821, vanished without trace after his fall. *The Dictionary of National Biography*, usually rather expert at innuendo, restricts itself to noting merely that he was 'deposed for a scandalous crime'.

Yet what can even the kindly-disposed say? There were no good works to report, nor were there any sermons to collect. He never married. He owed his rise and his great fortune entirely to family connections. The grandson of the Lord Chancellor of Ireland, he was the brother of the second Earl of Roden, and uncle to the third.

The third of four sons, Percy entered the Church as younger sons did. Ordained after leaving Trinity College, Dublin, his career progressed comfortably. In due course he was appointed the Rector of Tamlaght, Treasurer of Cork Cathedral, Archdeacon of Ross, Treasurer of Armagh, Prebend of Lismore . . . but why prolong the list? How seriously he took his divine mission can be gathered from some early letters written by an old university friend, Thomas Hore, another Irish clergyman. They are almost all we have of him in writing. They are not encouraging. 'You most idle of all Reverend idlers,' Hore calls him at one point. 'Do you ever write a sermon? Most worthy Rector of Creggan – not you.'

They do not tell us if Jocelyn was a man with any interest in religion at all. I am intrigued by the question of whether such men believed in God, or in the truth of the religion they must have known they were disgracing. Perhaps Percy never asked himself such questions. But, as was his birthright, in 1809 he was appointed the see of Ferns and Leighlin. In 1820 he was elevated higher still to the Bishopric of Clogher.

And then in July 1822 he was discovered in the back room of the White Lion, public house, in St Alban's Place, off the Haymarket, with a soldier named John Moverley. The exposure brought the disgrace and subsequent exile of the 84th Bishop of Clogher.

It is possible to reconstruct the fateful encounter. After a day in the House of Lords the bishop met the soldier at the White Lion. It is clear this was no casual encounter: the two had arranged to meet at around nine o'clock in the evening on Friday 19 July. Jocelyn, aged 58, was dressed in black, with 'the appearance of a gentleman'. The 22-year-old soldier was wearing his uniform. They retired to a back parlour. Rather unsurprisingly, 'they were immediately suspected'.

In the ensuing drama the landlord's son-in-law, James Plant, a shoemaker, played a key role. His suspicions aroused, he crept out into the back yard and peered through the window. He saw the bishop and the soldier 'in the state of Achilles as far as nakedness was necessary to their purposes'. Plant informed the landlord, Mr Lea, who ordered his son-in-law to fetch a watchman. Soon Plant, Lea, the watchman and about eight pub regulars were gathered around the window. George Dawson at the Home Office picks up the story in his (until recently embargoed) letter to Archbishop Beresford of Armagh ('Excuse me, my dear Archbishop for offending your eye with the following detail, I blush while I write it...').

> The unfortunate Bishop and the Soldier at last became so indecent, so horribly profligate in their proceedings, by taking every liberty with each other's person, by using every unnatural provocative, and by having recourse to licentiousness only human by the descriptions in the most abandoned writers of the French school, that the party assembled could no longer curb their indignation, but broke into the room at the very moment that the soldier was about to consummate the crime upon the prostituted and exposed person of the Bishop.

'You're a pretty shepherd of a flock,' Plant recalled saying; to which a startled Jocelyn declared: 'What have I done? What have I done? Nobody could see anything. Nobody can hurt me.' When

Witnesses interrupted Jocelyn and Moverley at a critical moment.

he was told what they had witnessed, and perhaps suddenly realising that he was half naked, he cried out: 'Oh God, good God! That I should come to this – I am undone, let me go – could you let me go?' We may guess that by now the burly landlord had a firm grip on the distraught bishop. The diarist Charles Greville reports that 'if his breeches had not been down they think he would have got away'.

'It was truly ludicrous,' a witness wrote, 'to see a Bishop, and a Peer (for such he is represented in the Calendar), fighting his way through a host of carpenters, butchers, &c. in order to escape exposure.'

But they could not escape. Jocelyn and Moverley were dragged to the St James's watch house. As this improbable procession moved by, Jocelyn still in a state of partial undress, a mob gathered which grew larger and more violent. Much of the account of what happened we owe to a pamphlet later published on the affair, *The Bishop!!*

It seems that as they passed Carlton House Jocelyn made a last, unsuccessful bid to struggle free. There appeared a real possibility that the bishop might be killed by the mob – but he got away with a black eye, a cut lip, and the ripping of his remaining clothes. 'The reverend hat was kicked about with contempt,' records one report. 'The soldier also received a sound drubbing.'

As yet, the crowd did not know Jocelyn's identity. He hoped to keep it that way. Clogher refused to give his name and once in the Vine Street watch house took a letter from his pocket, ripped it up and threw it into the grate – pointlessly, as there was no fire. The watchman, John Latchford, pieced it together again and found it addressed to the 'Bishop of Clogher' from the Bishop's nephew, the Earl of Roden.

His identity now known, Jocelyn dashed off a desperate note to a friend, and gave it to Latchford to send. It read:

ST JAMES'S WATCH HOUSE, VINE STREET –

JOHN; – COME TO ME DIRECTLY, DON'T SAY WHO I AM, BUT I AM UNDONE. COME INSTANTLY, AND INQUIRE FOR A GENTLEMAN BELOW STAIRS, 12 O'CLOCK – I AM TOTALLY UNDONE.

P.C.

TO MR JOHN WARING,
21, MONTAGUE-STREET,
PORTMAN-SQUARE.

The letter never reached Mr Waring. The watchman folded it up, put it in his pocket, and kept it as evidence.

Jocelyn passed the entire night in his cell on his knees, groaning, in fervent prayer – 'His supplications and ejaculations throughout the night were loud and unceasing.' In the morning the pair were taken by hackney-coach to the Marlborough Street magistrates.

Jocelyn is described as being about six foot high, stout, with powdered hair, a pointed nose – and a black eye. He stood in a corner, holding a handkerchief over his face. Moverley was of 'effeminate appearance', and dressed in military uniform. Both wept. The *Observer* described the scene:

During the examination the accused appeared sunk in the deepest mental agony; he did not utter a word. He was attired in an old great coat, and had worn his clerical hat, which was much torn; he had evidently been roughly handled.

Jocelyn had at least one cause for gratitude: as it was later put at his trial (which he did not attend), because he had been 'providentially arrested, before he had perpetrated the last foul act' (that is to say, before any penetration had taken place) he could not be charged with sodomy, a capital offence; but only with a misdemeanour, which was bailable. England's last execution for sodomy was still 14 years ahead. He was released on surety of £1,000, and bound over to appear at Clerkenwell sessions in September. Having paid up, and leaving by a back door to escape a waiting mob, he promptly fled to the Continent.

He left behind a country in uproar! 'The affair of the bishop has made a great noise,' wrote Greville in his diary on 30 July. Not the least distressed were the 'West End nobility'. All that they had heard was that a bishop, of noble stock, had been disgraced, but at first no one knew his name. Since virtually everyone who mattered in the West End was in some way related to a bishop the news was greeted 'in the greatest alarm'.

'At length the names of the parties concerned were soon spread about in every direction, especially on Sunday and Monday, when all the horn-boys in the metropolis were furnished with "full particulars" of the horrid transaction, with names and situation, &c,' said *The Bishop!!* Mr Lea, landlord of the White Lion, started charging a shilling for people to see the parlour where the bishop and the soldier were discovered. Soon wags dubbed Jocelyn 'the Arsebishop'.

The collateral damage extended to the rest of the clergy. The author of *The Bishop!!*, unconsciously echoing the Archbishop of Canterbury's remarks, wrote:

The mere appearance of a clergyman in the streets of our metropolis causes him to be pointed out and laughed at by the hardened, while others seem to gaze on him with a look of suspicion. It seems to have the effect of keeping this class of society indoors, for we missed those whom we were in the habit of seeing in the daily habit of their usual promenades. Such is the effect of the dreadful transaction.

But even though the news was tearing through the taverns and coffee-houses of London, with Jocelyn's name 'in the mouth of the meanest little boy', for the moment the newspapers were keeping a lofty silence (only the *Observer* mentioned the case in any detail, and even then named no names). One reason, of course, was that the whole business was monumentally embarrassing: Jocelyn was a bishop of the Established Church, a luminary in the Society for the Suppression of Vice (or 'spreading of vice' as it now began to be called), and the uncle of the Earl of Roden. Worse, the event had occurred (as it was phrased in the trial) in a 'common ale-house', and 'with a private soldier, wholly beneath him in rank and station'. The whole thing was positively subversive.

It was left to penny pamphlets and the radical press to keep the public informed, which they did with gusto. Over the days which followed a ferocious war of words raged – Jocelyn's disgrace being the cue for attacks on not just the Church but the entire political establishment including the 'so-called respectable part of the press'.

The Government set about trying to limit the damage. With the soldier Moverley still in prison and unable to raise bail, there was a danger that the case would come to trial, thus giving the whole scandal a thorough and public airing. The only solution was to get Moverley out of the country too. The really astonishing thing is that this suggestion came from the Home Secretary himself – or at least from George Dawson, Robert Peel's private secretary, whose letter to the Archbishop of Armargh spoke of 'this excusable connivance at his escape': 'of course you will not mention this hint as coming from me'. In his turn, the Archbishop wrote to Lord Roden, suggesting that 'someone' tender bail for Moverley, 'removing him out of the way'. No sooner said than done – and the soldier was not heard of again.

But there was perhaps another reason the Government was eager that the case be suppressed. At exactly the time the bishop's downfall was causing such a stir, the Foreign Secretary, Lord Castlereagh, was implicated in a homosexual scandal. Historians have speculated that the Cabinet Minister was being blackmailed for a crime remarkably similar to Jocelyn's: he had picked up a

# A CORRECT ACCOUNT

### OF THE

## *HORRIBLE OCCURRENCE*

Which took place at a Public-house in St. James's Market,
in which it was discovered that

## *The Right Rev. Father in God*

### THE

# BISHOP OF CLOGHER,

Lately transferred from the Bishopric of Ferns,

##### WAS A PRINCIPAL ACTOR WITH

# A Common Soldier!

To the disgrace not only of the Cloth, to which he was
attached, and as a Commissioner of the Board of Education, and a Dictator of Public Morals, but as a Member of that Nation which gave him Birth!

◆

### LONDON:

PRINTED AND PUBLISHED BY & FOR J. L. MARKS,
23, RUSSELL COURT, COVENT GARDEN.

#### *Price Sixpence.*

Title page from a contemporary pamphlet.

soldier, and had been caught. He had claimed he thought the soldier was a woman. For a bishop to be toppled by a homosexual scandal was unfortunate; for a cabinet minister to suffer the same fate would have been disastrous. The Foreign Secretary became unhinged. 'In his ravings,' wrote Mrs Arbuthnot in her diary, he 'actually accused himself of the same crime [as Jocelyn's], said everybody knew it, that a warrant was out against him and that he must fly the country.' Pushed (as Castlereagh's biographer, John Derry, writes) by 'a fear of some public disgrace as grievous as the bishop's', the Foreign Secretary cut his throat on 12 August.

The press – respectable or otherwise – could keep quiet for only so long, and there was a limit to the deference of editors. Once enquiries had been made into Jocelyn's more distant past, silence became impossible.

For Jocelyn's past was an outrage. It was discovered that while Bishop of Ferns and Leighlin he had been accused of exactly the behaviour in which he had been caught in London. His accuser then, James Byrne, a coachman, had detailed the allegations in a letter sent to Jocelyn's brother, the Honourable John Jocelyn, and to the Lord Mayor of Dublin. For his pains Byrne had been prosecuted for malicious libel.

The trial had been a disgrace. Held in Dublin in October 1811, Jocelyn was the sole witness for the prosecution. It had thus been a poor coachman's word against a bishop's. Asked whether the contents of Byrne's letter were true or false, 'his Lordship rose, and in the most impressive and dignified manner, placed his hand upon his breast, and said – "False".'

The bishop's word had been believed, of course. The trial is worth studying carefully, not least for the extraordinary arguments used by Jocelyn's counsel, the Right Honourable C. Kendal Bushe, Ireland's Solicitor-General. The first claim was that Ireland, being so far from the 'corrupted manners' of the Continent, remained untouched by any homosexual practices. 'There is no instance of its existence in the memory of any professional man,' Kendal Bushe declared. The 'contagion' not having reached Ireland, Jocelyn must be innocent. Counsel for the Prosecution intimated darkly that in England, from its 'proximity. . . to the Continent of Europe', 'the instances there are not a few'.

Another line of defence was to celebrate the supposed virtues of Percy Jocelyn, 'an exalted and venerable character, who, though raised to one of the highest dignities of the Church, is still less exalted by his rank than he is by the uniform piety of his life'.

Eleven years later a witness to the trial wrote, in a bitter open letter to Bushe, 'I well recollect the effect produced upon the Court, the Jury, and the auditory, by your powerful appeal to their feelings.'

Poor Byrne had hardly bothered to defend himself; he never even cross-examined Jocelyn. The inevitable 'guilty' verdict was reached and then it was the judge's turn to rouse himself to righteous fury. It was, he raged, 'so wicked a calumny that no idea is too horrible to be informed of you'. He warmed further to his theme. 'You have sought to asperse a Clergyman of the Established Religion, raised by his Sovereign to the highest station in our Church – elevated still higher by those virtues which are not made known by the casual ebullition of a day or years, but by the whole period of a life devoted to the enormous exercise of duty which becomes a man and a Christian...'

Thus had Percy Jocelyn – more familiar to his pals as 'most idle of all Reverend idlers' – been idealised by an affronted Establishment. Regretting that he could not pass harsher judgement Mr Justice Fox sentenced Byrne to two years' imprisonment and ordered that he be whipped three times through the streets of Dublin. The following week Byrne was duly stripped to his waist, tied to a cart, and flogged between Newgate and the Royal Exchange, and back again – a distance of over a mile.

Instead of the public executioner carrying out the sentence, as was usual, a six-foot drummer from the barracks, procured specially for the occasion, flogged Byrne with a cat-o'-nine-tails which broke under the force of the beating. Byrne served the full two years, and 85 days more – he could not be released until he had raised the money for the sureties of his good behaviour. On the eve of the second flogging, an emissary of the bishop visited Byrne in jail, and offered to remit the corporal punishment if he would withdraw the charge, which he duly did.

Buggering a soldier might to some have seemed unfortunate; but having a man whipped to within an inch of his life for speaking what everyone now realised must have been the truth, looked like a horrible miscarriage of justice.

A full week after Jocelyn was caught *The Times*, like a volcano erupting after long dormancy, exploded against 'this mitred reprobate'. With 'mingled feelings of sorrow, humiliation, and disgust,' the paper wondered whether to be relieved or outraged that Jocelyn had jumped bail 'and quitted forever the country which his presence has polluted...We know not whether to rejoice or grieve that he has fled from justice; we know not whether the trial of such a criminal, for such a crime, might not have cost more in the way of corruption, than even his death by law could have paid in the way of satisfaction to good morals...It is...dreadful to think how the Church of God has been scandalised and disgraced.'

Others followed suit. 'If the Church be in danger, who can wonder?' asked the *Morning Chronicle*, which seemed to have been waiting for the right moment to reveal some further surprising instances of recent clerical misbehaviour. 'First, there was a drunken Divine, who wanted to play the pugilist in the pulpit, in the face of the whole congregation; – next came the account of a rector, who in broad-day ran naked after a carriage in which females were taking the air: – and now comes forth this Mitred Miscreant, making one almost ashamed of our nature with his unutterable depravities. But it is not a subject on which we chuse to dilate...' The radical William Benbow compiled an entire volume of clerical scandal in Jocelyn's honour. Much of his research was carried out while serving a sentence in prison, where 'I am surrounded by guilty and infamous persons, who but for my incarceration would have remained hidden...'

Jocelyn's fall was the occasion for James Byrne's rehabilitation. At first everyone assumed that the coachman was either dead or driven to exile in the Antipodes. *The Times* had demanded that 'a diligent search be made for this injured being, and, when found, that an ample indemnity be insured to him' – perhaps, it was suggested, from the estate of the Bishop of Clogher.

Soon he was found: alive and well and living in Ireland. Preparations were put in hand for a triumphant entrance of the 'martyr of the unnatural bishop Jocelyn' into the capital. He became a sort of mascot for the radical movement. A great dinner was held in his honour, attended by 200 people, at the Horns' Tavern in Kennington. Its date coincided with the anniversary of Byrne's flogging. 'Great good will come to us all from the heroic conduct of this humble man,' declared William Cobbett (who presided over the occasion) when, to noisy and prolonged applause, a toast was drunk to the female sex. A public subscription set up for Byrne raised £300.

Meanwhile mechanisms for humiliating disgraced bishops were being put in place. In October 1822 the Metropolitan Court of Armagh convened for his trial. Citations for Jocelyn to appear were posted on doors of his palace and cathedral, on the doors of his house in Dublin, and given to his colleagues, family and friends. 'So extensive was the enquiry for him, and great the efforts to serve him with process, and to certify the commencement of proceedings, and its necessity and import, that his Grace, on the 8th of September last, was pleased, and according to law, to declare him contumacious, and in contempt for non-appearance.'

At the end of the proceedings he was called for three times, and, when he did not show, 'the absolute deprivation of Doctor Percy Jocelyn from the Bishopric of Clogher, and of his Episcopal Order and Authority' was formally passed, 'on account of divers crimes and excesses and more especially for the crimes of immorality, incontinence, and sodomitical practices, habits, and propensities.' Somehow, however, Jocelyn seems to have managed to auction off, beforehand, the whole contents of his episcopal palace. As the court ruefully put it: 'that splendid appendage of his dignity has been left as naked as a ruin.'

Two years later, the former Bishop of Clogher was officially declared an outlaw:

On Sunday last, after a sermon had been delivered by the Reverend Dr. Busfield, Evening Lecturer at Marylebone Church, and as the congregation were on the point of departing, a well-dressed man arrested their attention, by reading, in a very loud tone, the following words from a paper he held in his hand: 'O yes, O yes, O yes – Come forth (calling on the Right Reverend Father in God) and surrender yourself to the Sheriff of Middlesex, in the octave of St Hilary, for a certain misdemeanour, or you will be outlawed. W. M. Kemp, Bailiff to the said Sheriff, Marylebone, Dec.19, 1824.'

The congregation were astounded, and as many could not distinctly hear, it was a considerable time before the church and its spacious yard could be cleared. The notice is now to be seen posted on the principal door of Marylebone church.

And where was Jocelyn all the while? What was his state of mind? It is only after Jocelyn's disgrace that we hear his voice for the first time in a series of letters to his sister, the Countess of Massereene, sent from France. His tone is penitent if self-pitying. He thanks God that his mother never lived to see his disgrace – 'the bitter bitter Annunciation of the Disgrace and Ruin of her Child' – and rues the disloyalty of his friends who have 'flown with the wealth I once possessed'.

'Oh, could I describe to you the severe infliction I hourly suffer at having so degenerated from what I ought to have been,' he laments in one letter. In another: 'Every hour, nay every moment of my shameful existence, there is nothing left to look to in this life but the extreme of misery – nor can any event occur which can in the slightest degree diminish the weight of my calamity.'

Of course, he was writing in exile, when his disgrace was still fresh and hardest to bear, but he never again resumed any public position in society.

Jocelyn moved quietly to Scotland, under an assumed name. He lived with his sister, masquerading as a butler: one story circulated of an embarrassing occasion when, as he was serving, he was recognised by a former acquaintance. Later he moved to the banks of the Clyde – this time 'dressed in the rustic Highland garb' (according to the *Northern Whig*, reprinted in *The Times*) before finally moving to Edinburgh, where he lived out the remainder of his life incognito.

On Saturday 30 December 1843, the *Scotsman* announced that 'an individual died here a short time since who obtained an unenviable celebrity twenty years ago'. Jocelyn had been living at No 4 Salisbury Place, Edinburgh, under the alias of 'Thomas Wilson'.

His mode of living was extremely private, scarcely any visitors being known to enter his dwelling, but it was remarked that the post occasionally brought him letters sealed with coronets. His incognito was wonderfully preserved. It was only known to one or two individuals in the neighbourhood, who kept the secret until after his death.

The application for interment was made in the name of Thomas Wilson. There was a plate upon the coffin which he had got prepared some years before, but without any name upon it. It bore a Latin inscription, the sense of which was as follows: – 'Here lie the remains of a great sinner, saved by grace, whose hopes rest in the atoning sacrifice of the Lord Jesus Christ.' The preparation of this inscription years before shows that he was deeply penitent.

He was very anxious to conceal his true name, having got it perfectly obliterated from his books and articles of furniture. He gave instructions that his burial should be in the nearest churchyard, that it should be conducted in the most private and plain manner, and at 6 in the morning. His directions were complied with, except in the selection of the ground. His body was drawn to the new cemetery in a hearse with one horse, followed by five mourners in a one-horse coach, at 7 in the morning.

Such was the obscure and humble death of the honourable Percy Jocelyn, the son of a Peer, who spent the early years of his life in the society of the great, and held one of the highest ecclesiastical dignities in the empire. He was uncle to the present Lord Roden.

# JOHN ATHERTON

## 'The first of my profession that ever came to this shameful end'

Percy Jocelyn was lucky. As contemporary newspapers pointed out, by skipping bail he cheated the gallows. Protected – behind the scenes – by an Establishment eager to minimise its own embarrassment, Jocelyn could slip back into the country without much fear of arrest.

John Atherton, another Irish Protestant bishop caught in

compromising circumstances with a male person of inferior social class, was less fortunate. Predeceasing Jocelyn by two hundred years, the Bishop of Waterford and Lismore offended so many people, grand and humble, that when he fell there was no safety net. Convicted of displaying 'too much freedom with his own steward' (his tithe collector John Childe) he was hanged in Dublin in December 1640.

But, at the gallows' edge and in a style which would have done justice to Oprah Winfrey, he redeemed himself for posterity by a thoroughly modern virtue: public contrition. Atherton was a great sinner and admitted as much. In the seventeenth century as much as our own the crowd could find sympathy for a big man who confessed. The 1990s are not the first era to be swept by a fashion for saying sorry.

For the historian there is something unsatisfactory and something mysterious about the whole affair. Though a renowned scandal at the time, it is shrouded in infuriating obscurity. Widely mentioned in contemporary reports, the story seems to have caught the attention and imagination of the age and made a huge impression; yet only the flimsiest details survive – and they have invited fanciful embellishment: one printer spiced up the charges by adding the crime of 'bestiality with a cow and other creatures'. When just 70 years after Atherton's death a Waterford gentleman tried to establish the truth he could unearth little. Most of the papers had been destroyed the year after in an Irish rising against restrictions imposed by Ulster Protestants and Charles I.

Atherton was clearly of litigious spirit, enormous pride and had a huge estimation of his own abilities. It is also clear he was not liked. 'That he had many enemies and few, or no, friends, is plain,' wrote a biographer. Physically 'a proper strai[gh]t person' (according to the only account which mentions his appearance) with dark brown, almost black hair and a fine beard, there seems to have been something about him which inspired neither love nor loyalty: many of his accusers were the same men, he complained, who regularly feasted at his table.

He had a reputation as a philanderer. He admitted reading obscene books, drinking and swearing. On his own final self-assessment, and from the particular slurs of his enemies, he seems to have been a boor of the first order.

The son of a canon of St Paul's, Atherton was born in Somerset in 1598. Educated at Oxford, he was appointed rector of Huish Comb Flower after being ordained. Catching the eye of Thomas Wentworth, later Lord Strafford, Lord Lieutenant of Ireland (who also died at the hand of the executioner), he went over to that country at a turbulent time. After a stint as prebendary of St John's, Dublin, and then as Chancellor of Christ Church, he was created Bishop of Waterford and Lismore in 1636 at the relatively young age of 38.

This was a time when the Church was experiencing something of a financial if not spiritual malaise. The See of Waterford yielded a mere £60 a year: much of its land had been appropriated by locals. Atherton set about reclaiming God's property most effectively. Too effectively, if we are to believe one source which reports that he increased the annual revenue of Waterford twenty-seven-fold, to £1600. Doubtless a measure of ruthlessness was needed: even as Atherton climbed the scaffold one man was waving lease papers at him and protesting loudly.

None of this made him popular. One day near the end of 1640, after prayers in the Cathedral, he was arrested and accused of buggering his tithe-collector, John Childe. Nothing is now known about where or when or in what circumstances he was said to have been caught or who was supposed to have caught him.

The charges were put before Parliament and Atherton was tried by jury. Again we get the sense that there was something unlikeable about him – but without amplification. He defended himself in a manner which was 'by all condemned'. Later he admitted that the possibility that he might be convicted had never occurred to him. On 28 November he was found guilty, and sentenced to death. Deprived of his bishopric by a separate ecclesiastical council he spent the last week of his life incarcerated in Dublin Castle.

If we know little about what really happened to bring Bishop Atherton to this pass then we are better served when it comes to his last days in the condemned cell – thanks to his final confessor and spiritual companion, the Dean of Ardagh, Nicholas Bernard. This morose puritan, later Oliver Cromwell's chaplain, effected a reform in the bishop which for those who knew him seemed little short of miraculous.

Dr Bernard's strategy was simple: terror. He prescribed a strict regime for Atherton. His cell was darkened. He was deprived of all company except the morally elevating. He wore mean clothes. He fasted, and was even urged to scourge himself. For good measure, Bernard declared that Atherton should have his coffin made, and placed in his room.

With three visits a day from the brooding Bernard, Atherton began to be tormented by thoughts of the Last Judgement, experiencing terrifying visions of the furies of the Damnation awaiting him. He noted down all the sins he could think of and as he did so his past crowded in upon him. He rued his love of pornographic books, his drunkenness, and his theatregoing.

From overweening haughtiness Atherton became, it was said, extravagantly penitent. He considered asking to be beheaded (one of the more bizarre privileges of the aristocracy) but decided that a dog's death would be too good for him and so asked to be thrown into the sea with a millstone round his neck. Perhaps deeming this impracticable he then amended his instructions: he was to be buried in the furthest corner of the churchyard where the rubbish was kept. 'Speak no good of me,' he told Bernard, 'only what may abate the scandal.'

The day of execution arrived on 5 December 1640. Having bidden farewell to his wife, children and servants the night before, he read morning service to the other inmates. As the hour approached, the noise of the crowds outside grew louder. Taken from the prison he was greeted by a small army of halberdiers and the (Catholic) sheriff, who pinioned him with notable violence. His carriage pressed its way through a vast crowd, with the bells of Christ Church tolling his passing-bell, at his own request. Finally he caught sight of the gallows. 'There is my Mount Calvary from which I hope to ascend to Heaven,' he told Bernard.

And as one would expect at Calvary, Atherton found waiting for him there a scoffer – a fellow perched at one end of the gallows, heckling. It must have looked extraordinary. Above the noise of this man (and after the interruptions of the aggrieved leaseholder) Bishop Atherton, still wearing his episcopal robes, delivered a final, impromptu speech.

'I am I think the first of my profession that ever came to this shameful end,' he said. 'I pray God I may be the last. You are come hither to see a comedy turned into a tragedy, a miserable catastrophe of the life and actions of man in this world...'

Frontispiece of a 1641 pamphlet.
'Speak no good of me, only what may abate the scandal,' Atherton told his confessor.

He expressed repentance, acknowledged that he had neglected preaching sermons, catechising and even personal prayers. He criticised himself for his 'roving thoughts' in church. He denied the main charge in the indictment but 'confessed there were divers other heinous sins he had committed, the declaring of which would rather increase the scandal he had given than repair it'. Although he protested that some of the judges at his trial had been 'hot against him' he accepted that this was for their 'zeal against vice, which did deserve it'. His penitential tone struck a chord with the mob, and many who had come to gawp stayed to weep.

He finally climbed the ladder (we do not know whether his heckler was still in place) looked round and, seeing the tears, cried, 'I thank God I dread not death.' He told the hangman he was ready, tipped him, and quietly said 'Have mercy, have mercy.' His arms rigid by the sides of his cassock, the ladder was pushed away. Atherton, says the report, was 'turned off'. After three-quarters of an hour his body was cut down and removed to the coach in which he had arrived. The appalling Dr Bernard accompanied the corpse in order, he wrote, 'to feed my thoughts with mortality'.

Later in the day and by popular demand, Bernard preached a funeral sermon. There is a standard professional reaction to a professional misdemeanour: that the sins of one professional do not reflect on the profession itself. The Church is as eager to insist upon this as the Law, Politics, Insurance Broking or the Scouting Movement. We hear it today, and they heard it from the Reverend Doctor in 1640. 'A Church ought not to be judged by the lives of a few professors, but by the doctrine professed,' intoned Bernard.

Then, unable to resist the temptation to take a swing at Rome, he undermined the logic of his own position by adding 'Let not the Papists object this scandal to our church, least we return them such foul stories from the Holy See, which we have mind to raise . . .'

John Childe, Atherton's co-accused, was hanged the following March. The chief prosecuting witness, a servant, was himself executed a short while afterwards for an unrelated offence – confessing on the scaffold, it was said, that he had fabricated his evidence against the Bishop.

# JOHN CHURCH

## 'Yea! They had forgotten me in the *Sunday News!*'

'It was the sin of Rehoboam, that he regarded the counsel of the young men, and forsook the advice of the aged.' Thus and not for the first time John Church cited scripture to explain away wildly scandalous accounts of almost the entire course of his ministry. His critics cited scripture too: mostly the sulphurous end to Sodom and Gomorrah. It was to the Reverend Church's great notoriety that, beyond seeking the counsel of young men, he could not keep his hands off them.

There was never anything less than biblical in John Church's conception of himself. In his autobiography, modestly entitled *The Foundling; or, the Child of Providence,* he identifies himself with, amongst others, Moses, Jeremiah, John the Baptist, Joseph, Samson and Jesus Christ - as well as Rehoboam. At one point he finds an analogy between his own life and the fate of the nation of Israel. He compares his opponents variously to Herod, Nicodemus and Balaam, Philistines, Pharisees, and most of the various vile beasts which inhabit the pages of the Old Testament.

> I arrived safe at Achor Vale, glad enough I was to rest from the long strife. I was delivered from the noise of the archers, the sounding of the mountains, and the horns of rams blown by goats, the braying of asses, and the grumbling of bears...

The pious do have a tendency to adorn their language with biblical rhetoric. But this is Church describing his arrival in prison after he had been found guilty of attempting to sodomise a nineteen-year-old apprentice potter.

John Church was a dissenting minister who subscribed to the Antinomianist creed which freed Christians from the necessity of having to obey the Mosaic Law. This was a freedom particularly

REV.ᴰ J. CHURCH.

Frontispiece of John Church's defiant autobiography claiming to set the record straight.

convenient for Mr Church. His Antinomianism was proof enough for many that his life was dedicated to depravity. But remarkably, given that his notoriety (in his own words) had 'been sent to the four winds of heaven, to Wales, Ireland, Scotland, America, the East and West Indies, and to almost every country and village in England in twopenny, fourpenny, and sixpenny pamphlets', he withstood imprisonment, public vilification and even, on one occasion, being burned in effigy, and retained a large and devoted following. He was pleased to point out that the publicity so swelled his congregation that he eventually had to move out of one chapel and build a grander one. Inevitably he made rivals envious. The asses, goats, bears, rams and archers were assembling.

An early intimation that Church's ministry would be controversial came in June 1808, when the 25-year-old was a newly-appointed minister at Banbury, in Oxfordshire. The trouble was boys. According to one pamphleteer he made friends with 'several buckish young men', whom he would watch bathing naked in rivers and ponds. There were rumours of a dalliance with a hairdresser and with a porter and of a failed attempt to seduce a grocer from Warwick.

And now began the braying of the asses. What scandalised the people of Banbury was the revelation that, when he preached outside the town, he would stay the night in a host's house and take a young man to bed with him. He was not particular when it came to companions. In the neighbouring village of Kingham where Church often stayed with a friend, he was accused of having seduced his host's son and, when the son got fed up with Church, a male servant. 'I don't like to sleep with Mr Church because he always ****** on me in bed,' the son was reported as saying. 'I don't like sleeping with Mr Church because he ****** me so much,' said the servant in a similar vein. The passage of time has drawn a veil over what the asterisks stood for.

When the news spread in Banbury, townspeople attacked Church's meeting-hall, and scrawled the word 'sodomites' on the walls, doors and window-shutters.

Church was confronted with the charges on his way to preach in Birmingham. He ignored them, but on return was barred from entering Banbury and members of his church gathered in Chipping Norton to question their minister. He did not deny the truth of the accusations but put a novel spin on them. If he had behaved improperly, it was entirely by accident. 'I own that I have been too imprudent,' he explained, 'but I am not conscious of having done the actual crime; if anything of that nature has been of which they speak, it must have been without my knowledge, when I was asleep and supposing I was in bed with my wife.'

Banbury was unconvinced. 'Unknowing transgressor! What would society say of a female, who, acknowledging that she had been seduced, should pretend that her seduction was effected in her sleep?' Church was not allowed back into Banbury and moved to London, his wife (he appears to have had a wife) and possessions being sent after him. 'I had some scandal while at Banbury,' Church later recalled, 'but this was chiefly on account of my principles.'

Regency London was no place to restore a reputation. Church's autobiography skips lightly over these early years but if rumour-mongers and pamphleteers are to be believed they were among the most colourful. He became a preacher at the Obelisk Chapel in St George's Field's, taking an attendant at the Chapel as his lover and dodging blackmail threats. Church took refuge in what was (for him) the not uncongenial role of minister at the Swan Hotel in Vere Street. The Swan was a homosexual brothel, and Church officiated at transvestite weddings there. He also carried out funerals for men executed for sodomy, including two of the Vere Street coterie. This made him a gay cult hero.

But 200 years ago it began the grumbling of the bears. The 'Vere Street brothel' caused a sensation when its proprietor, James Cooke, and five others, were tried in September 1810 for what *The Times* called 'detestable practices'. They were sentenced to be pilloried in the Haymarket and condemned to two years in prison. When Cooke was released at the end of 1812 he confessed to the journalist and lawyer-baiter Robert Holloway who researched the scandal thoroughly and wrote up his findings in a pamphlet *The Phoenix of Sodom; or, the Vere Street Coterie*, published in 1813. Here he reveals that regulars were given female nicknames: 'Black-eyed Leonora' was a drummer, 'Pretty Harriet' a butcher, 'Lady Godiva' a waiter, and 'Miss Sweet Lips' a country grocer.

He also revealed that in the Swan there was a room known as the 'Chaple' where transvestite weddings took place 'sometimes

*Second Edition.*

# RELIGION & MORALITY
## VINDICATED,
### AGAINST
# *Hypocrisy and Pollution;*
OR,

AN ACCOUNT OF THE

# LIFE AND CHARACTER
OF

# John Church
THE
## OBELISK PREACHER,
WHO WAS FORMERLY A FREQUENTER OF
## VERE-STREET,
AND WHO HAS BEEN CHARGED WITH
## *UNNATURAL PRACTICES*
IN VARIOUS PLACES.

TO WHICH IS ANNEXED,

## *A Fac-simile of a Letter,*
WRITTEN BY HIM TO JAMES COOK, WHO KEPT THE
INFAMOUS HOUSE IN VERE-STREET.

'I heard the defaming of many, fear on every side,' wrote Church,
who frequently denounced the pamphleteers.

between a female grenadier, six feet high, and a petit maître not more than half the altitude of his beloved wife'. The nuptials, Holloway went on, 'were frequently consummated by two, three, or four couples, in the same room, and in the sight of each other'.

Holloway's pamphlet did not mention Church by name but a portrait of the minister was placed on the front cover. With the braying of the asses and the grumbling of the bears (not to speak of the goats blowing on rams' horns) already on record, the storm clouds (Church would probably have said locusts) were gathering. So was the imagery. At this point he quotes the prophet Amos: 'I fled from a lion and a bear met me, I went into the house, and leaned on the wall and a serpent bit me.'

One lion from which he was fleeing was the father of a young man, William Clarke, whom Church had attempted to seduce in a barn in Colchester the previous year. Church first heard about this new threat to his reputation when Clarke's father stormed into the Obelisk Chapel armed with two loaded pistols, intending to shoot him. Fortunately the man fainted, and Church's life was spared.

The lion evaded, Church was now met by the bear – or bears. His infamy brought in the crowds and in 1813 he opened a new, larger and more profitable Obelisk Chapel. Now the pamphleteers really started to lay into him. Church believed up to 20,000 leaflets and broadsheets were printed denouncing him. 'I heard the defaming of many, fear on every side,' Church wrote, quoting the prophet Jeremiah, of this period of his life. He describes one alarming day at the beginning of 1813 when walking down Blackfriars Road he passed a bookseller's window stocked with a pamphlet containing the Vere Street accusations. 'Soon after this every corner of the streets and every lamp-post had a placard posted, with these elegant words, in capital letters, JOHN CHURCH, INCARNATE DEVIL.'

A particular enemy at the time was Robert Bell, the editor of the *Weekly Dispatch*, who week after week listed Church's misdemeanours. He interviewed Church's former landlady. He printed love letters Church had sent to a tradesman by whom he was smitten, called Ned. All this appeared in a pamphlet, *Religion and Morality Vindicated against Hypocrisy and Pollution*. Copies were sold outside the Obelisk, where large crowds had started to gather daily to protest against Church.

Eventually the fuss died down and Church was left in peace. 'A little more than four years rolled away, while the enemy took breath. We were so quiet, that my name did not, for a long time, occur in the daily papers; yea, they had forgotten me in the *Sunday News!*' But it was not to last. Having contended with the lion and the bear he should not have leaned against the wall. The serpent bit him.

This serpent came in the form of the apprentice potter, Adam Foreman, and led to a second trial in August 1817.

Church's offence was the by now familiar one of failing to seduce yet another young man. In the witness stand Foreman describes how he had been startled out of his sleep 'by some one putting his hands under the bed clothes, and laying hold of my private parts . . . very tight'. When the apprentice potter asked who was there he heard a feigned woman's voice reply, 'Don't you know me, Adam? I'm your mistress.'

Fatally for his defence, Church admitted that he had been in Foreman's room, without giving good reason why. The attempted seduction could hardly be called subtle but surprisingly Church was prosecuted on a charge of having 'with force and arms' attempted to assault Foreman 'so that his life was greatly despaired of', with the intent of committing 'that most horrid, detestable and sodomitical crime (among Christians not to be named) called Buggery . . .'. Church was found guilty, and on 24 November (after preaching a sermon on the passage, 'Rejoice not against me, Oh mine enemy; though I fall, I shall rise; though I sit in darkness, the Lord will be a light unto me!') he was sentenced to two years' imprisonment.

He consoled himself with the thought that 'Samson's locks have grown again and John the Baptist has risen from the dead', and that Israel had been taken into bondage. 'Surely I discover the analogy: I have been dealt with in a similar way.' John Church's optimism was not ill-founded. He emerged from prison after 730 days with a devoted following (especially among young men, wrote one miffed commentator) and preached for the next five years giving by his own estimation thousands of sermons.

It is hard not to have some admiration for Church, who as a baby was discovered abandoned by his mother on the steps of a London church (hence his surname), educated in a foundling hospital, branded on the back of one hand by a hot wire in the manner of all orphans and at the age of 11 taken in as an apprentice to a master who treated him harshly. He survived to tell his tale in his autobiography, published in 1823, which for all its egomania nonetheless has the charm of a man apparently genuinely puzzled that such strange things can have happened to him – and all, it seems, beyond his control!

Thereafter, Church disappears from view, and – we can assume from the silence of the pamphleteers, not to say the goats, asses, bears and serpents, ended his days unmolested by the Balaams and Philistines of London – or, as he preferred to call the metropolis, Zion.

# ANGLICANISM AND HOMOSEXUALITY: RECENT AGONIES

## 'Can you tell me how you got hold of this?'

When the term as Bishop of Durham of the controversial theologian, David Jenkins, came to a close in 1994, members of his diocese could be forgiven for looking forward to a period of tranquillity during which Durham might drop from the news.

The arrival of an incumbent not reputed to doubt the Resurrection was greeted by traditionalists with a sigh of relief.

They sighed too early. Days before the inauguration of the Right Reverend Michael Turnbull, the *News of the World* splashed 'Bishop of Durham in Gay Sex Scandal' across its front page. The paper had discovered that the 58-year-old clergyman, married with three grown-up children, had a conviction for gross indecency.

Undercover police had caught the cleric committing what the

*Above*, 'The Arse Bishop' by George Cruikshank (1822) imagines the moment of Percy Jocelyn's capture. 'If his breeches had not been down they think he would have got away,' wrote Charles Greville in his diary.
*Below*, 'The vindication of James Byrne' (1822) depicting the coachman Byrne, 'victim of the unnatural bishop Jocelyn'. Flogged through Dublin for libelling Jocelyn in 1811, he subsequently became a hero of the radical cause.

*Left,* The Rector of Stiffkey, Harold Davidson, pictured with an actress. The photograph was produced at his trial. *Below,* Harold Davidson, the landlady Flora Osborne, and an actress on the lawn of Stiffkey rectory. Behind the shrub is Mrs Davidson. 'Does she always go about like that?' asked the Chancellor at Davidson's trial. *Right,* 'I do not know what the buttock is,' insisted Davidson. He claimed that this picture with 15-year-old Estelle Douglas, taken on the eve of the trial, was a set-up.

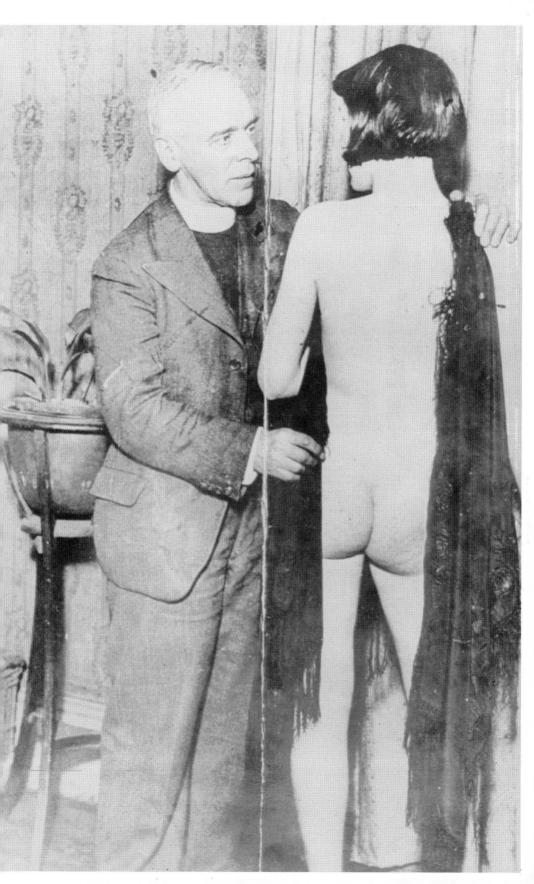

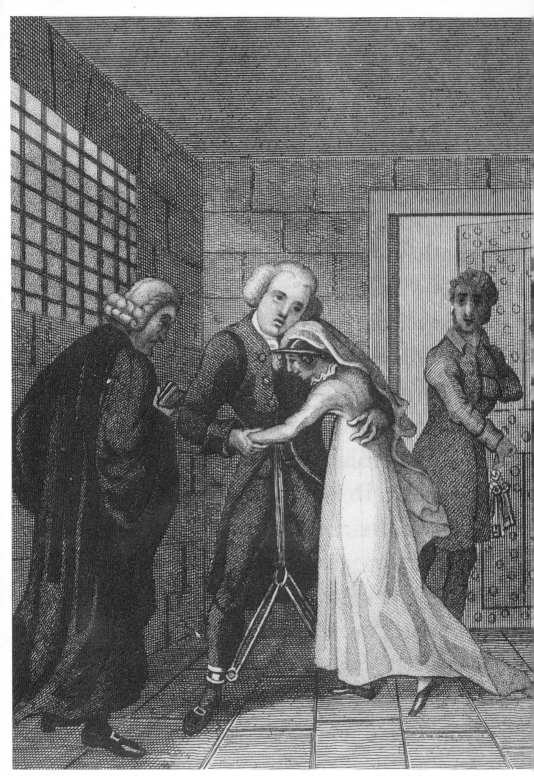

The Reverend Dr William Dodd leaving his wife on the morning of the execution. 'He is to be hanged for the least offence he ever committed,' remarked the Bishop of Bristol.

'A Sandwich' from Henry Angelo's memoirs shows John Montagu, fourth Earl of Sandwich and notorious philanderer, walking between two women. The Reverend James Hackman murdered one of his mistresses; Dr Dodd married another.

*Above*, Pope Joan giving birth in the Vicus Papissa ('street of the woman pope'), from A Present For a Papist (1785), one of the many Protestant rants on the subject.

*Right*, After declaring himself the Messiah, the Reverend Henry James Prince retired to the Agapemone, surrounded by 'soul brides'. Although claiming immortality, he died in 1899 and was succeeded by the Reverend John Hugh Smyth-Pigott. He named his children Glory, Power and Life.

Agapemone (Abode of Love) Spaxton, Som.
« Birthplace of Glory »

The author photographed in Lambeth Palace. Behind is a list of charges against the Reverend Dr Edward Drax Free, deposed by the Court of Arches in 1830 for numerous offences.

paper called 'a sordid gay sex act with a farmer'. He had pleaded guilty at Hull Magistrates' Court to a charge of gross indecency. His accomplice, a Yorkshireman, had also pleaded guilty. The pair had received a conditional discharge for 12 months.

Shocking? Perhaps, but some way into the story of this incident, the more alert among the readers of the *News of the World* will have realised that it had actually occurred more than a quarter of a century ago, in August 1968. Turnbull had only been a chaplain to the Archbishop of York at the time, having married his wife Brenda, a churchwarden's daughter, five years earlier. His 'cottaging' conviction had been 'hushed up' by the Church, said the paper – a rather dramatic phrase for an incident which will hardly have been considered sensational. He recovered. No one has suggested he ever reoffended. But his *Who's Who* entry listed 'family life', alongside cricket, as his interest. Never do this. There is no surer way of offering editors an opening paragraph and a 'public interest' defence than listing 'family life' among your interests in *Who's Who*.

They would have run the story anyway. The paper used the charge of hypocrisy to justify its front-page splash. The church admitted to knowing all along about his conviction, yet when they appointed him Bishop of Durham in February 1994, Turnbull had been asked what he thought of gay priests. 'Such a lifestyle is incompatible with a full-time stipendiary ministry,' he answered.

The *News of the World*'s revelation caused a terrific shock. The night before publication, as the newly appointed bishop was moving into his palatial seat, Auckland Castle, Co. Durham, the paper contacted him. 'Ah . . . I've nothing to say,' he stammered, 'can you tell me how you got hold of this?'

The farmer – by then in his late 60s – was more forthcoming. Reportedly 'stunned' when the *News of the World* revealed the identity of the man he had 'fondled' all those years ago, he allegedly told reporters: 'Oh, bloody hell. I knew he was a cleric of some sort. It was a strange sort of going-on . . . The other gentleman put his what-you-call-it through the wall and I touched it and two police came down from the roof . . . They'd got holes bored in the roof and all things like that. That's not police work as far as I'm concerned.'

After his conviction Turnbull had left his post at York Minster for the more humble role of rector at nearby Heslington. He also became Chaplain to York University. Seven years later his rise began again in earnest. The post of Archdeacon of Rochester followed eight years as Chief Secretary to the Church Army. In 1988 he became Bishop of Rochester. Before his promotion to Auckland Castle his most prominent job was as chairman of the Archbishop of Canterbury's commission into the reorganisation of the Church of England's senior hierarchy.

After the news broke it quickly became clear the Church intended to hang on to Turnbull. A spokesman for the Archbishop of York confirmed that the conviction had been known at the time and that the Archbishop of Canterbury, Dr George Carey, had been aware of it when Turnbull was appointed Bishop of Durham. 'We regard it as entirely uncharacteristic of the man we know, in whom we have the greatest confidence. I deplore that something which happened twenty-six years ago is now being publicised long after it has been forgiven.'

Turnbull himself described the incident as a 'mistake' and denied ever being homosexual. He was persuaded against stepping down. A friend, the Dean of Durham, the Very Rev John Arnold, said 'It's been a kind of hell. The awakening of old nightmares is one of the worst things that can happen to you.' It is good to know we shall have Mr Arnold's sympathy at the Last Judgement.

Happily, Turnbull survived. But the Church was damaged – not least because of forces beyond its control. A few months previously Parliament had voted to lower the age of consent for homosexuals to 18, but not, as many had hoped, to 16. Angered by what they saw as injustice, some in the gay rights movement began collecting information on senior figures in public life who were secretly homosexual. They were led by Peter Tatchell, founder of the Outrage lobby group. 'We were angry because he had publicly condemned gay clergy,' Mr Tatchell said. Ironically, Tatchell had himself found his sexuality splashed across the nation's press more than a decade earlier, when he had stood for Parliament.

Their activities caused great alarum. Tatchell made it clear that the Bishop of Durham was not alone. 'The Church is storing up trouble. They should come out of the closet.' Names were not revealed but hints were made that they might be. It was enough to send a collective shiver up cassocks across the land.

In the meantime, Outrage resolved that they would attempt to disrupt the new bishop's enthronement at Durham Cathedral, planned for Saturday 22 October. On the day, a crowd of about 150 gathered. As the new bishop emerged into the daylight he was initially greeted by cheers. They faded to angry jeers from protesters who had mingled with the crowd. A chant began: 'Turnbull is a hypocrite! Sack the bishop!' A banner was unfurled: 'From cottage to cathedral'.

It was at this point that the police noticed Peter Tatchell sprinting across Cathedral Green, hurdling headstones as he ran in the direction of the startled bishop. Television cameramen refocused their sights in time to capture frames of a burly policeman rugby-tackling Peter Tatchell, kneeling on him face-down in the grass. He was handcuffed and arrested, but later released without charge.

Inside the Cathedral the bishop told the congregation he had been 'through a private and now public process of repentance... I am deeply sorry that so many friends, and especially new friends in this diocese, have shared some of the consequences. The people of the north east have a right to be shocked.'

The papers managed to keep the story going a little longer. Among the numerous clergy of the Church of England, it is always possible to find a few censorious voices, and the *News of the World* did its homework. The parish priest for Turnbull's new home, Auckland Castle, the Reverend John Marshall, boycotted the service and urged the bishop to resign. 'It's a miserable situation,' he said. Another accused him of 'making a mockery of his ministry'. The Reverend Nicholas Beddow, of Escomb and Witton Park, said Church leaders 'failed to realise deceit does not fade with age. It festers and becomes ever more poisonous.'

Speaking shortly afterwards Turnbull said he had seriously considered resigning, but had come to the conclusion that it would have been 'a denial of the gospel and a victory for the forces of darkness'. He urged gay clergy who had been dismissed for similar offences to his own to ask for a review of their cases if they felt they had been unfairly treated. 'I would want to encourage people who still feel a sense of injustice to go back to the bishops and say: "Look, this happened to me, and I want it reviewed".'

As to his statement at the height of the storm denying that he was or ever had been homosexual, he said: 'I was responding at the moment to the charge of hypocrisy; and I was trying to make a distinction between an incident and a lifestyle.'

Michael Turnbull was frank, though at a point when it was in his interests to be so. Other senior figures in the Anglican Communion remained unwilling to talk publicly about the subject of homosexuality. A meeting in London of the General Synod was looming, with the likely prospect of further protests.

A 33-year-old parish priest from Roehampton, Surrey, chose his moment to announce he was gay – and living with a long-term lover. Reverend Niall Johnstone, as head of an unpublicised network of lesbian and gay clergy, had been quietly briefing the press for some time. He telephoned his bishop, Roy Williamson of Southwark, and told him he intended to go public. 'He didn't try to stop me,' Johnstone says. 'He just made sure I knew what I was doing.'

Johnstone claims he did this because he was feeling generally fed up with the church, though not with his own diocese. There was talk at the time about the loss of his first lover in a motorcycle accident, and his agonies (after meeting someone new) about whether to resign. He attracted personal sympathy.

Niall Johnstone's life is hardly scandalous. Yet his decision to be open about his sexuality – a path followed by others since 1994 – presents the Church of England with a larger dilemma than any number of the scandals catalogued in this book. To be caught and to repent, or indeed to deny all, is one thing. To deny the sinful nature of the thing of which one is accused is quite another.

At the end of November 1994 Outrage carried out their threat to 'create a crisis in the Church of England'. Delegates arriving at Church House, Westminster, for the second day of the General Synod were greeted by a small band of demonstrators, including one man dressed as a nun, and a larger number of reporters, photographers, cameramen and police.

With the 'stiff, half-grinning shuffle of shepherds in a school nativity play' (said the *Independent on Sunday*) Outrage secured the Church House steps. Beneath an exhortation to 'Tell the Truth' their placards bore the names of ten Anglican bishops, among them Michael Turnbull. Two were members of the General Synod, four had already retired. Five were or had been diocesan bishops.

Many Synod members walked past the activists without taking

a leaflet but some found it hard to ignore the demonstration. One greeted a protester with a kiss. Tatchell claims another cleric paused to read the names then turned to him and said 'no surprises there then'. The Reverend Roger Arguile from Stafford described the action as 'filth'. 'This preoccupation with sex is absurd,' he said.

The next day's press poured scorn on the quality of the group's evidence, none of which was or ever has been produced. Only the *Guardian* printed any of the names. Church House officials knew in advance of the demonstration and had their legal staff on hand to serve injunctions. But they failed to do so – Outrage too had taken legal advice. Their call for the bishops to 'tell the truth' fell short of an actionable statement.

Jack Nicholls, suffragan Bishop of Lancaster, who was named, put out a statement: 'Having known something of the pain which comes from homosexual feelings, I have spent a considerable amount of my ministry supporting gay people. I have tried to help the Church become more accepting and less judgmental towards them.'

Another bishop named was the retired former Bishop of Southwark, Mervyn Stockwood. A controversial liberal figure throughout his life and a campaigner for social justice, Stockwood had held the Southwark episcopate from 1959 until 1980. His biographer, Michael De-la-Noy, a former press officer to the Archbishop of Canterbury, believes Stockwood was homosexual but 'all the evidence suggests he led a life of total celibacy'. The bishop had spoken in favour of the decriminalisation of homosexuality in 1967. He even blessed a gay relationship although he felt that calling it a 'wedding' was 'a contradiction in terms'. In 1979 Mervyn Stockwood wrote to a friend:

I regret much of what is done by the Gay Liberation Movement, especially in the Church. If two men believe they are justified in living together, and if they wish to ask God's blessing on their commitment, I think it best for a priest to say prayers with them privately. The time may come when the Church will take a different attitude, but at the moment a public ceremony can do nothing but make a difficult situation even more difficult. It is true we have a duty as priests towards homosexuals, but we also have a duty to those who sincerely take a different point of view.

In retirement he added: 'as you know, I did a lot to help but never appeared in print or joined a campaign'. His failure to go public seems to be the reason Outrage took the unkind decision to include Stockwood in their campaign.

It is probably true that Stockwood failed to promote priests who he feared might bring the Church into disrepute – some would argue that is a bishop's job. Hugh Montefiore, a later Bishop of Birmingham, was one of his suffragans in Southwark. He has said that Stockwood 'didn't mind his clergy having it off as long as there wasn't a scandal'.

Mervyn Stockwood was alone at his home in Sydney Buildings, Bath, when the local bishop, James Thompson, phoned him with the news of that morning's activity at Church House. Stockwood replied, with some bravado 'I couldn't care tuppence. And if the press get on to you, tell them I've had a lot of women too.' Six weeks later Mervyn Stockwood died. He was 81. There is no evidence that the outing played any part but his friends remain angry at what they see as a unwarranted attack on a very old man.

Stockwood's death did not signal the end of the outing campaign. Perhaps unsettled by all the fuss, the Bishop of London, Dr David Hope, the third most senior bishop in the Church of England, stated that his sexuality was a 'grey area'. The House of Bishops was later persuaded to deliver a denunciation of homophobia. This caused a large grouping of traditionalists to issue the threat (so far no more than a threat) to break away from the Church for good.

This author takes the other side in this dispute. I do, however, like many outside the Church, have a slight personal difficulty with the appeal for our *sympathy* (as distinguished from understanding or support) for gay churchmen; and a larger difficulty with their call upon any sense of public outrage. I can well see how a gay man might join the Church (or Army, or Conservative Party) and hope either to keep quiet and get away with it; or alternatively take a stand once accepted as a member and work from within for change. I admire people who do the latter; while understanding those who prefer to keep quiet.

But outrage on anyone's part seems to me hard to justify. The terms of their employment cannot have turned out to be very different from what must have been anticipated at the outset. I am also uncomfortable with the argument that because a great many churchmen are gay, that *in itself* would be reason to alter doctrine. One surely needs to establish that the doctrine is wrong – not that it is awkward. A pacifist, convinced that pacifism is the teaching of Christ, should surely not be impressed by the objection that many in the church are soldiers?

This does not seem to me a debate which non-believers are entirely equipped to enter.

And it is possible to dislike almost every party involved in the wretched, tawdry controversy described in this chapter: the strident and self-righteous voices of Church 'traditionalists', strangers to any sort of kindness; the self-serving bleating of those found out (but only once found out), all their rigour and judgement suddenly collapsing into a preference for amnesia and fudge; the shrill, too-shrewd self-advertisement of gay campaigners, as ready as any *tricoteuse* to knit other people's wrecked lives into banners for their own causes; the maudlin and intellectually confused presentation of bereavement, personal tragedy and implicit calls for sympathy as though these were moral or theological arguments; the dogged refusal of the conservatives to notice their Church's teaching on mercy and the dogged refusal of the liberals to notice their Church's teaching on sexual licence; the persistent conflation of self-pity with reason; and, through it all, the simpering Anglicanism which, fearful of losing anybody, wants to have its cake and eat it – and just wishes everyone would shut up.

It would be too theatrical to see in this sorry saga fresh and compelling evidence of the moral confusion of the Church of England: the Church's moral confusion is ancient, widespread and famous, and needs no modern illustration. What does strike this observer as, if not new, then more compellingly evident than of old, is the pitiful *intellectual* calibre of the voices and arguments coming from within the Church. A noble, powerful, lucid case can be put honestly and without unpleasantness for moral conservatism; and a fine, philosophically formidable case for qualified moral relativism can be opposed to it.

But where are these voices? Where are the *minds*? All we observe is intolerance, low censoriousness, circumspection, self-pity, sniping, whimpering and special pleading – and, always and forever, the grinding of axes.

# RUNAWAY ROMEOS

## EAMONN CASEY

## 'Off with the collar and off with the nightie!'

'It has come to our attention,' wrote Dublin's *Phoenix* magazine on 1 May 1992, 'that a clergyman of some considerable eminence will soon be catapulted onto the front pages of the public prints.' The language was old-fashioned, almost quaint. But then so was the sin.

The cleric, the article went on, 'has been named by a respected but greatly disillusioned lady of middle years as the father of her 14-year-old son. The cleric's position in the Church and his high media profile are said to be certain to cause a scandal which will make the affair of the Aranmore parish priest and the sergeant's wife look positively boring.'

It was the first hint of what was to become one of Ireland's greatest modern clerical scandals – and there is some competition. Save for the age of the child (17, not 14), the magazine's prophecies were proved correct in every respect. Within a week, Bishop Eamonn Casey had resigned as Bishop of Galway and fled, it was presumed, to South America. On the streets of Dublin people wore T-shirts with the pun, 'Wear a condom, just in Casey'. It was a dreadful end for one of Ireland's most gifted and popular prelates.

Bald, rotund and 65, Eamonn Casey looks like a self-indulgent pope. With a penchant for fast cars (his lover claimed she was whisked in a Lancia to the scene of their son's conception), fine wine and good food, his only previous brush with scandal had been a drink-driving conviction in London a few years previously. This, far from discrediting the bishop, boosted his popularity in

Ireland after a heartfelt apology was read out from all the pulpits in his diocese. It was only *drinking* and his prosecutors had been British for heaven's sake!

Casey combined his high-life with a real devotion to humanitarian work. A founding member of the homeless charity Shelter when a young curate in London, as an Irish bishop he was a formidable and controversial campaigner for the alleviation of poverty in Latin America, though also a noted opponent of contraception. A more stuffy character would have fared less well when news of his affair broke. As it was, the revelation was greeted with great sympathy. The 'human face of the Irish Church' – as Casey was known – had revealed another weakness of the flesh.

Temptation for the bishop had come in the form of a comely young American, Annie Murphy, to whom Casey was distantly related. She arrived in Ireland in April 1973 to recuperate from a 'bad divorce'. The temptation was obvious, and from Murphy's account of the affair – she wrote it all up at merciless detail later seventeen years after its conclusion – the Bishop of Kerry (as he then was) did not put up much of a fight. He wrestled with his conscience for a fortnight after his American visitor's arrival at his home – and then went wild.

One night he appeared in Murphy's bedroom, solemnly divested himself of his brown flip-flops, undid the cord of his dressing gown, unbuttoned his faded blue pyjamas and stood, quite naked, before her. 'I looked on mesmerised as he hardened below a black fringe of curls,' recalls Murphy, before going on to recount, in pitiless detail, the story of their first forays in physical love. 'There stood the bishop, my love, without clerical collar or crucifix or episcopal ring, without covering of any kind... witnessed a great hunger. This was an Irish famine of the flesh...'

For most of the following year the two were ardent lovers. They groped and fondled everywhere – in the Bishop's Palace, in the back of his chauffeur-driven car while Church officials sat in the front, and on his hearth-rug. Murphy would sometimes await the bishop's return from church perched and purring on top of his piano, dressed in a negligée. She once waved from the window of the bishop's bedroom, naked, towards a convent. She says he told her to wear zip-up clothes 'for easier access'. On one occasion late at night in Dublin, Murphy thought that she was being kerb-crawled when a car sidled alongside her. It was the bishop in his sports car, newly imported from Italy. She was whisked off to a gravel pit outside the city where, Murphy claimed, their child was conceived.

In July 1974 she gave birth to a son, Peter. At this point the bishop's ardour seems to have deserted him. He packed Murphy off to a convent where the nuns joined him in pressurising her to have the child adopted, denying her medical attention when she refused. Rejected, she returned to America as a single mother.

Over the next 17 years she received meagre handouts from the bishop, who was soon moved to the see of Galway. In July 1990, through her lawyer, she negotiated a 'final settlement' payment of $125,000. Casey, whose episcopal salary was £8,000 per year, paid up promptly. It later transpired that the money had been removed from diocesan funds.

A year later, Casey was in New York on Church business. For the first time in 16 years he and Murphy met, in the Grand Hyatt Hotel, where Murphy was working as a receptionist. 'Time would rub out mountains but not us, not Eamonn and me,' Murphy writes in her dreadful book. They went to the bar. To capture the moment Murphy had strapped round her waist a tape recorder; concealed behind a pot plant were her son and a friend with a video-recorder. After a few drinks the old ardour rekindled; the Bishop of Galway and his discarded mistress left the Hyatt and spent the night in a cheaper hotel. Murphy thoughtfully records that the bishop was wearing 'showy' underpants. The next morning they parted on the platform of the Grand Central Station, the last time the couple saw each other.

In fact, neither the video nor the tape recording were used to expose the bishop – although Peter had managed to shoot footage of his parents kissing. Instead, at the beginning of 1992, with Casey still refusing to make a public acknowledgement that Peter was his son and having only ever met him for four minutes in the offices of a New York lawyer, Murphy contacted the *Irish Times* on a 'highly charged political and religious matter'. As she relates it the decision to go public was made by Peter, who resented the fact that Casey had never acknowledged him. Further payments from the bishop failed to mollify him.

The *Irish Times* broke the story on 7 May 1992. By now Casey had flown to Italy and handed in his resignation to the Vatican. The following day he fled to New York from Shannon Airport in an empty first-class cabin; other passengers had been cleared out. He was whisked through Customs at JFK into a black limousine and vanished into 'hiding'.

Reaction in Ireland was confused. 'A bishop's personal life is very much his own,' said Cardinal Daly, the Primate of All Ireland, a novel doctrine if the Cardinal meant the remark to be taken as broadly as it was couched. Annie Murphy rushed out her book, *Forbidden Fruit: the True Story of My Love for the Bishop of Galway*, capitalising on the immense public interest the affair generated in Ireland. Saccharine in tone, but sparing nothing, it went straight to the top of the Irish book-sales charts.

But she was given a surprisingly hard time by (and on) the Irish media. This was more than a matter of the Church protecting its own: indeed much of the Catholic Church took a more serious view of the matter than the Irish laity appeared to. There was a good deal of affection for Casey whom many saw as a lovable old roué cruelly pecked at by a hatchet-faced American harpy.

By now the 'disgraced' bishop was ensconced with 14 nuns in a Mexican convent, only to be tracked down by a reporter, Gordon Thomas, with a copy of Murphy's book in hand. But the Irish Catholic establishment weathered the storm. Casey after 'treatment' from the Church remained in South America. He is now a priest in Ecuador, though no longer a bishop. He retires soon and plans to write a book. It is reported that he is anxious to come home. Annie Murphy has returned to the United States. The Saw Doctors had a hit with their satirical ballad:

Now when he was up and going and taking in the church
  collection
His lover was busy writing down her recollections
How she loved the Bishop and he loved her just as well
Only God knows whether they go to heaven or to hell

Oh Mighty, Mighty Lord Almighty!
Off with the collar and off with the nightie!
Jesus, Mary, and Holy St Joseph
The beads are rattling now...

Must be funny in the morning he'd be doing the consecration
After long nights of long and passionate unbridled
　　fornication
Sitting in the Chapel, attending exposition
Dreaming Kama Sutra and his favourite positions

Oh the blind, faithful followers are worried and distraught,
And the only thing that's bothering them is that poor man he
　　got caught

Oh Mighty, Mighty Lord Almighty!
Off with the collar and off with the nightie
Jesus, Mary, and Holy St Joseph
The beads are rattling now...

# RODERICK WRIGHT

## 'There are no more women.
## Just these two'

Once, when a bishop broke his vows and fathered a son, the boy
could expect a great deal. Cardinal Wolsey made his natural son
Thomas Wynte Dean of Wells, Provost of Beverly, Archdeacon of
York, Chancellor of Salisbury, Prebendary of Wells, York,
Salisbury, Lincoln and Southwell, Rector of Rudby, Yorkshire
and St Matthew's, Ipswich – and all while Thomas was still a
schoolboy.

Not today. At least one schoolboy in East Sussex waits in vain
as I write for even a portion of such preferment. Modern morals
and modern prurience can sometimes seem almost less civilised
than the mellow degeneracy of our forbears.

In Wolsey's time moral failure in the higher levels of the English

Church called first for concealment and secondly for the buying off of all concerned. And then, hopefully, silence. Today there is only noise. When a bishop is revealed to be subject to the same human weaknesses as his fellow men, this becomes the cue for an orgy of a different kind: a frenzy of soul-searching, TV chat-show sermonising, national debates on celibacy, the mobbing of individuals by journalists and cameramen and absurd predictions of the demise of the Papacy. As modern as all this may seem, it has the simplicity and inevitability of the dramas of ancient Athens: the spurned mistress playing the Furies; the gods of Vengeance represented by the tabloid press; and the Chorus by the churchmen and columnists (like me) who chant the same platitudes. It is Greek tragedy rewritten as a twentieth-century Christian morality play.

Never more so than in the events which followed the disappearance in 1996 of Roderick Wright, the Catholic Bishop of Argyll and the Isles. He left his grey-walled bishop's palace in Oban for the last time in early September. For five days no one seemed to notice the 56-year-old clergyman's absence. Then the BBC picked up the story. A 'divorcee' from the town, it suggested, had gone missing at about the same time. Wright, famous for his charm and chain-smoking was (in his younger days) nicknamed 'Bishop Starsky' because of his televisual good looks. And his Volkswagen car had become a regular sight outside the home of the missing woman.

Journalists with O-levels in Geography remembered that among the scattered islands of his diocese was one called Muck. Inevitably, Roderick Wright was then dubbed by the papers the 'Bishop of Muck'. Less erudite journalists stuck to puns about Dyno-Rod or cracked jokes about the new rules in Scottish chess: the bishop jumps anything.

In a statement issued through the Catholic Church in Scotland on Monday 16 September – when his whereabouts were still a mystery – the bishop confessed he had eloped. 'I am physically and spiritually unable to sustain the responsibilities of a diocesan bishop. I ask your forgiveness.' Cardinal Winning, head of the Catholic Church in Scotland, expressed the hope that Wright would remain in the ministry.

The Scottish press preached 'compassion' for the 56-year-old bishop, and preached it often and at length, on the front and inside pages, and over many editions. Space was also found for speculation and pop psychology. The rules on celibacy were blamed for placing intolerable demands on the clergy. 'If I was fifty years younger, I'd have run off with him,' sighed one old lady outside Oban Cathedral.

Roderick Wright had, it seemed, given up everything to be with Kathleen MacPhee, a 44-year-old married auxiliary nurse with whom he had been conducting an affair for over a year. The couple had met when Wright buried Mrs MacPhee's stillborn child. 'Roddy was just a really nice man ... very approachable and could give a damn good service,' she said.

Days passed. Bishop Wright remained in hiding. Then a bombshell: several hundred miles away, near Eastbourne, an entirely different woman emerged voluntarily on the BBC News to declare that she had thought it was she who was the bishop's mistress. What's more 48-year-old Joanna Whibley revealed that she was the mother of Kevin, his 15-year-old son.

I can report parts of this story quite directly as I met Joanna Whibley and her son at their home in East Sussex and interviewed her for a radio series on media intrusion.

The press, tipped off by rumours in Oban, had been camped outside her door near Eastbourne since the bishop's disappearance. But until she agreed to tell her story herself they dared not publish. And they did not know about Kevin.

The Church did. After he ran away Wright had forewarned Cardinal Winning about both his mistresses and his child. But nobody had expected Whibley to proclaim the affair. The Church may have entertained hopes that this part of the truth would never emerge. It hoped, perhaps, to arrange a partial rehabilitation for its former bishop.

Now Joanna Whibley had put her head above the parapet, however, the Church seemed to affect surprise. Catholic spokesmen changed their tune. Wright was officially denounced for behaving like a 'second Lord Lucan', and the Archbishop of St Andrews and Edinburgh fretted on television that more mistresses might emerge.

Still tucked away at a secret address, Roderick Wright became Britain's temporary Most Wanted Man. He had chosen a bad time of year: the tail-end of the summer lull in real news, and a week before Party Conferences could provide any alternative entertainment. The hunt for Wright became something of a national preoccupation. 'WANTED' wrote the *Mirror*. 'RANDY ROD FOR SERIAL VIOLATION OF CELIBACY. *Call the Mirror if you see him. (PS lock up your wife and daughters first.)*'

But it was the *News of the World* which got the scoop. Tipped off by a neighbour that the bishop was closeted with Mrs MacPhee in a Lake District town, the paper dispatched two reporters to find him. 'We knocked and Bishop Wright came to the door,' Phil Hall, the paper's editor, told me. 'And we asked, "Are you interested in talking to the *News of the World*?". He said, "Yes, would a fee be involved?"'

Roderick Wright has said that he would have let the Devil in through the front door, such was the pressure on him to talk.

The two reporters spent Saturday evening with the bishop and Mrs MacPhee eating a Chinese takeaway and drinking a bottle of cheap whisky. Wright provided the paper with next morning's 'World Exclusive – Runaway Bishop Confesses all to the *News of the World*: Why I Sinned'.

Rumours circulated that he had agreed to talk for £300,000. The sum turned out to be much lower, £15,000, and was due to be paid to MacPhee's children but the news that he had sold his story lost Wright what public sympathy remained. Call-girls and cast-off mistresses were expected to sell their stories to the *News of the World*. But a bishop?

Joanna Whibley never did sell her story. This was not for want of scrawled offers pushed under her door by the media throng outside, some of which she showed me. When direct offers of cash failed to tempt her journalists tried proposals of donations to charity or to a trust for her son's education. When she refused these too, journalists enquired how she could be so heartless as to deprive others of the money. Whibley had no private funds of her own but was determined that she and her son should not use this affair to enrich themselves. When she did eventually agree to talk she chose the BBC, who do not pay, because she believed they would handle the matter responsibly. I have much respect for Joanna and Kevin Whibley.

At this point in the story they were under siege: on one occasion they feared the windows of their house would collapse under the weight of journalists pressed against them. The pair communicated by writing notes to each other, afraid that the press had placed listening devices in air vents. They suspected that their phone had been tapped and removed light bulbs from rooms at the front of the house to prevent photographers snapping their silhouettes through the thin curtains. Journalists, crowded outside, floodlit the building. Joanna Whibley described the press pack in the garden as a vast and terrifying tidal wave, about to engulf her house.

She had met the bishop 20 years before. He had instructed her when she converted to Catholicism. An affair began and Kevin, their son, was born in 1981. Wright, then a curate with a promising Church career ahead of him, told Whibley he would leave Britain for Peru if she revealed that he was the father (she says). He is not mentioned on his son's birth certificate. For the next 15 years he occasionally paid maintenance. In July 1996 Wright, who was on a stipend of £6,000 a year, sent Whibley a cheque for £2,031 – which she refused to cash. Some money was, however, paid in £200 cash instalments. Mrs Whibley thinks cash was preferred so that the Child Support Agency could not trace the father. Later he had sent her a postcard from Lourdes. He also talked, Whibley told me, of resigning from his diocese to come and live with her and Kevin.

The week before he vanished, she says, Wright had telephoned her to say that in the next few days she could expect to see him on her doorstep. She stocked up the freezer and prepared the house for a visitor. When she heard on the radio that the Bishop of Argyll had disappeared she thought he was on his way down to East Sussex. He had said nothing of any other woman, she says.

The next thing Joanna and her son heard was the bishop's statement apologising to his Church and his parishioners – and declaring his love for Kathleen MacPhee. Even after resigning he did not mention his son.

'I wanted the fact to be known and retain the dignity for myself,' she told me. This is what prompted her to speak. 'I didn't do it for revenge, but coincidentally his failure to acknowledge Kevin was avenged.' The press-pack in her garden meant that Wright could no longer deny his son's existence. 'So I was delighted, in some ways, that they had come.' The *Daily Mail* summed up a general feeling and possibly Joanna Whibley's with its front-page headline: 'Just How Many More, Bishop?'

As to the former bishop's debut in the *News of the World*, it was

Rupert Murdoch and Roderick Wright meet in the *Guardian*

something of a let-down as kiss-and-tell splashes go. The two
questions on prurient minds – had the two made love? and were
there any more mistresses? – received unsensational answers. We
learnt that their relationship had not been consummated. Wright
said it had been confined to kisses. 'Kathleen insisted on that.'
And no, 'there have been no affairs with any other women. Just
these two.'

The former bishop and his second lover fled to France in
'getaway cars' provided by the *News of the World* in the small hours
of the morning on which these revelations appeared. On their
return they announced at a press conference that they planned to
marry and, yes, the relationship had been consummated. Press
conferences are becoming strange affairs.

Cardinal Wolsey never had to put up with anything like this. It
is hard not to feel some sympathy for all the parties concerned.
Mrs MacPhee's marriage collapsed. Whibley was let down in a
quite astonishing way. And Wright discovered that three years as
a bishop don't qualify you for much. Door-stepped by a journalist
from *The Times* he admitted he was occupying his time
redecorating the house.

I doubt (having spoken to him) whether Kevin wants to be
Dean of Wells, Provost of Beverly, Archdeacon of York,

Chancellor of Salisbury, Prebendary of Wells, York, Salisbury, Lincoln and Southwell, Rector of Rudby, Yorkshire and St Matthew's, Ipswich – and all before his A-levels. I simply ask whether this might not have been a better way of dealing with the affair.

# FEET OF CLAY

## SAINT GEORGE OF CAPPADOCIA... OR WAS IT ALEXANDRIA?

## Purveyor of Pork and Patron Saint of England

It says something about the English that not even our patron saint is free from allegations of sleaze and that the defence of the character of a man whose very existence is in doubt and whose legend is, on even an optimistic view, a tissue of myth, has become a patriotic duty. Hesitating between the claim that St George was the vicious parasite whom enquiry has uncovered, and the claim that that was another George, his defenders over the centuries have mostly chosen the view that there were two Georges.

St George of Cappadocia (complained the historian and theologian Peter Heylyn in 1633) has been martyred twice: once in his person, and once in history. The patron saint of England, martyr for Christ, first knight of the garter, slayer of dragons and one of the Seven Champions of Christendom has – almost since the day he died – been bedevilled by accusations that he was a low-born and corrupt administrator who as Archbishop of Alexandria in the fourth century was so brutal that he was murdered by the mob he had oppressed. It is all a distressingly far cry from the traditional picture of the young, well-bred Christian officer in the imperial army tortured and executed for defying the emperor's edicts against Christianity.

It must be allowed that apologists for the Saint – and they are legion – have dispensed with some of the more unbelievable

190

trappings of his claimed life. No one now maintains that he was born in Coventry (as suggested by Richard Johnson in his *Seven Champions of Christendom*). And even in the seventeenth century Peter Heylyn did not suggest that the story of the dragon was anything other than an elaborate allegory.

However without these tales the traditional St George is a sadly diminished figure, resting on uncertain historical ground. Two fifth-century hagiographies containing gruesome accounts of St George's martyrdom were condemned as impossible fantasy by Pope Gelasius almost as soon as they were written; the Pope was reduced to saying that 'George's deeds are known to God only' – a tactful way of saying that we know nothing about him at all.

The best shred – and it is only a shred – of historical evidence for England's St George is one paragraph in the fourth century historian Eusebius's *Universal History*, in which an unnamed, wealthy young man from Nicomedia tears up an imperial edict against the Christian Church and is duly executed. This nameless martyr has traditionally been seen as the historical kernel of England's St George. The paragon (Tennyson wrote):

> Whose glory was redressing human wrong,
> Who spake no slander, no, nor listened to it;
> But through all the tract of years
> Wore the white flower of blameless life.

Such claims are at least fanciful, at most seriously misleading. For there is another George – the infamous Archbishop of Alexandria – whose existence is not in question and whose deeds are better documented by his contemporary, the historian Ammianus Marcellinus. This 'human snake' (as Ammianus described him) is, the sneerers claim, the man we now revere as patron saint of England.

The attribution was known in Heylyn's time and he indignantly denounced those, including the Bishop of Norwich, who besmirched the saint's reputation. However, it was Edward Gibbon, the unreservedly anti-clerical historian, who made the definitive attack: in the 23rd chapter of *The Decline and Fall of the Roman Empire*, in memorable prose. *Daily Telegraph* leader-writers who ascribe the debunking of St George to the modern fad for besmirching virtue and patriotism overlook the grandest besmircher of all. George's reputation never quite recovered.

In every detail the deeds of this other George seem calculated to assault English dignity. Far from being of noble Christian stock Gibbon insisted that George was born in a fuller's shop in Cilicia. 'From this obscure and servile origin,' Gibbon remarks with magisterial disdain, 'he raised himself by the talents of a parasite.'

Worse, his first job was as a bacon-supplier to the Egyptian army – and of all the charges this is the one which has thrown the defenders of George into the most violent apoplexy. 'It is inconceivable,' spluttered the Dean of Cape Town in 1888, author of *The True History of St George*, 'that the Church of Christ, and emperors and kings of nations, would pay homage to a defunct pork-purveyor.'

Gibbon based his account on that of Ammianus, and other contemporary sources. The rest of his account, rich in invective, is worth quoting in full:

His employment was mean; he rendered it infamous. He accumulated wealth by the basest arts of fraud and corruption; but his malversations were so notorious that George was compelled to escape from the pursuits of justice. After this disgrace, in which he appears to have saved his fortune at the expense of his honour, he embraced, with real or affected zeal, the profession of Arianism. From the love, or the ostentation, of learning, he collected a valuable library of history, rhetoric, philosophy, and theology; and the choice of the prevailing faction promoted George of Cappadocia to the throne of Athanasius. The entrance of the new Archbishop was that of a barbarian conqueror; and each moment of his reign was polluted by cruelty and avarice. The Catholics of Alexandria and Egypt were abandoned to a tyrant, qualified by nature and education to exercise the office of persecution; but he oppressed with an impartial hand the various inhabitants of his diocese.... Under the reign of Constantius he was expelled by the fury, or rather by the justice, of the people; and it was not without a struggle that the civil and military powers of the state could restore his authority and gratify his revenge. The messenger who proclaimed at Alexandria the accession of Julian announced the downfall of the archbishop. George, with two of his obsequious ministers, Count Diodorus, and

Dracontius, master of the mint, were ignominiously dragged in chains to the public prison. At the end of 24 days the prison was forced open by the rage of the superstitious multitude, impatient of the tedious forms of judicious proceedings. The enemies of gods and men expired under their cruel insults; the lifeless bodies of the archbishop and his associates were carried in triumph through the streets on the back of a camel; and the inactivity of the Athanasian party was deemed a shining example of evangelical patience. The remains of these guilty wretches were thrown into the sea.

So this was the 'martyrdom of St George': the murder of a heretical, tyrannical prelate by the righteous fury of an oppressed populace. Gibbon, concluding his account, twisted the knife:

> The odious stranger, disguising every circumstance of time and place, assumed the mask of a martyr, a saint, and a Christian hero; and the infamous George of Cappadocia has been transformed into the renowned St George of England, the patron of arms, of chivalry, and of the garter.

More than any other, Gibbon's onslaught stirred the patriotic furies of Englishmen of his day. As George himself rescued the lady from the dragon, so the patriots set about rescuing St George from the Gibbon. Almost as soon as Gibbon's account appeared, the Reverend J. Milner, writing for the Royal Antiquarian Society (patron: St George) published a *Historical and Critical Inquiry into the Character of St George* which fully exonerated the man.

The scandal rumbled on through the nineteenth century. 'For six hundred years we have borne his banner of the red cross into every corner of the globe,' wrote William Hepworth Dixon, a Victorian journalist and enthusiast for odd causes of all sorts. 'We have placed his badge on the noblest breasts; we have kept his day as our special feast; we have given his name to the most regal chapel in our land; we have dedicated to him a hundred churches; and while we have been doing all these things in his honour we have been indolently content to allow our greatest historical writer to describe him as one of the lowest scamps and darkest villains who ever stained this earth with crime.'

At the turn of the twentieth century, the Royal Society of St

George commissioned Edward Clapton to compose a *Life of St George*, which takes 50 pages to accept that we know virtually nothing of St George of the Garter, but concludes with the faint hope that perhaps somewhere in the Middle East an early, authentic history of the Saint may yet emerge. 'All honour to this tutelary saint of Old England!' he writes. 'May the English race throughout the world continue to revere his memory as of yore, and ever flourish under that red cross banner which is the symbol of our patriotism!' A pamphlet-sheet published by the society in 1937 warms darkly, in bold type, that England's St George must not be confused with Gibbon's St George.

Today, however, the Royal Society of St George, whose patron is Her Majesty the Queen, appears to have forgotten Gibbon's attack. A call to their London offices elicited no defence of the Patron Saint; they preferred to affect surprise that his character had ever been called into question.

After 1,500 years of relentless abuse George deserves a little peace. In this author's view the most bombproof way of defending him may be to accept that St George is a myth and to revere the myth.

# WILLIAM JACKSON

## 'Doctor Viper'

On 23 August 1773 the *Morning Chronicle* published a list of seven of the most scandalous parsons in England. It is a frustrating document for the author restricts himself to the clerics' initials and only some of their identities can be discerned.

They are a splendidly dissolute crowd: the 'apostate patriot, the late Brentford-parson H. The ravishing, duelling, forging, Fleet-street parson G. That bullying, boxing, Vauxhall parson [Henry] B[ate] [see p235]. The pilfering plagiary, the Bloomsbury parson

T. The assassinating parson P. That libelling, lanksided, lately-whipt Welch parson L...' These are a mere prelude to the real object of the writer's scorn, 'the lying, swearing, drunken King's Bench [prison] parson Jackson!' 'If to sit in alehouses, to brawl in taverns, to frequent brothels, and to inebriate in public gardens be virtuous, that reverend divine, Mr William Jackson, is a miracle of modern goodness.' To be singled out so was high praise indeed. But who was this deviant divine?

The Reverend William Jackson gets scant attention in histories of the period and – so far as I can discover – no biography has been published. He deserves a more careful account especially of his influence in Anglo-Irish history, but this is no place for that. Jackson is part of a notable company in British history (Lloyd George and John Wilkes spring to mind) of considerable rogues who were also undoubted idealists.

Jackson's clerical career came to little. He was educated at Oxford University, where he made a 'rapid proficiency in all branches of clerical and scientific knowledge', according to a profile published in *Hibernian Magazine* of 1795. After leaving university, he became private chaplain to the Earl of Bristol ('with a handsome salary annexed; his circumstances about this time having become much strained'). Jackson was a fine firebrand preacher and this post offered much promise. Had his patron, the earl, entered government, he would have made Jackson an Irish bishop. But he remained outside the administration and Jackson was forced to make his own way in London.

He did so in a spectacular fashion. Jackson played a prominent and wholly discreditable role in the most sensational society scandal of the eighteenth century, and helped encourage the great resurgence of Irish nationalism in the 1790s. A ferocious polemicist and a libertarian who staunchly supported reform in England and revolution in the American colonies, he was born in Dublin in about 1737, and died there in 1795, committing suicide in the dock of the High Court in Dublin after having been found guilty of high treason. Not even his assailant in the *Morning Chronicle* could have foreseen such an ending back in 1773.

Jackson's notoriety – he was dubbed 'Dr Viper' – stemmed from the fact that, like the Reverend Henry Bate, he was a journalist who specialised in vituperative prose. A colleague writing after his death compared Jackson's work to 'the darts of the savage, barbed and poisoned with the most refined art and rankest venom.'

His most celebrated flurry of invective came when as editor of the radical *Public Ledger* he defended the Duchess of Kingston from her critics. This was no mean task; in her youth the duchess (said court gossip) had been the mistress of George II. She attracted notice by arriving at a masquerade clad in a short skirt and a transparent veil. In 1769 she married the fabulously wealthy and conveniently ancient Duke of Kingston. She seems to have overlooked the fact that she was already married. Fifteen years earlier she had wed a Lieutenant Augustus Harvey – a union which (though Harvey was keen to overlook it too) had never been dissolved. The story surfaced two years after the death of her second husband the duke.

The duchess was charged with bigamy in March 1775. Tongues wagged and scandal-sheets tittered and Lady Kingston needed a publicist. Here began the Reverend Dr Jackson's role as her literary henchman. Her ladyship had discovered she was to be lampooned by the playwright Samuel Foote in a new comedy, *A Trip To Calais*. Jackson was employed to launch a counter-attack in print. He seemed untroubled by any conflict between his role as a bigamist's hired character-assassin and his calling as a priest.

The fightback began in his *Public Ledger* where, almost daily, Jackson heaped opprobrium on the playwright. After weeks of unrelenting abuse Foote wrote to Kingston stating that he would drop his plans to publish the play 'PROVIDED the attacks made on me in the newspaper do not make it necessary to act in defence of myself'. But the duchess was in no mood to compromise. Jackson (writing in her name) began insinuating that Foote was a homosexual. Foote offered a ceasefire.

He replied (still in her name): 'I shall keep the pity you send me until the morning before you are turned off: when I will return it by a cupid, with a box of lip-salve; and a choir of choristers shall chant a stave to your requiem.'

Thus was war joined. 'Pray, madam,' Foote replied, 'is not Jackson the name of your female confidential secretary; and is not she generally clothed in black petticoats made of your weeds?' Then he rewrote *A Trip To Calais* as *The Capuchin*, replacing 'Lady Kitty Crocodile' with a lecherous monk, 'Dr Viper', described as the 'doer of the Scandalous Chronicle', who 'mowed down reputations like muck' and 'push'd yourself into the pay of Lady Deborah Dripping'. The dispute was rapidly moving from an attempt by a lady to preserve her reputation to a feud between a parson and the playwright. Of the two, the parson proved the more savage.

Kingston was found guilty of bigamy at the end of April 1776, deprived of her title and – seemingly unbothered by the irony of the destination – made the trip to Calais. Stripped of one title she by lucky chance acquired another: the previous year her lawful husband's brother, the Earl of Bristol, had died childless. The former duchess now became the Countess of Bristol. She stayed abroad, leaving the poisonous parson to battle on her behalf.

Jackson's persecution of Foote began in earnest. The clergyman tracked down a sacked servant of Foote's, John Sangster, who was prepared to allege (probably for a bribe) that the playwright had attempted to bugger him on three occasions. Sodomy was a capital offence so Jackson's actions were at the very least intended to destroy the playwright's reputation and perhaps to kill him too.

Foote's trial began in December. His defence counsel argued that 'the whole charge was a scandalous lie, originating in the foulest malice, and supported by the most wicked and wilful perjury'. This was almost certainly true. Lord Mansfield, the trial judge, echoed these sentiments in his summation. 'The indictments appear founded on conspiracy, and a prosecution supported by perjury,' he said. 'Who is that man? Is he a friend to justice, or an enemy to Mr Foote?' It took the jury just two minutes to acquit Foote.

But the stress broke his health. He died in Dover the following year – on a trip to Calais. The priest had accomplished his task. Dr Viper headed for St Petersburg (where the Duchess-turned-Countess was cavorting with Catherine the Great), returning to England 'with a considerable sum of money, as the FINAL reward of his services'.

For the next few years he vanishes from our view, but Jackson's involvement in scandal and intrigue was not at an end. In 1788 the countess died and departs our tale. Jackson quit the country. It was announced in the London press that he was dead, a view Jackson did nothing to discourage. He was on the run from his English debts.

Feigning death may also have been a means of preparing the ground for a covert return. In the years after the duchess's trial Jackson became ever more enthusiastic in his support of the American and French revolutions. In 1794 the priest returned to England – this time as a French agent masquerading as an American businessman. His brief was to assess the chance of a successful French invasion of either England or Ireland. He found Ireland the more fertile territory and began sounding out potential allies and informants in Dublin. It was not long before he was arrested and charged with high treason.

He spent a year in prison, during which time idealism seemed to overtake this cynical man. He resisted all efforts, including bribery, to persuade him to inform. The jury found him guilty. Judgement was set for four days later, and on 30 April 1795 Jackson made his way to court in a coach. On the way he was seen vomiting violently out of the window. This was attributed to nerves. But once in court it was clear that he really was unwell. He sweated profusely. When he took off his hat, steam rose from

Detail of Rowlandson's *A Theatrical Chymist*, 1786,
depicting Jackson when he edited the *Morning Post*.

his head. As he went up into the dock he whispered 'We have deceived the Senate.' This was a quotation from Thomas Otway's *Venice Preserved*, in which a character who is about to be executed persuades a friend to kill him before mounting the scaffold.

In the dock, Jackson struggled to raise his right hand to take the oath but it quickly fell. His defence counsel argued that he was too unwell to receive sentence and then proceeded to quibble on a legal technicality. All the while Jackson's condition was visibly worsening. The judge ordered the windows to be opened. Defence counsel continued talking. Jackson slumped into his chair. Now it was the judge who suggested that he was too unwell to receive sentence. Jackson started to froth at the mouth. A doctor examined him. 'Can you say you understand your profession sufficiently, so far as to speak of the state of the prisoner?' the judge asked the doctor.

'I can,' the doctor replied. 'I think him verging towards eternity.'

Deemed incapable of hearing sentence, the clergyman was ordered to be taken away. Too late. Jackson was dead. When examined his stomach was found to be corroded by a pint of arsenic. In the end he had acted with nobility. He had refused to name his co-conspirators; and, by killing himself before his sentence, he had saved his estate for his wife. Had he died on the gallows the estate would have been forfeit.

As befitted the former Doctor Viper, William Jackson's role in Irish history was concealed but deadly. His was the first treason trial in Ireland for over a century, but from then on there would be a wave of arrests, convictions and executions. A man of whom one contemporary wrote that, had he been content to rise within the clergy to the level of bishop, he would have been 'an adornment to the Church' became, instead, what some historians have seen as a precursor and exemplar of Irish revolutionary values.

The Reverend Dr Jackson started his career as a mercenary rogue and ended it as an idealist. You may judge for yourself which was more dangerous.

# JAMES CANNON

## A Methodist on the
## Stock Exchange

Bishop James Cannon was fired by Methodist principles. Secretly a loose cannon, he kept his powder and his country dry. So dry that it is fair to call him the most formidable crusader against alcohol in American history.

He was viewed with universal awe. 'If he were to sprinkle baptismal water upon the head of a child,' said one Republican senator of this terrifying man, 'I should expect its scalp to be scalded rather than hallowed. If he were to preach a funeral sermon over my corpse, I believe that like Lazarus, I would throw aside the cerements of the grave and come back to life in indignant resurrection.'

Cannon's biographer, Virginius Dabney, views his subject's life as a series of 'instructive warnings'. When, at the pinnacle of Cannon's fame and influence, news broke that he had engaged in bucket-shop gambling, had conducted an adulterous affair with his secretary while his wife lay dying of cancer and – worst of all – that he had hoarded flour in wartime, Cannon emerged from the storm unabashed, unapologetic and (so far as he was concerned) unscathed. By the time he died in 1944, a few weeks short of his 80th birthday, even his oldest enemies viewed him with a kind of stunned respect. A particularly potent cocktail was named after him.

Had James Cannon Jr lived in seventeenth-century Salem, he would have been an enthusiastic burner of witches. Had his career coincided with McCarthyism he would have been a hot Cold Warrior. Were he alive today he would undoubtedly be hunting down computer pornography and exposing paedophile rings in the Outer Hebrides. But in Cannon's lifetime the Devil's temporary residence was in rum – and every other kind of potable alcohol. One of those puritanical zealots whom the United States specialises in producing, Cannon fought the fight against liquor as a holy war.

Born in Virginia in 1864, Cannon was ordained a Methodist minister in his twenties and soon afterwards founded a girls' school. Its motto, 'thorough instruction under positive Christian influence at lowest possible cost', gave early intimation of Cannon's knack for keeping one eye on Calvary, the other on the cash register. Rising rapidly through the ranks of the Methodist Church and the Anti-Saloon League, which campaigned for a nationwide ban on the sale and consumption of alcohol, he soon found himself in a position of power in both. In 1918 he was (in the way of American Methodists) elected a bishop.

The implementation of nationwide Prohibition at midnight on 16 January 1920 demonstrated the power of the Methodist Church – described by President Grant as the 'third party' in US politics. No one more clearly exemplified that power than Bishop Cannon. Having succeeded in America, the bishop turned his sights to the world. He helped found the World League Against Alcoholism.

During presidential elections in 1928 Bishop Cannon cracked the Methodist whip. Chinks in the 'noble experiment' of Prohibition were showing. In Chicago Al Capone was one of many gangsters making a fortune from bootlegging. There was a mood, if not for an end to Prohibition then at least for its modification. Alfred E. Smith, Governor of New York and the Democrats' presidential nominee, was standing on a moderate 'wet' platform (and was accused by his enemies of drinking eight cocktails a day).

Like most Prohibitionist Southern Methodists, Cannon, a lifelong Democrat, was appalled. 'Democracy will be better served,' he declared, 'by Governor Smith's defeat.' With his usual energy he set about convincing the Democrats' natural supporters that on this occasion they should cast aside lifelong loyalties and vote for the Republican candidate, Herbert Hoover.

Happily for Cannon Governor Smith was a Catholic. Summoning up the anti-Catholicism of the Southern states (helpfully fostered by the Ku Klux Klan) Cannon commenced another holy war. He used church funds to finance Republican candidates. This was an illegal practice which led, eventually, to protracted Congressional hearings. On the hustings he inveighed against the double threat of a Catholic and a wet, and succeeded in turning around the Southern Methodist vote. The result was a huge victory for Hoover.

The effect of Governor Smith's defeat (in Dabney's words) 'rocketed Cannon into a position of prestige and influence never before equalled by a cleric in the history of the United States'. The *Christian Herald* nominated him 'the American who during 1928 made the most significant contribution to religious progress'. The *Herald* awarded him a trip to the Holy Land.

Cannon took his widowed 'secretary', Mrs Helen McCallum, on the trip. This was a detail destined for closer scrutiny. For it was precisely at the moment of his greatest triumph that everything started to unravel. On 20 June 1929, a paper revealed that for the previous two years Bishop James Cannon, bone-dry moral arbiter of the nation, had engaged in bucket-shop gambling through Kable & Co., a seedy stockbroking firm whose directors were shortly to be indicted for conspiracy and fraud. For the modest investment of $2,500 the bishop had made a $9,000 profit. The news was greeted with glee by much of the New York press (which had consistently opposed Cannon's Prohibitionism) and dismay by his fellow-Methodists.

Characteristically, Cannon lashed out, claiming there was a Catholic and 'wet' conspiracy to undermine him. In a blockbuster of a pamphlet he launched a vigorous defence to all press charges – which soon included flour-hoarding during the First World War, and the misuse of Methodist funds in the Smith-Hoover election campaign. Cannon insisted that although brought up to believe that 'all trading in Wall Street was gambling' he had merely invested a modest sum in what he believed to be a reputable stockbroking firm presided over by 'business men of reputation and standing, not only in the community, but in the Churches'.

Cannon's defence persuaded the Methodist Church not to press for a trial. Others were less convinced. 'No one else could have painted a harsher picture of him than he paints of himself between the lines of this casuistical apologia,' wrote one commentary.

It soon became clear that Cannon's defence had missed a few facts: his financial relationship with Kable & Co., for example. Letters written by Cannon to his stockbrokers found their way into the press. The letters showed that Cannon had been heavily involved in speculation and remarkably greedy. He had secured an advance on his episcopal salary to cover any potential losses; he had received daily updates from his broker while on missionary work in Brazil, Mexico and Cuba; and on several occasions he had communicated with Kable & Co. on Sunday. This from a man who condemned Sunday newspapers as unjustifiable on the grounds that 'those who publish them do it because they only want to make money'.

An intriguing new version of Cannon began to take shape: of a bishop who at the same time as gathering souls for the Lord in the wilds of South America was in a frenzy of anxiety about what his shares were doing back in New York. It was all most undignified, though if the bishop felt embarrassment he never let it show. Even staunch supporters began to waver. The *Christian Century* attacked him in a front-page editorial. Such universal hostility would have finished a feebler man. But the bishop ignored calls for his resignation (both from within and outside the Methodist Church) and set nonchalantly off for a holiday in Europe.

The next the world heard of his movements was through the Press Association's London correspondent who broke the news that he had married his secretary, Mrs McCallum, in a ceremony in Pimlico in London. Given that both were by this time widowers (Cannon's wife had died two years previously, of cancer) there was no obvious impropriety. However he had failed to mention his intentions to anyone before setting off. A man who, according to a friend who knew Cannon over forty years, had never once been known to laugh and who smiled only rarely, was thought unlikely to have succumbed to an impulsive holiday romance.

As the newly-wed couple honeymooned through Europe (the 65-year-old bishop only wresting his attentions from a bride twenty years his junior to deliver speeches on behalf of the World League Against Alcohol) odd details of their courtship began to emerge in the American press. The fact that when Cannon had first met McCallum he had done so under an assumed name and occupation – 'Stephen Trent, a writer' – struck some as strange. Newspapers reminded readers that Mrs McCallum had accompanied Cannon to the Holy Land the previous year (shortly after his wife's death) and that even during the first Mrs Cannon's last illness Cannon had spent much of his time with his secretary in New York.

'Their friendship was temporarily interrupted one night,' wrote the *Los Angeles Examiner*, with a hefty nudge, 'when Bishop Cannon, in McCallum's apartment, received word of the serious illness of his wife, the former Luru Virginia Bennett. The bishop rushed to her bedside.' After the funeral 'he returned to Mrs McCallum for consolation'. The newspaper also revealed that Cannon had been providing McCallum with $200 a month. The implication was that even before his wife's death McCallum had been the bishop's kept mistress.

This was more than tittle-tattle. Indeed the source was impeccable: Mrs McCallum herself. She had provided the newspapers with copies of her correspondence with Cannon. Later the explanation emerged. McCallum had read an erroneous report in a newspaper that Cannon had married someone else. In revenge she had contacted the press.

Cannon stepped from the boat in New York harbour to find his reputation being shredded. His response was in character. Cannon announced that he would sue William Randolph Hearst, the newspaper tycoon whose titles had been raking up the dirt, for $5,000,000. This was one of a number of suits filed by Cannon against newspapers, none of which ever found their way to court but which served the purpose of quietening friends and foes alike.

Many of Cannon's colleagues in the Church were unimpressed by his bluster. Four of them pressed for a trial, on charges of gambling, flour-hoarding, lying, 'gross moral turpitude' – and now adultery. In February 1931 a 'committee of investigation' was held, *in camera*, to determine whether any trial was necessary. To universal incredulity, it was decided that there was not. Cannon had escaped again.

And this was just about the end of the affair! Congressional hearings were held to decide on the legality of Cannon's actions during the 1928 election but despite treating the proceedings with contempt, once walking out of a committee (the first person ever to do so), he was finally cleared of all impropriety. Though he was discredited in many quarters, Cannon's bishopric was never prised from his grasp. He retired in 1938.

James Cannon's bucket-shop adventures should have been a great scandal. Instead, they never amounted to more than a sensation. Here is to be found none of the hubris of a great man tripped by his flaws. His star only really waned with the repeal of Prohibition. Not even Cannon could have prevented the failure of that costly experiment.

His will seemed a calculated rebuke to critics who accused him of reckless profiteering. His nine children and one grandchild received just $25 apiece.

The glib advice offered to the guilty when cornered by the press – to 'come clean' – is not borne out in this case.

# HENRY WARD BEECHER

## 'A dunghill covered with flowers'

Henry Ward Beecher liked to boast that he 'preached the truth just as fast as he thought his people could bear it'. Brother of the novelist Harriet Beecher Stowe, an advocate of women's suffrage, Darwin's theories of evolution and scientific Bible criticism, he was an outspoken opponent of slavery and, in a series of lectures in England during the American Civil War, won over many to the Yankees who at first supported the Confederate cause. In 1884 Beecher helped Grover Cleveland achieve the majority in New York State which made him the first Democratic president for 30 years. His sermons attracted thousands. His preaching could move crowds to frenzies of grief or fits of laughter. He was one of the great men of his age. He was also a lying womaniser and a faithless friend.

On the public platform, as in the bedroom, he was a hugely persuasive man. They called him 'the Shakespeare of the pulpit'. Beecher had a splendid voice and great dramatic power. His Sunday sermons in Brooklyn needed specially chartered 'Beecher Boats' to ferry worshippers across the East River. The Plymouth Hall, where he preached, was more like a vast concert hall than a church and still features in tourist guides to New York. The pulpit

Beecher satirized in *Puck* magazine.

was made from olive wood from the Garden of Gethsemane and the income from pew rentals was $100,000 a year.

All of which was too much for some. His detractors mocked him as 'a dunghill covered with flowers' and decried his 'religion of gush'. Oscar Wilde (who visited as Beecher's scandal was brewing) thought him a clown.

But he was no brainless prairie-preacher. As an advocate of freedom of all sorts – of the press, of speech, of opinion – Beecher used his deft eye for publicity to work for the abolition of slavery. He held a mock auction of a slave girl in his church to stir the congregation into supporting the cause. When, towards the end of the civil war, Abraham Lincoln was asked whom he thought was the greatest living American, he replied after only a moment's hesitation, 'Beecher'. His father, Lyman Beecher, another preacher, was known as 'the father of more brains than any other man in America'. Three of his children – Henry Ward, Harriet and Catherine – achieved fame, the other three distinction. All of them were radical liberals.

Still, it is not Henry Ward Beecher's good works which have earned him a chapter in this book but the scandal which nearly swamped him. In 1872, a decade after the abolition of slavery, when Beecher was a moral guide to the nation, he was publicly accused of committing adultery by the first-ever woman candidate for the Presidency of the United States, Victoria Woodhull.

The sin was small enough. But it caused what American historian Paxton Hibben described as 'a terrific battle that for years filled whole pages of newspapers daily, obsessed the thoughts of millions of men and women, disrupted churches, shook the very foundations of the established order, and destroyed individuals as ruthlessly as if they had been thrown into the machinery of a stamping mill'. A guilty verdict, Beecher's defence counsel argued when the matter came to trial, would be 'a blow at the dignity and credit of human nature amid the civilisation and purity of American life'.

The lawyer chose his argument shrewdly. His client avoided public disgrace – just. Woodhull's claims proved too painful a psychological leap for many of Beecher's followers to accept. But he was never again taken seriously by the millions of Americans who had once respected him as the country's foremost ethical progressive.

One of these was the woman who so nearly brought him down, Victoria Woodhull. She was an amazing figure: a feminist a generation before it became fashionable, a spiritualist (she claimed Demosthenes as her 'muse') and a Communist. Woodhull published the first American version of the *Communist Manifesto*.

She was also an ardent advocate of 'free love' (her phrase), the 'inalienable, constitutional, and natural right to love whom I may, to love as long or short a period as I can, to change these lovers every day if I please'. Marriage, said Woodhull, had 'outlived its days of usefulness'.

It was Beecher's misfortune that this remarkable, volatile woman, with such dangerous views, claimed him as an ally. It was his tragedy that she knew him to be an adulterer. His utterances on progress, his talk of love, and his admirable role during the Civil War made her see in Beecher a formidable fellow-liberal. What sealed it was his adultery: this only encouraged her.

A Christian minister, he had for some years been conducting an affair with the wife of his best friend. Mrs Woodhull, sensing a conflict, sought, in private, to persuade Beecher that if he came clean, and declared himself a 'free lover', his moral stature would carry with him the rest of America. Instead he vehemently denied the accusations and she 'outed' him. The storm that followed took 'Mrs Satan' (as Woodhull was dubbed) by surprise. At one point Beecher was called upon to commit suicide.

On 2 November 1872 Victoria Woodhull first announced in print what had already been circulating as rumour in the women's movement in her own journal, *Woodhull and Claflin's Weekly*. 'I am reliably assured that HENRY WARD BEECHER preaches to at least twenty of his mistresses every Sunday,' she wrote with breezy exaggeration. 'I intend,' she went on, 'that this article shall burst like a bombshell into the ranks of the moralistic camp.' One hundred thousand copies sold out within hours. The article claimed to be the 'commencement of aggressive moral warfare on the social question'. It was a cogently argued case against the 'organised hypocrisy' of those who 'act upon the new doctrines while professing obedience to the old'.

Woodhull revealed that Beecher had conducted an affair with Elizabeth Tilton, wife of his best friend and literary protégé, Theodore Tilton. Both the Tiltons were members of Beecher's congregation and Beecher's relationship with Theodore was longstanding. He had handed over the editorship of the *Independent* newspaper; both men had campaigned for the Northern cause during the Civil War and both were supporters of the women's movement.

Their friendship had been jeopardised in July 1870 when Elizabeth Tilton confessed to her husband that for the past two years she had been having an affair with the preacher – a result, she said, 'of long moral resistance and repeated assaults'. At first Tilton sat on the news and appeared to forgive Beecher. But six months later tensions opened in the management of the *Independent*. Tilton had written a leading article advocating the relaxation of divorce laws. It was a subject pressing on his mind: Elizabeth had left him to live with her mother and rumours were circulating about the state of their marriage. On Christmas Eve Tilton met the *Independent* proprietor, Henry Bowen, to discuss them. He revealed to his boss what Elizabeth had confessed six months previously. It must have shaken Bowen whose own wife had made a similar confession on her deathbed. Both men had been cuckolded by a greater man, upon whom both in some measure relied. Tilton immediately wrote to Beecher:

> Sir: I demand that for reasons which you explicitly understand, you immediately cease from the ministry of Plymouth Church, and that you quit the City of Brooklyn as a residence.

Bowen delivered the letter by hand. But when Beecher greeted him with indignant denials Bowen accepted the word of the famous preacher. Instead of insisting that Beecher resign he sacked Tilton.

In private, Elizabeth Tilton made a written confession of adultery. Then, after talking to Beecher, she wrote another letter which categorically denied an affair. She continued to vacillate between the two positions until 1878, when, in a letter to a newspaper, she categorically admitted to the adultery. 'The lie I had lived so well the last four years had become intolerable to me', she wrote. But by then she had changed her mind so often that no one really cared.

Beecher, who did not lack conscience, seems to have felt very badly about the betrayal of his friend and the abuse of Elizabeth. Yet all the parties involved had an interest in keeping the story quiet, and they agreed to do so. In return Beecher produced a limited private admission of guilt. On New Year's Day, 1871, Beecher dictated a letter to a mutual friend.

My Dear Friend Moulton:

I ask through you Theodore Tilton's forgiveness, and I

humble myself before him as I do before my God. He would have been a better man in my circumstances than I have been. I can ask nothing except that he will remember all the other hearts that would ache. I will not plead for myself. I even wish that I were dead; but others must live and suffer.

I will die before anyone but myself shall be implicated. All my thoughts are running towards my friends, towards the poor child lying there and praying with her folded hands. She is guiltless, sinned against, bearing the transgression of another. Her forgiveness I have. I humbly pray to God that he may put it into the heart of her husband to forgive me.

I have trusted this to Moulton in Confidence,

H.W. Beecher

The uneasy truce was sweetened by $5,000 that Beecher paid Tilton to help set up a new magazine, *The Golden Age*. It looked suspiciously like hush money. But Tilton and his wife talked. In particular, Elizabeth Tilton unburdened herself to two women in the suffragette movement, Susan Anthony and Elizabeth Stanton. The rumours reached Victoria Woodhull. ('Oh! What have I done!' Stanton later wrote.)

Victoria Woodhull did not act immediately, though she signalled her knowledge of the affair in a letter to the *World*. 'I know of one man, a public teacher of eminence, who lives in concubinage with the wife of a teacher of almost equal eminence... I shall make it my business to analyse some of these lives, and will take my chances in the matter of libel suits.'

She had another motive, beside the encouragement of free love. Several pro-Beecher newspapers were running a smear campaign against her, including Bower's *Independent*, which saw her as a dangerous maverick harming the women's movement in America. Harriet Beecher-Stowe, Henry's sister and the author of *Uncle Tom's Cabin* joined in the criticism, as did another sister, Catherine Beecher.

Woodhull's definitive response ('Victoria Woodhull's Complete and Detailed Version of the Beecher-Tilton Affair') came out on 2 November 1872. It was well-timed to attract attention – Woodhull was the candidate of the Equal Rights Party in the presidential election, which took place on 5 November. Equally eye-catching was Woodhull's unexpected arrest on the charge of sending obscene mails through the post. The arrest came a day after her revelations about Beecher and had been engineered by a leading member of Beecher's church. Woodhull spent the following three months languishing in Ludlow Street jail, which she colourfully called the 'American Bastille'.

Eventually the 'obscene mail' charge was heard before a jury, which refused to convict. Liberated, she began a lecture tour of the entire United States, spreading the gospel of free love and drawing attention in particular to Henry Ward Beecher's generous freedom with his own love. She packed halls wherever she spoke.

But Woodhull's maverick reputation ensured that press reaction was muted, or at least chary – while Beecher and Tilton stayed absolutely silent. For most of the next two years they managed to avoid any public mention of the affair and cobbled together a 'tripartite pact' lubricated by more money from Beecher. Although Woodhull was raising hell across the nation she was more or less dismissed as a lunatic.

And Beecher's popularity increased! A pew sale in Plymouth Church raised a record sum, and more people than ever flocked to Plymouth Church to hear – and see – him.

There were those in the congregation who now began blaming Theodore Tilton for originating the rumours. Poor Tilton was dropped from the rolls of the church for bringing 'open dishonour upon the Christian name'. A subsequent church council set up to investigate Tilton's dismissal concluded that there had been nothing untoward in Plymouth Church's actions. Further ignominy was heaped on the man Beecher had cuckolded when a Congregationalist minister from Connecticut, Leonard Bacon, in a series of lectures on the affair, concluded that Tilton was a 'knave' and a 'dog'.

The worm turned. A furious Tilton now published Beecher's 'apology'. A rift between the two men, unbelievably long-postponed, had come at last. It was open war.

Forced to respond, Beecher (who still denied everything) declared that a 'trial' would be held in Plymouth Church to settle the charges once and for all. A committee of six men, hand-picked by Beecher, listened to the evidence. The faithless Beecher described Tilton as 'a reckless schemer, pursuing a plan of mingled greed and hatred'.

The press, which had remained quiet up to now, worked itself into a frenzy. Newsmen climbed trees outside the room where the committee sat, to catch indications of what was going on. To nobody's surprise the church wholly exonerated their preacher.

Even before this was known Tilton had filed a suit against Beecher for alienating his wife's affections. He claimed $100,000 damages. His wife, who had long withdrawn her confession of adultery, supported Beecher during the Plymouth Church trial. Tilton's suit came to court in January 1874. 'Nothing since the outbreak of the Civil War had excited such interest,' says one historian. Victoria Woodhull's mud-stirring had ensured that the American public were fully versed in the details of the scandal, and eager for a thorough airing of the case in open court.

Newspapers throughout the country reported the proceedings in depth, and they lasted a full six months from January to July. The jury deliberated for eight days in sweltering heat, but was unable to reach a verdict. Beecher and supporters hailed the non-result as a ringing victory. Some press commentary was less sure. 'Mankind fell in Adam, and has been falling ever since, but never touched bottom until it got to Henry Ward Beecher,' remarked one paper.

Beecher though let off the hook never quite regained his earlier standing. On lecture tours he would sometimes be greeted by hoots and jeers. But in Brooklyn he retained a large, loyal and lucrative following. When he died in 1887, 50,000 people turned out to pay their respects.

Tilton heard the news of Beecher's death in Paris, where he had emigrated after the case – without his wife. He was playing chess in the café, heard the news, said nothing, and turned back to his game.

The strangest twist was in the career of Victoria Woodhull. After years of raising hell she moved to England, disowned her past, and married a millionaire banker, John Biddulph Martin. Biddulph Gardens (in the Potteries), a fantasy-theme park of a garden, are open to the public these days. Victoria mellowed somewhat, but did sue the British Library for holding pamphlets about her which she believed to be defamatory. With her husband's money she became the patron of numerous philanthropic causes, including offering $5000 to the first person to fly across the Atlantic. She died in Norton Park, Worcestershire, in 1927, aged 88.

# A LIAR

## TITUS OATES

## A Shame to Mankind

From time to time the English go mad. In retrospect these episodes appear embarrassing, even sinister; out of context, high emotion can look lunatic. But at the time madness seems sane and the mad and bad carry all before them. Such a fellow was the Reverend Titus Oates.

'He was a man of an ill cut, very short neck, and his visage and features were most peculiar. His mouth was the very centre of his face, and a compass there would sweep his nose, head, forehead, and chin within the perimeter,' wrote the Tory pamphleteer, Roger North of Oates. Others mention a purple complexion, a red beard and a wart over one eyebrow. Titus Oates was not a pretty sight.

The first thing people noticed was his chin. 'He has the largest chin of any clergyman in Europe,' wrote one observer. Another recalled that 'his chin was almost equal in size to the rest of his face.' His chin figures prominently in every contemporary portrait. Even friendly artists working when Oates's star was bright and it was prudent to flatter, were unable to dissemble. This unpleasant first impression survived closer scrutiny. Everyone who ever made Titus Oates's acquaintance seems to have come to regret it.

But for a while England worshipped him.

The England Oates both fostered and spoke for became a rather brutish little country, a place of mob hysteria and raw injustice. On the word of one mythomaniac Anglican clergyman – uttered in an atmosphere of paranoid bigotry – the people, Parliament, the courts, the Church and the King were content to watch at least 35 innocent men led to their execution, and cheer as they went. For a while the nation was possessed; and though the tide whose high-water Titus Oates marks swept out as fast as it swept in, it was to return in smaller surges. A residue of prejudice persisted for centuries.

In the end no one, absolutely no one, had a good word to say for Titus Oates. 'He was a most consummate cheat, blasphemer, vicious, perjured, impudent, and saucy, foul-mouth'd wretch, and, were it not for the Truth of History and the Great Emotions in the Public he was the cause of, not fit to remember,' recorded Roger North. But for two years Oates was hailed as the 'saviour of the nation': a Protestant cleric who had discovered a heinous plot to subvert the Kingdom.

He was born in Norfolk in 1649, the year Charles I was executed. A biographer writing three hundred years later described these events as 'two national tragedies'. Oates's father, Samuel, was a dissenting minister during the Civil War and Interregnum who, after the Restoration, switched to Anglicanism and finally died a Baptist. His life foreshadowed his son's in this respect and in others: in 1646 Samuel could be found in Colchester gaol; in 1654 he was arrested in Scotland for 'stirring up sedition in the army'; in 1674 he was expelled from the Rectory of All Saints in Hastings – for 'disgraceful practices'.

Sent to Merchant Taylors' school in 1665, the young Titus did not impress his tutor, William Smith. Smith recalled that 'the first trick he served on me was, that he cheated me out of our entrance money which his father sent me...' Later, during the Popish Plot, Oates had Smith arrested and forced him to testify in court to imaginary Catholic conspiracies.

This was one of the hazards of associating with Oates: sooner or later former associates were dragged into the Popish Plot. The choice they usually had to make was between the dock (facing a death sentence) and the witness box, perjuring themselves to secure the death of another.

Oates lasted no longer at Merchant Taylors' than he was to last at so many of the other organisations he joined. As soon as people got to know him they came to distrust him. He was expelled from the school in his first year and sent to a smaller school in Hastings. He did not prosper there either.

In 1669 he went up to Gonville and Caius College, Cambridge.

'The plague and he both visted the University in the same year,' wrote a contemporary at the college, Adam Elliot. Later Oates brought Elliot to trial on a trumped-up murder charge. His tutor declared him a 'great dunce' and after just two terms the college expelled him. After moving to St John's College where his 'malignant spirit of railing and scandal was no less obnoxious' he left Cambridge in 1669 without a degree.

This failure did not stop Oates entering the Church. One of the mysteries of this man's rise to prominence is that he progressed through a string of communities, any one of which could soon have sworn to his villainy had they been asked. But nobody pieced together the picture it would have been so easy to assemble. Of such a man today, a modern *Private Eye* reputation-pricker with a telephone directory and a couple of well-placed informants could construct a devastating column in an afternoon. But in seventeenth-century England Oates's notoriety somehow failed to cohere until it was too late. Nobody joined up the dots.

His first clerical appointment was as curate in Sandhurst. He was expelled after parishioners complained of his drunkenness and his habit of robbing them of their pigs and hens. He became vicar of Bobbing in Kent but did not last long. Perhaps aware that he was unemployable anywhere else he retreated to All Saints, Hastings where his father hired him as his curate. In Hastings Titus Oates honed a skill at which he would later excel – perjury. In an attempt to steal a local schoolmaster's job he accused the incumbent, a certain William Parker, of sodomy with 'a young and tender man-childe'. For good measure he accused Parker's father of High Treason.

Here is early evidence of Oates's utter lack of scruple, for both charges carried the death penalty. The Privy Council (which four years later was to eat out of Oates's hand) heard the latter charge and dismissed it as ludicrous, while the younger Parker proved he had been nowhere in the vicinity at the time of the alleged offence and that the supposedly abused 'man-childe' did not exist. Caught out, Oates was arrested in an action for £1,000 damages and gaoled first in Hastings and then in Dover Castle. He soon escaped.

The young clergyman now fell back on an expedient which has so often beckoned a priest in trouble: he became a chaplain in the Navy. The Reverend Chaplain sailed to Tangier on HMS *Adventure*. During this first voyage he was accused of sodomy and expelled from the Navy. Back in England he was arrested on a charge of perjury, and once again incarcerated in Dover Castle. Again he escaped.

On the run in London Oates began mixing with Catholics despite being an Anglican clergyman. One, an actor named Matthew Medburne, introduced him to the Pheasant, a louche club in Holborn and a gathering place for underground Catholics (though club rules forbade talk of religion on pain of a fine). With depressing reliability Oates was later to accuse Medburne of complicity in the Popish Plot. This led to Medburne's gaoling in the King's Bench Prison, where he died. But for the moment the connection with Medburne served Oates well. It was apparently thanks to him that he was hired as chaplain to the Protestants in the household of Henry Howard, sixth Duke of Norfolk. The Duke was one of England's grandest Catholics. Oates soon began leaking the names of his master's friends to government spies.

When Oates came to describe the train of events that led to his 'uncovering' of the Popish Plot he presented these dalliances with Rome as part of a systematic attempt to infiltrate English Catholicism in order to expose the papists' wicked designs. Another explanation is suggested by John Kenyon in his book on the plot: underground Catholicism offered Oates the opportunity to indulge his homosexuality. The Pheasant club, Holborn, was a pick-up joint.

In 1677 Oates's career took a decisive turn. He met the Reverend Israel Tonge, a man described by Kenyon as a 'mental casualty of the Civil Wars'. The Rector of St Mary in Stayning, Tonge was obsessed with Catholicism to a degree unusual even for that febrile time. That he was in some degree mad is beyond doubt. His life was given over to constructing supposed Jesuit plots which he would outline in books with such titles as *The New Designs of the Papists Detected*, and *Jesuitical Aphorismes, or a Summary Account of the Doctrines of the Jesuits*. Yet it was not long before Tonge's pamphlets and dozens like them seemed sober by comparison with the frenzied speculations Oates unleashed.

It is worth inserting a word here about the background against which this blind terror of Catholicism was mushrooming. Madmen like Tonge and Oates would not have been believed unless large numbers of people wanted to believe them. Oates should be understood partly as a cause of the national hysteria but partly as a product of it. And the hysteria, though irrational, was not without its own causes. In seventeenth-century England fear of Catholicism was understandable.

This was the century in which Guy Fawkes tried to blow up Parliament. Across the Channel Louis XIV showed the militant face of Catholicism, forcing hundreds of thousands of French Huguenot Protestants into exile. Many came to England with horrifying stories to tell.

Comparisons may be made with an era when similar forces were at work, though at a much lower pitch. After 1945 and all through the Cold War, fear of the Soviet Union, a fear which was not wholly unreasonable, was stoked by the presence in the West of emigrés from behind the Iron Curtain with much that was disturbing to relate, and their own reasons for playing up the horror. From time to time stories of communist plots would emerge from both sides of the divide. Some of the Soviet conspiracies touted by the 'hawks' of the day were imagined, but not all of them. Once in a while, proof would be found of the truth of one or another anti-Soviet allegation and this would seem to lend credence not only to that allegation but to the whole demonology of what Ronald Reagan called the 'Evil Empire'. Cooler heads, who had doubted some of the wilder claims, appeared to have been discredited and were denounced as dupes. Such was the atmosphere in which a Joseph McCarthy could flourish, unchecked by the critical examination for which the succeeding age sees so obvious a need.

And the England of the latter part of the seventeenth century was infinitely more volatile. Information was harder to test, rumour was fleeter of foot and fears grew faster. The Great Fire of 1666 was popularly supposed to have been the work of Catholics. The King's heir and brother, James, Duke of York, was not just a Catholic, but a convert, which was doubly alarming. Since Charles's wife had failed to produce an heir, a possibility frightened the nation: that he would be succeeded by James.

He was, in the end, after his brother had sought financial help from France in return for promising to convert to Rome. Apologists for the terror which swept English Protestants might quote the modern quip: 'Just because you're paranoid doesn't mean they aren't out to get you.'

'The people thought their enemies were in their bosom',

recorded the Scots philosopher, sceptic and historian, David Hume. 'Each breath and rumour made them start with anxiety. Like men affrighted and in the dark they took every figure for a spectre... common sense, and common humanity, lost all influence over them.'

This was fertile ground for Tonge and Oates. They moved into an apartment and began to piece together their picture of what would become the Popish Plot. It is unlikely that either man envisaged the final consequences of their speculations and fabrications; indeed, it would appear that Oates, until now half-starved and homeless, was primarily desirous of the food and warmth provided by Tonge in return for his 'revelations'.

No commentator has dealt to this author's satisfaction with the question of whether Oates himself believed in the Popish Plot. It is certain that he lied prodigiously to persuade others, and he must have known that many of the Plot's ramifications which he claimed to uncover were fictions. Beyond question, too, is the fact that Oates made a very good living out of his lies, achieving wealth, fame and the status of demagogue. It is only a small step from these premises to the conclusion that Oates knew the Plot was as fanciful as the evidence he constructed for it; but it *is* a step. I hesitate to make it. It seems possible to me that he was personally convinced about the threat from Rome; and that his crusade to alert England to the threat sprung in part from that conviction. I have known so many crusaders against the European Union, the Soviet Union, Socialism, Capitalism – even Apartheid – whose principled horror of these things has not (to them) seemed inconsistent with an unprincipled willingness to distort or invent the evidence needed to persuade others. The more sure we are that our cause is good, the more evil we feel emboldened to risk in achieving it.

Titus Oates almost certainly sent to the executioner men he knew were innocent in pursuance of his crusade to awaken his countrymen to a foreign plot. But I am unwilling to say he did not believe in the plot.

To lend his allegations plausibility Oates needed to build on the inside knowledge of Catholicism he had acquired in the Duke of Norfolk's household. So with encouragement from Tonge he concentrated on what was becoming his forte: religious espionage. He left the employ of the duke and in April 1677 'joined' the Roman Catholic Church. He was sent to the Jesuits' English College at Valladolid in Spain. After four months he was expelled. This did not stop him claiming later that during this period he had been created a Doctor of Divinity by the University of Salamanca. Thenceforward he insisted on being called Dr Oates. The title lent him an authority which was the more spurious because even on his own account his winning of it would have been a trick.

Undeterred by rejection from Valladolid, in December he entered St Omer's college in Flanders. This institution was effectively a boys' school. Oates was now 28. He must have horrified the younger students for later (after he was disgraced) many proved willing to journey to England and testify in court to his bad character. 'We had a pretty fellow at St Omers, that went sometimes by the name of Lucy, and sometimes by the name of Oates, a minister of the church of England,' recalled one, sarcastically.

The reader may not be wholly surprised to learn that on 23 June 1678 Titus was expelled from St Omer's College. He returned from the Continent with absolutely no evidence of a Catholic conspiracy – yet armed with enough inside knowledge to brew up the essentials of a believable plot. With England nervously watching the growing strength of Louis XIV's France, Oates tapped a rich vein of anti-Catholic fear.

He knew too that he could rely on the support of the nascent Whig party in Parliament. This group encompassed dissenters, low-church Anglicans and opponents of the Royal Prerogative. They wanted to exclude the Catholic Duke of York from the throne. Against them were ranged the King's high-church and Catholic supporters, men soon dubbed 'Tories'. The term, originally an insult, is often attributed to Oates.

In the vast Jesuit conspiracy which Titus Oates (through an intermediary) alleged, the King would be assassinated and his Catholic brother James placed on the throne. There were plans, he claimed, for a gruesome massacre of English Protestants. Oates said he had 'proof' that the Great Fire of 1666 was a Popish conspiracy. He spoke of mysterious men lurking in the park with daggers, pistols or bludgeons to assassinate the King.

He had 'overheard' treasonable words uttered by his old tutor, William Smith, and his former friend, Matthew Medburne. He

TESTIS OVAT

Titus Oates in the pillory: the most famous view of him.

had 'seen' a papal Bull which, in anticipation of the plot's success, drew up appointments to the chief ecclesiastical posts in the country. There were 6,000 Catholics in Scotland ready to rise when the call was sounded. All over London there lurked Jesuits disguising themselves as merchants, 'scriveners' and tobacconists. And he named names.

An alarmed Charles II ordered his Lord Treasurer, the Earl of Danby, to investigate. At first Oates stayed behind the scenes. He had been busy inventing new twists to the Plot, all communicated to Danby; but it harmed the Plot's credibility that the key informant remained in the shadows. So on 6 September 1679 Oates swore before a popular London Justice of the Peace, Sir Edmund Berry Godfrey, to the truth of the allegations; and soon after made his debut before the Privy Council.

It was a triumph. (Oates was not, however, grateful: in time three Privy Councillors were to find themselves in prison, charged with treason.) That evening five men named as the King's potential assassins were arrested; all were later executed. The following day warrants were put out for the arrest of eight more men.

The nation's first Catholic was of course the King's brother, the Duke of York, and Oates was keen to implicate him. So he named the Duchess of York's private secretary, Edward Coleman, among the plotters. By a fluke he mentioned letters to Pierre de la Chaise, a French Catholic priest who heard Louis XIV's weekly confession. When Coleman's papers were inspected there were indeed letters to la Chaise. They were incriminating. Referring to Protestantism as a 'pestilent heresy', Coleman expressed the opinion that 'there were never such hopes of success since the death of our Queen Mary, as now in our days'.

One can imagine, of course, that a Catholic might well write a private letter to another in such terms, given that the sect to which they belonged was under siege in England, its adherents living in hope that a Catholic might succeed to the throne; but it was possible to place a much darker construction upon the letter – though Oates can only have guessed at its contents. The discovery was dynamite. Coleman was charged with treason.

The arrest of Coleman after the revelation of his letters gave a huge boost to the 'Plot'. Soon there was another. Sir Edmund Berry Godfrey, the magistrate before whom Oates had sworn the truth of his charges, was found dead: he had been strangled and then run through with his own sword to make it look like suicide.

We can see how compelling the evidence must now have looked – or felt, at any rate. Oates was surely right! There *was* a Catholic conspiracy to murder Protestants everywhere.

Or so it seemed. Deciding who killed Godfrey is one of those historical parlour games English historians like to play. Possible culprits range from Oates himself, to unnamed Catholics, to genuine suicide. Joining such speculations we quickly find ourselves in the psychological territory Oates himself inhabited – but on the other side. Would it not have suited the *Protestant* inventors of a Catholic plot to contrive the apparent murder by Catholics of a popular magistrate?

For news of Godfrey's murder was electric. The death was an event which, if it did not cause the subsequent hysteria, focused it. A young Catholic man, Miles Prance, was dragged from the silversmiths where he worked and tortured into confessing to the crime. On his evidence three men were hanged.

On 23 October 1677 Oates appeared before Parliament. For the Whigs led by the Earl of Shaftesbury (a former member of Oliver Cromwell's Council of State) Oates's claims seemed heaven-sent. MPs at once pushed through a Bill excluding Catholics from both Houses: an Act which remained on the statute books until 1829. The Whigs also took the opportunity to introduce a Bill excluding the Duke of York from the throne in favour of Charles's Protestant but illegitimate son, the Duke of Monmouth. This was one step too far for the King, who dissolved Parliament.

However Charles had been dependent on Parliament for his income. Without the Commons he needed another source of funds. So he contacted the King of France and invoked a secret clause to the Treaty of Dover negotiated eight years earlier. The clause allowed for a substantial private subsidy from French coffers if Charles agreed to convert to Catholicism before his death. Seldom has there been a neater demonstration of self-fulfilling prophecy. Initially unfounded fears of a Popish Plot had actually caused a Popish Plot.

Titus Oates knew nothing of the King's treacherous behaviour but he was riding high in Protestant esteem. Events seemed to have established his credibility as a witness. One after another, people fingered by Oates were brought to the dock and sentenced to death. Installed in Whitehall apartments and protected by a small army of bodyguards, Oates was now receiving a huge pension from the government. On top of this he submitted an enormous £678 12s 6d bill for his 'expenses' in uncovering the Plot. It was paid on the instant.

He dined with bishops (and dressed like one). He had, if not the sympathy of the King then at least his horrified attention. Publicly adored as the saviour of the nation, he enjoyed ever more extravagant epithets. His servants vied for the privilege of washing him in the morning. He appeared in heroic guise on the reverse side of playing cards. Perhaps for the first time in his life he was in demand as a fashionable preacher.

Emboldened by his new-found status, Oates expanded his charges to include five Catholic peers. All five were arrested and thrown into the Tower. Incredibly (before the Bar of the House of Lords) he also accused the King's Catholic wife, Queen Caroline, of plotting to murder her husband. Oates referred to her as 'Dame Short-arse'.

A London militia was established with powers to stop funeral processions and examine coffins for arms. By the month's end the Commons had resolved that:

> ... this House is of the opinion that there hath been and still is a damnable and hellish plot contrived and carried on by the popish recusants for the assassinating and murdering of the King, and for the subverting of the government, and rooting out and destroying the Protestant religion.

It was a sign of how wide the hysteria had spread, that citizens who – even on their accusers' own account – had no connection with Oates's accusations, now fell under suspicion. The first man to be executed under the terms of this new Commons definition of a 'Plot' had nothing to do with Oates's alleged conspiracy. On Monday 25 November a Catholic banker's son, William Staley, was sentenced to death after he had been heard saying in French that the King was a rogue and that if no one else would stab him then he would. It was not credibly suggested that Staley was in touch with any 'plotters' at all, or aware of any Plot, but the Lord Chief Justice ordered that his corpse be exhumed, his quartered body stuck on the City gates and his head displayed on London Bridge.

The trial of the Duchess of York's secretary, Edward Coleman, followed the next day. Oates, appearing as the principal witness, lied brazenly. Repeating the allegations that he had first made before the Privy Council he invented further details in the witness stand: among them that he had himself *heard* Coleman say that the plot to kill the King was 'well contrived' and that he had himself *seen* Coleman handing over a guinea to one of the 'four Irish ruffians' supposed to kill the King.

Lord Chief Justice Scroggs, who appeared to take pleasure in sending Catholics to their deaths, pointed out that it was the habit of Continental Catholics to thirst after Protestant blood. 'Remember that the Plot is on foot, and I do not know what arts the priests have, and what tricks they use...' he remarked before pronouncing sentence: 'You shall return from prison, from thence to be drawn to the place of execution, where you shall be hanged by the neck, and be cut down alive, your bowels burnt before your face, and your quarters severed, and your body disposed of as the King thinks fit; and so the Lord have mercy upon your soul.'

The Roman Catholic Archbishop of Armagh, Oliver Plunkett, head of the Church in Ireland, was among those sentenced to death in the following weeks. He went into the dock facing the trumped-up charge of conspiring to bring the French Army to Ireland. Nearly three centuries later Plunkett was beatified by Rome. I worked on the Foreign Office desk dealing with the Vatican at the time and remember, even then, that Protestant sensitivities about this beatification had to be answered in Britain, particularly Northern Ireland.

The slaughter did not end with Plunkett. In the summer of 1679 14 Catholics were executed. The only crime of one, an Irish Franciscan named Charles Mahoney, was to have been shipwrecked off England. In November 1680 Viscount Stafford was tried and convicted by his peers (among them seven members of his own family, who voted for his execution). As a special favour Charles allowed him to be beheaded, for which Stafford appears to have been genuinely grateful. As the summer of 1681 arrived, the 35th victim of the plot was executed.

The politics of the period remained unstable. In the two years after 1679, in what became known as the Exclusion Crisis, the

King dissolved Parliament three times to stop Shaftesbury from introducing his Bill to block the accession of the Duke of York. This growing polarisation began to spell trouble for the man who had done so much to bring it about. Oates was at the height of his success but the mood began to turn. There had arisen a significant 'King's party' and the clergyman found himself pitted against more than Catholicism: against monarchy itself.

And, all at once it seems, the anti-Catholic engine ran out of steam. The first sign came in 1679 when the Queen's physician, Sir George Wakeman, was acquitted, although Oates had given evidence against him. And as imitator after imitator piled in to add details to the plot in the hope of matching Oates's status the whole thing began to look dubiously over-egged.

In retrospect it is possible to explain this apparently mysterious shift. Both the rhetoric and the logic of Oates's imaginings had pointed to the imminence of events which would confirm them. People waited. But there were no Popish risings in Scotland. Protestants did not have their throats cut. Not a single person, even on the block or gallows, ever confessed to the truth of the Plot. And Oates himself started to come under unpleasant scrutiny. His past at last began to catch up with him. His early indictment for perjury surfaced. The consistency of the witnesses pitted against his conspiracist view was becoming ever more plain.

And in 1682 the ambassador of the Emperor of Morocco, Hamad Lucas arrived in England. His visit would have been no surprise – but for the fact that Titus Oates had told everyone that his Cambridge contemporary Adam Elliott had murdered Lucas. Now it was clear he had lied. Elliott sued Oates, who was gaoled. Though bailed by his friends Oates was soon back in prison. He was no longer the public hero of the hour. On 29 April 1682, the 22nd anniversary of the Restoration of the monarchy, an effigy of Oates was burnt in Covent Garden.

Suddenly this was a man no one wanted to be associated with. In 1684 he was charged with slandering the Duke of York and tried by 'Hanging' Judge Jeffreys – a man who, not long before, had been an enthusiastic persecutor of alleged plotters. The clergyman was found guilty and fined the fabulous sum of £100,000, a sum Jeffreys well knew he could not pay. Oates languished in prison, in irons.

The following year Charles II died and his brother succeeded him as James II. With Shaftesbury dead, James on the throne, no pogrom of Protestants and the Popish Plot discounted, Oates was utterly discredited. Possibly England felt slightly foolish. No longer protected (as in the past) by the adoration of the mob, he became vulnerable to all the enemies he had made in high places. He was charged and tried on two counts of perjury.

It is difficult not to feel *schadenfreude* at the reports of Titus Oates's trial. Once again Judge Jeffreys presided. Perhaps sensitive to his own injustice in having sent innocent men to their deaths on Oates's say-so, Jeffreys was merciless. 'Hold your tongue; you are a shame to mankind,' he interrupted the accused.

Remarkably for so blatant an enemy of the King, he escaped execution: perjury, the crime for which he had been found guilty, was not punishable by death. Oates was fined 2,000 marks and unfrocked. But a week of punishment was drawn up which, it seems, *was* supposed to kill the rogue priest.

On the Monday morning following his conviction he was to be set in a pillory in Westminster Hall. On Tuesday he was to be pilloried in the Royal Exchange. On Wednesday he was to be flogged from Aldgate to Newgate. Thursday was a day off. On Friday the whip was to be picked up again at Newgate, and dropped at Tyburn.

And there was more. 'Mr Oates, we cannot but remember, there were several particular times you swore false,' announced Jeffreys, cruelly savouring the moment. 'Therefore, as annual commemoration that it may be known to all people as long as you live, we have taken special care of you for an annual punishment.' For the remainder of his life Oates was to be annually pilloried on four days in April and August.

The following week's floggings and pillories were duly carried out. Oates appeared at Westminster on Monday 18 May 1685 wearing a sign: 'Titus Oates convicted upon full evidence of his two horrid perjuries.' He survived the whole ordeal – just – thanks to four weeks' treatment by a team of surgeons. There seems to have been a morbid appetite for keeping this human exhibition of shamefulness alive.

For the next four years he lingered in prison, only leaving to keep his appointments with the stocks. It was rumoured that he fathered a child with the prison bedmaker. It was unusual for Oates's name to be mentioned in connection with a woman but given the constraint of the prison walls the unfrocked clergyman may have found what port he could in the storm.

The experience taught the old dog other new tricks too, as we shall see in a moment. Remarkably Oates achieved something of a rehabilitation and even gained a sort of respectability, after the invasion from Holland of the Protestant William of Orange, who installed himself as King William II of England in 1688. Oates was released – and somehow worked his way back on to the government payroll. The Archbishop of Canterbury invited him to dinner. Oates announced that, like his father, he had become a Baptist. Though he renounced the Church of England (and it had renounced him) he continued to dress as an Anglican churchman and to title himself with the Jesuit doctorate he had awarded himself from Salamanca.

And then came the remarkable news of his marriage. The Reverend Doctor was joined in matrimony – with an heiress. Not until the wedding of the Labour MP, Tom Driberg, in 1951, at which Churchill remarked 'buggers can't be choosers', would so lost a sheep return so late to so unlikely a fold. 'Everybody stood amazed, and it was a considerable time before they could recover themselves from the astonishment,' wrote Tom Brown in his satire of the match, *The Salamanca Wedding*. Brown is arch:

> You know, for a person of his Constitution, that always expressed, and perhaps inherited an aversion to the Fair Sex, and besides, had found out a Back door to bestow his kindness and strength elsewhere, to confine himself at last to the insipid duties of matrimony, is as unnatural and unexpected a change as for an old miser to turn prodigal. The Doctor promises that he will never attack either in bed, or couch, or in stool, or table, the body of the aforesaid Mrs Margaret W— *a parte post*, but to comfort, refresh, and relieve her *a parte ante* . . .

As for the wedding night itself:

> . . . the Doctor resolutely marched towards the place of execution. . . . The bed continued in a trembling fit for most part of the night, which I suppose occasioned the report of an earthquake, which the next neighbours said they felt that

unbloody night. 'Tis not doubted but that the doctor behaved himself with great gallantry, since Madam O told her midwife that is to be, that the Doctor fought out all his fingers, and she already begins to Puke, and be out of Order, like women in a breeding condition. . . .

It need hardly be said that in due course the newlywed was to be expelled even from the Baptist order, after trying to defraud a wealthy widow of her inheritance. He squandered his wife's fortune and spent a spell in a debtors' prison. In July 1702 he was tried in Westminster Hall Quarter sessions, for 'scandalising and assaulting' a woman named Eleanor James.

And once again, Oates entered the market for invented plots. He claimed to have inside knowledge of a Jacobite conspiracy intended to put James II's Catholic son on the throne. Oates was essentially rehashing the Popish Plot for the new circumstances of the day – and throwing in an extended dash of self-justification and lamentation for his plight. But the public had lost its appetite for this sort of thing, at least for the moment. Jacobite plots took several years to become fashionable. Oates missed that tide.

He died in July 1705, in some obscurity. He was 58. He left a daughter, Rebecca Crisp Oates, born 3 October, 1700. I wonder if her descendants live today.

# A PIRATE

## LANCELOT BLACKBURNE

## 'The jolly old Archbishop of York'

A popular story was told of an old pirate arriving in England after years at sea, and asking what had become of his 'old friend Blackburne' – to be told he was now the Archbishop of York.

With Lancelot Blackburne, eighteenth-century scandalmongers were never sure where to begin. Successively an Antiguan pirate (by repute), Bishop of Exeter and Archbishop of York, he was – even by the standards of the prelates of the day – seriously tarnished. Much mud was flung and much stuck. It was said he secretly married George I to his German mistress and, more improbably, that he employed Dick Turpin as his butler. And no one doubted his powers of seduction: Blackburne was an ardent womaniser until his death.

The gossip was as widely believed as it is hard to confirm for Blackburne took care to ensure his private papers were burned after his death. Entrusted with this task was the man assumed to be his bastard son, Thomas Hyter, Bishop of Norwich.

Nevertheless rumour persisted. An eighteenth-century biographer remarked that 'there is something mysterious in the history and character of Dr Blackburne'. To Horace Walpole he was 'Blackburne, the jolly old Archbishop of York, who had all the manners of a man of quality though he had been a buccaneer and was a clergyman, but he retained nothing of his first profession except his seraglio.' A contemporary called him 'a most vile, scandalous, illiterate man', 'an atheist, a man e'er good for nothing'.

Born in 1658 and educated at Christ Church, Oxford, Blackburne was ordained in 1681. But the simple life of a parish priest was not for him. In December 1681 the records of Charles

II's secret service show that Blackburne was paid a £20 bounty 'for his transportation to Antego' – now Antigua. For an ambitious cleric the Caribbean was an unusual start. He joined a rabble of deadbeats and chancers. 'Please do not send any more Scotch clerics,' a contemporary wrote home from the islands, 'the people do not like them.'

The enterprise was risky in the extreme. One might drown on the way, or be raided by pirates. The climate was good but the state of the Church was hopeless. As to the salary – the good news was that it was generous; the bad news that it was paid in sugar. Most settlers seemed eager to leave.

Whether or not Blackburne spent time in Antigua we know he served as minister at St Paul's, Falmouth, a settlement on the island of Nevis. This is all we know, for a French invasion (another hazard of the job) ensured that the island's documents were destroyed in 1712. For the rest of his life rumours would abound that he had served as a chaplain on board a pirate ship and shared in bounty captured from Spanish galleons.

Parson or pirate, Blackburne did not stay long in the Indies. By 1683 he was back in England casting his eye around for dying clergymen with comfortable livings he could inherit. 'The incumbent, Mr Bonhomme, about 70 years of age, is at the point of death,' he noted of the Rector of Calstock, before succeeding him.

His eyes were on Exeter's Cathedral Close. In January 1694 he was appointed the cathedral's sub-dean. Little is known of his work as a dean – though a witchcraft trial seems to have engaged his attention.

And scandal was catching up with him. In 1702 a whispering campaign began. Poisonous letters were sent to 'the most distant places and to the greatest persons', including Bishop Trelawny of Exeter. They claimed that Blackburne was cuckolding one of the leading citizens of the town, a close friend, the aptly-named Mr Martyr.

The charges caused a sensation, not least (said his defenders) because of 'the artifice, the diligence, the violence with which this report was set on foot'. Blackburne's enemies waited until he had left town, then pounced, denouncing him at the town assizes. Tales were told of a secret passage constructed on his orders by a local carpenter, Mr Stibbs, leading from the study of his palace to Mr Martyr's house next door. A delegation inspected Blackburne's office. There was indeed a door leading into the Martyrs' home. But Stibbs indignantly denied constructing a passage. He said he would 'spit in the face' of anyone who claimed otherwise.

Mr Martyr wanted to trust Blackburne and was reported as insisting that he 'never gave him any just cause for believing that the great friendship contracted between them and their families was ever grounded on a wicked design'. However a little later, after an evening in the local tavern and perhaps stung by the taunts of fellow-drinkers, Martyr insisted on inspecting the sub-dean's study for a second time. Blackburne complained ruefully of Mr Martyr's 'after-whimseys'.

These charges were too serious and too famous to brush aside and Blackburne was forced to resign while an investigation took place. 'Though we do not think ourselves concerned to take notice of every defamatory report that may chance to be spread abroad of any of our body, yet in a matter of so heinous a nature so industrially propagated as that imputation hath been which one of our brethren, Mr Canon Blackburne, now lies under, we cannot but esteem it our duty to make some inquiry into the grounds of it,' concluded the bishop.

The Dean and Chapter of the Cathedral offered 'all manner of encouragement' for witnesses to Blackburne's misbehaviour to come forward. None did. Servants who had previously accused him changed their stories; a workman was produced to say the inter-connecting door had been sealed three years previously on Blackburne's orders. The Cathedral Chapter issued a report exonerating the sub-dean; but it was two years before he was reinstated.

The era's 'rage of party' was at its height. Blackburne now nailed his colours firmly to the Whig mast. He backed George I when he acceded to the throne in 1714 and did not waver during the Jacobite rebellion of 1715.

Far from it. He mercilessly pursued a former friend for printing a Jacobite pamphlet. Philip Bishop had published one of the sub-dean's sermons and Bishop's wife had stood up for Blackburne when he was suspected of adultery. But all this counted for nothing. 'A more vicious slander has never been written,' fumed Blackburne, deploying spies to track down Bishop. Captured, he languished in Newgate Prison, dying before his trial and presumed conviction. The sentence would have been the amputation of his hands and ears.

Popular with the new Court, in 1716 Blackburne accompanied the King as Anglican chaplain on a visit to the royal lands in Germany. As the King was neither Anglican nor an English-speaker and Blackburne had no German there was little obvious call for his services. Horace Walpole suspected Blackburne was close to the King for another reason. The new monarch was widely lampooned in England for keeping his wife confined in a Hanoverian castle for 32 years. His two mistresses were famous. Walpole alleges that Blackburne married George to one of them, the Duchess of Munster, in a secret ceremony. It was for this, thought Walpole, that Blackburne was elevated to the Bishops' bench in the House of Lords.

Walpole may be right. But I suspect that Blackburne's old habit of keeping careful watch on the failing health of clergymen in plum jobs mattered rather more. In November 1716, on his return to Exeter, Blackburne visited the bishop whom, he noted, 'a gangrene eats hourly'. Blackburne began plotting to succeed him, recording with evident relish that the bishop was not expected to live 'to the date of our meeting on the 8th of next month (for the gangrene has eaten above his knee and the surgeons dare not cut off the leg)'. Three days later, the bishop was dead. Blackburne moved fast with an obsequious letter to the Archbishop of Canterbury. He got the job.

Anglicanism and religious enthusiasm were not always coupled in the eighteenth century. Blackburne was rarely at Exeter Cathedral, preferring to spend most of the year in London. He carried out as few ordinations as was decently possible but remained a good Whig, which was what mattered. After seven years of comfortable idleness he was elevated to the Arch-bishopric of York. He was duly enthroned to the second most powerful post in the Church of England in 1724.

He was now 66. Grey hair and ecclesiastical eminence brought neither virtue nor modesty and did nothing to moderate his lust. As archbishop, Blackburne 'won more hearts than souls' recorded his biographer. In 1731 the Reverend Samuel Barber published a long poem, *The Farmer's Daughter; or, the Art of Getting Preferment* suggesting that clerics who tried to impress the archbishop with piety or learning would be wasting their time. To win Blackburne's favour, advised Barber, 'send your handsome wife'. Barber

Frontispiece of a contemporary satirical poem chronicling the
Archbishop of York's affair with a milkmaid.

suggests Blackburne lived the life of an epicure. Most of the poem
is devoted to the sordid tale of Blackburne's seduction of a pretty
milkmaid employed in his palace as 'secretary'. After two years, as
a favour, he appoints her idiot brother to a parish in his care.

A saucier story still was published in the year of Blackburne's
death, 1743. It suggests the Archbishop enjoyed three-in-a-bed
sex romps.

> *One had her charm below, and one above.*
> *So I together blended either bliss:*
> *Lydia lay on, Dolly had my kiss.*

We do not know that the archbishop ever bothered to respond to
any of this. Perhaps he was too idle to care for, as in Exeter,
Blackburne revelled in the property, stature and good living his
position brought him. He could afford to engage others to fulfill
his duties. In 1736 he engaged the Bishop of Gloucester to carry
out a Bishop's Visitation – apparently the only one he arranged
during his tenure. For the last decade of his life he failed to ordain
any new clergy at all.

On his death at 84, Blackburne's reputation was finally ceded
to the ballad-singers. They set to work at once. 'A thousand
weeping matrons wait his hearse,' wrote the author of *Priest-Craft
and Lust: or Lancelot to his Ladies*, a squib published to coincide
with Blackburne's funeral.

> *All the buxom damsels of the North,*
> *Who knew his parts, lament their going forth . . .*

There have been more dignified farewells for Archbishops of
York. Indeed there have been more dignified farewells for pirates.

Many of the figures in this book have been undone by some vast
misjudgement or huge folly; or by evil, madness, or terrible luck.
Blackburne was different – but typical of not a few eminent men
I have known, who were no better than they ought to be. He was
not so much wicked as without conscience, and combined the
ordinary vices with extraordinarily careful judgement in matters
affecting his own position.

# A JOURNALIST

## HENRY BATE

## 'I have stuck the fork in the dunghill, up came Mr Bate'

'Parson Bate, so celebrated in his day, is now almost forgotten ... he figured amongst the most prominent characters of the last reign,' wrote Henry Angelo, once a friend of Bate's, in his memoirs.

When Reverend Henry Bate, Prebendary Canon of Ely and Rector of Willingham, died in 1824 an obituary notice appeared in the *Gentleman's Magazine* which reviewed his life's work in glowing terms. His house 'was the seat of hospitality, but no prodigality'. 'His person was finely formed, and possessed all its symmetry beyond the age of 60.' He had been ennobled for his 'uncommon abilities as a magistrate of eleven counties'. Sir Henry Bate Dudley was, a casual reader would conclude, a consummate good egg.

Could this be the man who, in his youth, was hailed variously as 'Reverend Bruiser', 'Reverend Iago' and 'Reverend Reputation-Butcher'? Who fought five duels, founded two scurrilous newspapers, and wrote plays which caused riots in London theatres? Who was named as a correspondent in a notably sordid adultery trial and spent a year in prison for libel? The two characters seem so far removed from each other that we have trouble recognising them as the same person.

Henry Bate's was such an exuberantly eighteenth-century life that it could have been extracted from one of Sheridan's comedies. He belongs equally to histories of journalism, theatre, and duelling. It is easy to forget that he was a clergyman – though his contemporaries did not. William Benbow finds a place for him in his annals of criminal clerics; an anonymous writer in the *Morning Chronicle* called him 'that bullying, boxing, Vauxhall parson'. George III referred to him as 'that worthless man Mr Bate'. He was a scandal to the cloth until the grey dawn of the nineteenth century brought a sober respectability, and he succumbed.

Born in 1745, Bate inherited his father's living as Rector of North Fambridge, Essex. He claimed to have become a Doctor of Divinity at Oxford but there is no record of this. His career was so diverse and yet so colourful that it is hard to relate as a narrative. But if there was one thing that unified all his endeavours, it was his combative spirit. He was the 'Fighting Parson'.

He earned the soubriquet in 1773, soon after he had been appointed editor of *The Morning Post*, defending a lady's honour in Vauxhall Gardens. His companion was a celebrated beauty, the actress Mrs Hartley (Bate later married her sister), who was insulted by a group of 'Macaronies' – a stock term of abuse for a certain type of fop dedicated to Continental fashion. Among these macaronies was a certain Captain Croft.

According to a pamphlet written by Bate (I have modified it slightly) he shouted at Croft, who was mocking the couple:

Bate:  You are four dirty impudent puppies.
Croft:  *(In a menacing tone)* Did you call me a dirty puppy?
Bate:  Well that depends on whether or not you formed part of that group. If so, why then, Zounds sir!, you are a dirty, impertinent puppy!
Croft:  *(Looks Bate up and down in a supercilious manner)* Hah! You are indeed a good tight fellow, and therefore mean to intimidate me I suppose, because you are a boxer.
Bate:  If you speak three more impudent words I'll wring your nose off your face.

Croft wrote to Bate that night: 'I will meet you on your own terms; and if you do refuse to give me the satisfaction I require, I will hunt you up and down London till I find you, and will then *pull your nose, spit in your face, and pull the black coat off your back.*' Croft involved his friend, the Honourable Edward 'Fighting' Fitzgerald, a half-mad aristocrat who had lost part of his skull in the course of fighting numerous duels, and Fitzgerald in turn nominated his footman, 'a hired bruiser', to settle the matter in the Turk's Head Coffee House the following afternoon. Bate emerged triumphant. His adversary was sent home in a coach, 'his face a perfect jelly'.

The affair was quickly dubbed the 'Vauxhall Affray', and rumbled on throughout the summer in an increasingly ludicrous epistolary feud. Thoroughly chronicled in the *Post*, whose hallmark was gossip and sensationalist journalism, the whole affair did wonders for circulation figures.

The habit became addictive. From the Vauxhall Affray on, Bate used the *Morning Post* to goad public figures in the hope of provoking duels which would grip readers. Standards of journalism, often bewailed as low today, were far lower then. Scurrilous, witty and wildly inaccurate, it is to the *Morning Post* more than any other trailblazer that today's tabloid obsession with the private lives of public figures can be traced. 'Pity posterity, who will not be able to discern a thousandth part of the lies of Bate,' wrote Horace Walpole. Liar he may have been but Henry Bate was certainly one of the most gifted self-publicists to enter holy orders.

Given the number of enemies Bate had made in the course of editing the *Morning Post* it was hardly surprising that when the clergyman's head was on the block there were plenty prepared to take a chop. One opportunity came at the beginning of 1776. There had already been too many victims of his abusive journalism for Bate to be able to write and stage a play in London's West End, the heart of his newspaper territory, where most of his victims resided, without inciting a riot. And that was exactly the reaction to his musical comedy, *The Blackamoor Washed White*, produced at the Drury Lane Theatre and directed by his friend, the celebrated David Garrick.

Only one newspaper deemed the production an unqualified success, remarking that it 'was received throughout with universal applause' – the *Morning Post*, whose critic was in all likelihood Bate. 'If his enemies have now forgotten their personal resentment towards him, the opera promises to become a favourite entertainment.'

Despite such optimism, Bate took precautions. He recruited a number of his friends, including Angelo, to stand by in the event of disruption; he also hired professional boxers. Sure enough, as the production got underway there were catcalls, hisses and yells from the audience. Instead of ignoring this the management over-reacted. Bate, his friends, and the hired boxers leaped onto the stage and crossing from one side to the other made menacing gestures at the audience with their fists. 'This was the signal for a general charge upon Bate's party,' recorded Henry Angelo. 'The box in which we were crowded was attacked with showers of apples, oranges, and other such missiles.'

At the next performance one of the ringleaders of this attack burst into the theatre and challenged Bate to a duel. In less than a week the play was taken off.

Bate fought five duels, wrote about them all and never killed an opponent. But this does not mean they were rigged. Although the parson was never badly injured no one can doubt his bravery. On one occasion in 1776 his hat was blown off and his skull grazed by his opponent's pistol shot. This failed to satisfy the honour of either side and in the ensuing sword fight (conducted in the dark) Bate was left with a wounded thigh which put him out of action, but not out of the newspapers, for several days.

'The Theatrical Dispute, or the Parson Baited' (1776).

'A Baite for the Devil' (1779), depicting Henry Bate's roles as
clergyman, magistrate and hunter.

One attempt to spark a duel backfired, however, and led to Bate's resignation from the newspaper and a year's imprisonment.

In February 1780 he launched a brass-necked attack on the Duke of Richmond, a leading member of the Opposition and a famously volatile character. (During the American Revolution Richmond cheeked George III, sailing his yacht across the bows of the royal barge while flying the Stars and Stripes.) Bate accused Richmond of treacherously opposing increases in the country's military strength to ease the way for a French invasion of England. Like most newspapers of the day the *Morning Post* was shamelessly in the pay of a political faction. But even Lord North, the Prime Minister supported by the paper, thought that Bate was 'perhaps too warm on the part of the government'.

What Bate really wanted, of course, was a duel. Had Richmond behaved in character he would have got one. Instead, the duke sued for libel, a move welcomed by every establishment figure who had been abused by 'that infernal print the *Morning Post*' (as it was put at the trial). Richmond won and Bate was sentenced to a year's imprisonment, postponed until the prison, destroyed in the anti-Catholic Gordon riots, had been rebuilt. Eighteenth-century England was a wild place.

The correction alarmed the paper's proprietor, Mr Richardson. He worried that if Bate continued as editor, he too would end up on the wrong end of a libel writ. Bate called Richardson and his fellow proprietors a 'parcel of cowards'. Richardson challenged him to a duel unless he withdrew the remark; Bate refused and the next afternoon the two fought, with pistols. Richardson's arm was hit first and he was unable to return fire. Typically, their correspondence was printed by Bate in the paper, though of course 'only to prevent the least misrepresentation, to the disadvantage of either side'.

Within weeks Bate had resigned from the *Post*. He immediately founded a rival paper, the *Morning Herald*, which he continued to edit from prison. Conditions in gaol were not hard. 'Like many sons of the Church,' wrote Angelo (a regular visitor to Bate's cell) 'he kept a good table and was no mean professor of gastronomy.' The good parson was allowed to live with his wife. He also managed to keep a mistress, a Mrs Dodwell, who on one occasion bumped into and quarrelled with Mrs Bate on the prison landing.

Henry Bate's final blast of notoriety came in 1788, just as he

was in danger of achieving respectability. By then he had assumed
a double-barrelled name, attaching Dudley to Bate to comply
with the terms of a will. He began a career as a magistrate. And
the *Morning Herald*, which he continued to edit, was a far cry
from the scandal-sheet he had pioneered in the 1770s.

Henry Bate Dudley's new difficulties stemmed from his
mistress, Mrs Dodwell. He was not her only lover – these
included a French general, 'a healthy and alert old gentleman'
with whom she conducted an affair on a pleasure yacht. But to
secure a divorce *Mr* Dodwell, an amateur anatomist, needed to
prove at least one case. As he put it: 'I have stuck the fork in the
dunghill, up came Mr Bate, and it is his chance, and I cannot help
it.' In December 1788 Henry Bate Dudley was charged with the
'seduction of, and criminal conversation with, Mrs Dodwell'.

Mr Dodwell should have picked an easier target. Although Bate
effectively admitted his affair he insisted there had been no
'criminal conversation' for at least six years and he could not
therefore be convicted. He also argued that Mrs Dodwell could
hardly be blamed for straying from her husband, as he dissected
human bodies in a laboratory near his bedroom:

a practice he followed in utter disregard of her [Mrs
Dodwell's] repeatedly desiring he would desist; ... notwith-
standing her entreaties to the contrary he appproached her
with his hands covered with all the nauseous filthiness of
such pursuits; this might have furnished a delicate lady with
an apology for abandoning her husband.

Although a jury heard servants' evidence of stained sheets and of
jealous quarrels between Mrs Dodwell and Bate's wife, Bate was
acquitted. Parliament was unable to sanction a divorce and the
Dodwells remained man and wife.

The case received widespread attention in all quarters of the
press. Except, of course, for the *Morning Herald*, whose account
of the trial was limited to a paragraph. For once Bate had lost his
appetite for the limelight.

Thereafter Henry Bate ceases to be of interest to chroniclers of
clerical scandal. He became involved in a protracted dispute with
the Bishop of London over the sale of ecclesiastical office. In 1819
he wrote to George IV complaining 'that through the unceasing

hostility of the Bishop of London I was banished to Ireland.'

In Ireland, though, he made good once more. After excelling as a magistrate Bate moved back to Essex, was created a baronet and became Rector of Willingham where he lived in respectability until his death in February 1824. He had no children.

One man who knew him thought Bate 'constituted, both in mind and body, for the army or the navy, rather than for the church'. He is a curious figure. A friend of Garrick and Gainsborough, a patron of the arts, a convivial host, he was a more interesting figure than the swaggering, duelling burlesque with which the public were familiar and in which he seemed to delight. Perhaps too elusive for a full-scale biography, most accounts, like this one, have been diverted by his most colourful escapades. He probably deserves more considered analysis.

But I still find it remarkable that he was a clergyman.

# OTHER NEWS

## ASSORTED MISCREANTS

## 'They will come to see me prosecuted but not hear me preach'

In October 1987, under the headline 'The Filthy Vicars in Our Midst' the *News of the World* asked: 'Just what has happened to all the upstanding, God-fearing vicars and priests whose morals were once as clean as their freshly-laundered dog collars?' The paper published a list of all the scandalous vicars it had exposed in the past year. At this point, near the end of our book, it is worth waving before the reader a similar list, indicative rather than exhaustive, of other news snippets on which we lack the space to dwell.

In the News International archive at Wapping there are no less than 30 files covering half a century stuffed with newspaper cuttings concerning clergymen who have ended up in court, or who have been sacked or forced to resign after a scandal. Often the stories record nothing more than common misdemeanours – adultery and drink-driving convictions abound – but which made the news because the culprit was a clergyman. More than one curate has been caught dipping his fingers into the church collection box. And a very great number of cuttings show that the naughty 'vicar and choirboy' is more than a myth. Paedophilia is the most frequent cause of clerical scandal, if the archives are anything to go by, followed by a near-endless list of vicars caught by the police importuning in public lavatories. Bigamists are also well-represented.

From time to time there are stories so macabre that you could be forgiven for thinking they were invented by a tabloid night editor with a page to fill. In March 1985 a Welsh Methodist minister, the Reverend Emyr Owen, was sentenced to four years imprisonment after admitting that he mutilated corpses awaiting burial. It was his practice to sever the genitals from the bodies, photograph them and then feed them to seagulls. He would sometimes scorch the corpses' buttocks with electric fire bars. This gruesome tale has an eighteenth-century precedent in Henry Timbrell (see p20), who was gaoled in 1764 for castrating two of his apprentices – though the boys were alive.

A large number of drunk, foul-mouthed, abusive or simply eccentric clerics have ended up in the magistrates' court. In September 1977 the Reverend Maxwell Crosby Halahan, an Anglican vicar from the Isle of Wight, was fined £50 and bound over to keep the peace for a year after he became drunk at a Jubilee night party and began sparring with other guests. He took off his jacket and waved it like a matador attempting to enrage a bull, before taking off his shirt and dog-collar and running around the room in his vest and trousers. He pleaded guilty to 'using foul language, insulting people, assaulting a youth and behaving in a manner likely to cause a breach of the peace'. Another hothead, the Reverend Richard Allen, vicar of Williton in Somerset, was reprimanded in October 1994 by his bishop when instead of delivering an after-dinner speech at the Minehead Cricket Club he bellowed 'It's time for catching practice!' before bowling roast potatoes down the table.

In 1963 the Reverend Eric Weeks outraged his parishioners in Ashbrittle, Somerset, after whacking his dairymaid with a walking stick during an argument. In response, the dairymaid, Mrs Kathleen Mable Moon, threw a bucket of dirty water over the rector's head. Ashbrittle; dairymaid; Mable Moon ... if a junior reporter were (God forbid) to make such a story up, his editor would require more believable names and roles! Afterwards, Mr Weeks ruefully remarked of his flock 'They will come to see me prosecuted but not to hear me preach'. In January 1956 the Reverend Richard Henry Smart was reprimanded by his bishop after he undressed and spanked a bride-to-be in the vestry. He claimed he had been angered by her laxity in religion and was trying to remedy this.

Meanwhile in Holmfirth, in the West Riding, the Reverend John Fitzgerald was so unpopular that two churchwardens and the choir refused to attend his services. A fiery evangelical, he divided his congregation into the saved and the damned and made them sit on different sides of the aisle. Fitzgerald finally departed after he called one of his parishioners a drunkard and spat in her face. In April 1987 Canon Michael Dittmer offended 200 mourners at the funeral of a local farmer when he described the man he was about to bury as 'a very disagreeable man with little good about him who will not be missed'. In January 1994 the Reverend David Heron made the mistake of getting drunk before conducting the funeral of a late colleague. He called the deceased – a man – 'our late departed sister' before collapsing in a heap on the floor. He had to be carried out by the pall bearers.

Just one cleric is recorded as having organised a striptease show in his church, the Reverend Eric Henry Betteridge, a Baptist minister from Surrey. He was gaoled for three months – which seems a bit harsh. Another, the 74-year-old Reverend Hugh Proctor was given a six-month suspended sentence for playing strip poker with two boys. And the Reverend John Poole, vicar of Holy Trinity Church in Huddersfield, was gaoled for three years after holding a homosexual wedding in his church, followed by an orgy before the altar. Of course there was nothing new in this: performing gay weddings in the notorious Vere Street brothel was one of the many allegations made against John Church at the beginning of the nineteenth century (see p163).

America is another source of grisly newspaper snippets. In 1975 the Reverend Samuel Corey was sentenced to death by electric chair in New Orleans for murdering a prostitute, Patricia Gieseck. She had been pushed under the wheels of Corey's car by her husband as part of a conspiracy to claim life insurance. Corey had married the couple two weeks before the killing. Back across the Atlantic in Rome, a woman who admitted to adultery in the confessional found herself the victim of blackmail threats. When she left a sum of money in a dustbin for the blackmailer to collect the police swooped – and the blackmailer turned out to be her padre.

Some characters crop up in the cuttings files more than once. The Reverend Richard Mayes, a curate from Prittlewell, Essex, known fondly as 'Rick the Vic', first made an appearance in the press in December 1977 when he was gaoled for nine months for drugs dealing. He next made the news in September 1979 for assaulting a police officer, for which he was fined £50. The following month he was arrested after two girls riding on horseback through a wood in Essex encountered the former curate stark naked. On seeing the girls (it is alleged) he cried out 'Come over here darlings!' When police came to investigate he explained to them 'I've got this thing about primeval man. It's marvellous.' Rick the Vic was last heard of living in a teepee in the Rainbow Red Indian Tribe, near Aberystwyth. The *News of the World* quoted him as saying 'I no longer believe in the moral values of society. What is morality to the outside world, I consider prudery.' Readers may spot a similarity with seventeenth-century Ranter Abiezer Coppe (see p122).

Flashing is an ancient peccadillo of the clergy. It was one of the charges laid against the Reverend Edward Drax Free (see p109) when he was prosecuted in 1829, and as far back as 1476 court records show that the Reverend Thomas Ysakyr 'showed his private parts to many women in the parish'. In March 1952 the Reverend John James Stanley Whyte, a former Royal Naval Chaplain was prosecuted under the Vagrancy Act after he presented himself at his bedroom window stark naked to a plainclothes policewoman. His defence, which ran along the lines that 'we always did that sort of thing in the Navy', did not find favour.

The fall of a bishop is a solemn moment. Sensational cases such as the Bishop of Clogher (see p144) and the Right Reverend Roderick Wright (see p182) received massive coverage in the press of their day. A quieter tragedy was that of the Right Reverend Stephen Thomas, Bishop of Landaff, who was forced to resign in 1975 after an 'act of gross indecency', committed in a public lavatory with a fitter. The bishop, married with four children, was also fined £25. The magistrate noted that clerical misdemeanours 'are regrettably common these days' – which is something magistrates have been saying for centuries.

Some prelates fall in spectacular fashion, such as the Right Reverend Gordon Savage who shocked his flock when, soon after retiring as Bishop of Southwell in 1970, he moved in with a former topless dancer, Amanda Lovejoy. *The News of the World* caught up with the ex-bishop in 1982, when 'Sexanna the stripper', whose acts included simulating sex with a teddy bear, alleged that he had used an American Express card to pay for sex in a Belgian night club. The bishop (she said) had asked her 'to be his teddy bear'. Sexanna, the paper discovered, had been a chorister in Southwell Cathedral when Dr Savage was bishop.

Then there is the mass of minor but curious cases, such as the priest who told his wife that he was going to watch a cricket match but who instead went to Hyde Park to look at courting couples through binoculars. For this, the Reverend Hopkins Evans was fined £2 by Marlborough Magistrates' Court in June 1959. The following year Father Terence Patrick McDonnell found himself in court after approaching two 14-year-old boys and offering them three shillings if they took part in practical research. The boys took up the offer and accompanied McDonnell to the field where the priest whipped them. He was fined £40 and the canes and straps in his possession were confiscated.

Given the abundance of scandalous clergymen (and in spite of the title of this book) there have been surprisingly few formal unfrockings. A bishop's decision to depose a priest from holy orders, rather than merely insisting that he resign from whatever ecclesiastical offices he holds, appears to be an entirely arbitrary one. The Reverend William Bryn Thomas, Vicar of Balham, was unfrocked in May 1961 for 'open and notorious sin' after he was caught having an affair with a divorcee, as well as being found guilty of molesting his curate's wife. The Reverend Tom Tyler (see p32) remained in holy orders after being found guilty of a near-identical offence. In August 1972 the Very Reverend Eric Goff, Provost of Portsmouth was unfrocked even though no consistory court hearing ever took place. Goff had resigned after rumours of a relationship with a secretary working for the cathedral. In contrast, the Reverend William Ingram, Principal of the London Choir School, convicted of a series of assaults on children in 1954, remained in holy orders – despite the *Sunday Pictorial*'s stark headline: GO UNFROCK YOURSELF FATHER INGRAM.

To the best of this author's knowledge self-unfrocking is unheard of and probably impossible, the act itself depriving the agent of the authority to accomplish it.

# EPILOGUE

## ROGER HOLMES

## 'The Knicker Vicar of North Yorkshire'

'Did you capture a scandal on video?' asked an ad in the *News of the World* in March 1997. 'We'll pay £250 to tell YOUR story. Ring the newsdesk any day of the week. Don't worry about the cost, we'll call you straight back.'

The 1990s scandals industry is a sharp-clawed predator and naughty vicars are prized game, as Roger Holmes, vicar of All Saints Church in Helmsley, Yorkshire, discovered on Easter Sunday 1997. After preaching what was to be his last sermon at the 8:30 service that morning, he went home, to be greeted by a whey-faced parishioner with a copy of that morning's *News of the World*. On its front page were grainy stills printed from a video-recording of himself in bed with a woman who was not his wife, 'sneering' – so the paper reported – 'I'm the Knicker Vicar of North Yorkshire.'

I relate the tale not because it matters, or is unusual – but as an example of how a story which matters not at all, and is in no way unusual may temporarily grip, horrify and (let us be honest) entertain much of the nation.

For compared with some in this book it was hardly a scandal at all and certainly not news. Presumably vicars have been unfaithful since vicars began. But it was the end of Roger Holmes's clerical career. He was suspended from all 'priestly duties' that evening; a day later he resigned his living, apologising to parishioners for the 'hurt' he had caused them. 'Mr Holmes is not my favourite incumbent in any case,' said his superior, the Bishop of Whitby, when told by the tabloid of its exclusive, 'Cheating Vicar in Video Sex Outrage'.

The goings on in Helmsley were picked up with alacrity by the *Daily Telegraph* and the *Daily Mail*. The latter summed things up best: 'An Unholy Affair: Or how the RE teacher's wife was filmed in bed with their vicar while her husband ran off with a church warden.' 'I was dealing with what seemed to be more than a menage of trois,' added the Bishop of Whitby.

What the papers quickly dubbed 'the ultimate Aga Saga' began in 1994 when the Reverend Roger Holmes and his wife Lynn arrived in Helmsley from the Yukon, in Canada. He attracted notice as a forthright, muscular clergyman in a backwater parish dominated (says the woman who became his mistress) by 'miserable, carping old-timers'.

Two couples in particular became close friends of the new vicar and his wife; the Schofields and the Roberts. All had young children and a taste for religious discussion. Alison Schofield and Adrian Roberts became church wardens. Gillian Roberts joined them as secretary of the Parish Council and editor of the parish newsletter.

For Mrs Roberts, a specialist in medieval literature more at home in Bloomsbury than the Yorkshire Dales, it was an exhilarating time. She relished the companionship and debate. She had married Adrian, a fellow student, shortly before he took a post as a religious studies teacher at his old school, Ampleforth, the leading Catholic college. Though the couple bought a pleasant house, Ivy Cottage, just outside Helmsley and had two children, things did not go well. Their second child was diagnosed as having cerebral palsy. The life of a schoolmaster's wife did not appeal to Gillian. She took every opportunity to visit her old bookish haunts in London.

There have been claims and counter-claims about when the infidelities began and whose provoked whose – and who cares? – but nobody denies that in time both Mr and Mrs Roberts were seeing someone other than their respective spouse; and each knew about the other.

Certainly by the middle of 1995 Gillian and her vicar were in love. 'I felt like a teenager and all love-poetry suddenly seemed real,' she wrote later in the *Daily Mail*. 'Roger, the vicar, is a passionate sensualist and sex, when it began between us, was a reflection of that.'

Meanwhile her husband Adrian's affair – with her fellow

church-warden, Alison Schofield – had intensified. In February 1996 he left his wife and moved in with Alison. Roberts's behaviour did nothing to moderate the bitterness he felt at his wife's adultery. He and Alison went to the Bishop of Whitby, the Right Reverend Gordon Bates, and told him of the local vicar's sins. Summoned to explain himself, Roger Holmes denied everything. By now tongues were wagging in Helmsley. But few in the town were much exercised by what was going on. So Adrian Roberts rang the *News of the World*.

The paper dispatched three reporters from London and they met – while Gillian Roberts was away – in Ivy Cottage. They were not trespassing. When his marriage broke up Adrian Roberts retained not only a set of doorkeys but ownership of the house. He let the reporters in. They glued a tiny video camera to the inside of a bookshelf, in the master bedroom which by then was being shared by Gillian Roberts and the vicar. And somehow – no one quite likes to say by what route – they took away with them *verbatim* extracts from Mrs Roberts's diary entries. These described not only the course of the affair but intimate details. Soon they were to be read at breakfast tables throughout Britain.

Interviewing the couple later for a radio programme about press methods I called at Ivy Cottage. Mrs Roberts showed me the hole in the door of her bedside bookcase. It was no bigger than the head of a small nail. She told me she felt 'violated' by the existence of the videotape and by the publication of passages from her diary.

The paper had the evidence it wanted and on the eve of publication approached the couple. They were at home watching the boat race. 'I went outside after I'd had a bit of time to think and told the reporter what I thought of the *News of the World*,' Mrs Roberts explained to me. 'He wanted Roger to come out, he said "we know that's his car". What we wanted to avoid at that point was a photograph of him leaving the house.'

It was too late. On Easter Sunday the *News of the World* splashed its video nasty. 'Cheating Reverend Roger Holmes looked his Bishop straight in the eye and promised he was pure in body and soul ... and then carried on his debauched lust for wild sex and corporal punishment with his Church secretary ... the affair will devastate the pretty town of Helmsley, where parishoners lovingly tend their parish church.' Bathetically, the paper's main picture of the 'sex romp' showed little more than the vicar's bald head.

Helmsley was not devastated. Though the local newsagent had to order in extra copies of the *News of the World*, the scandal was a three-day wonder.

Except of course for those directly concerned. You might say that four lives have been hit by something like a hurricane. You cannot say they played no part in calling it into being but nor can you say that any of them expected or deserved what came to pass. I include the story by way of postscript to this book. I include it because it crystallises for me – and may for you – what is so very odd, so compelling, and so unfair about scandals in which men of the cloth fall from grace.

The tale of the Knicker Vicar seems to have all the elements. Sin – of a faintly exotic kind. A respectable neighbourhood, an appearance of propriety and an apparently pious churchman. And of course a shock disclosure and a mighty fall. In the words of George and Weedon Grossmith's Mr Pooter in *Diary of a Nobody*, 'Ho! What a surprise!'

Yet if you examine the building bricks from which this sensation is constructed – as I did – what have you but a handful or ordinary (and in this case rather pleasant) people whose behaviour – reprehensible or otherwise – has departed not a jot from that of millions of their fellowmen and fellow-women, since human history began?

So what is it about vicars? You cannot even say they stand as symbols for a faith in which most of their countrymen any longer believe. More than ten times as many people read the *News of the World* as follow any religion with anything that could be called conviction.

Some have suggested the pleasure people take in such stories is simply the glee with which the lesser see the greater fall. But this explanation does not suffice. Bigger figures than Roger Holmes – tycoons and newspaper editors – can tumble with a lesser splash than the errant vicar. Some of these great men may wag a more censorious finger at the common people than vicars ever do yet their disgrace has less capacity to amuse, less power to make others hug themselves with pleasure.

I am far from solving this riddle but end with one thought. Visiting and getting to know the Reverend Roger Holmes and

Gillian Roberts spoiled the fun for me in a way in which it would have done, I suspect, for almost every reader of the *News of the World*. Instead of comic caricatures one encountered real people, no larger than life, who bleed. I actually preferred the story when it was offered to me as a novelette might be. Enjoyment of a good read is in no way spoilt by the knowledge that none of the characters portrayed is intended to bear any resemblance to persons living or dead. It almost goes the other way; as the characters become more real those pseudo-scandals crumble in our hands.

Do churchmen provide, even in a godless age, pantomime representations of universal stereotypes: naughtiness and censure made flesh? Each of us fears and resents (a little) the Accusing Voice. To construct for ourselves pantomimes in which what we fear is represented as a figure of ludicrous hypocrisy who gets his comeuppance because in the end he is no better than us, is enormously reassuring.

So we seize on stories such as that which Helmsley sent the *News of the World* with a relish which tells us more about ourselves than about Helmsley, or anyone who lives, preaches or fornicates there. In a sense, Helmsley, Roger Holmes, Gillian Roberts, the cartoon vicars and cartoon choirboys, the Rector of Stiffkey, John Wakeford, Dr Dodd . . . all that cast of cartoon cats and cartoon mice, together with their cartoon landscape of kitchen tops, catflaps and mousetraps or altars, sacristies, prying eyes, newspaper presses and waiting gallows – do not exist save in the imagination of passing ages.

# AFTERTHOUGHT

## A RESEARCHER WRITES

On 25 October 1997 the old British Library closed. For a month a great tribe of British Library readers – dispossessed, unwillingly evicted from their homeland in the heart of the British Museum – was allowed to roam, unsupervised, before being relocated to a new site a few hundred yards north of Bloomsbury. Where did they go in the meantime? I personally found shelter in Lambeth Palace Library, a serene place looking onto a grassy courtyard with a small gurgling fountain, secretly relishing researching a book on religious scandal in the seat – so to speak – of the Archbishop of Canterbury.

Readers of this book will by now have realised that its researcher must have spent an unhealthy amount of time in the company of drunks, fornicators, adulterers, the mentally unbalanced – and British Library readers. In the somewhat ignoble cause of unearthing 2,000 years of religious scandal I spent the best part of a year in the old British Library, and two or three months more in the new one in St Pancras, and it is hardly surprising that, as I lifted my head from books about wicked bishops, transvestite methodists and mutilating nuns and looked up at a mass of people silently reading, frantically scribbling, quietly murmuring to themselves, or fast asleep, I should muddle the two and suspect that libraries are deranged places. The moral of Eden's apple is that knowledge is dangerous and here there were hundreds gorging the stuff; gorging it, digesting it and finally secreting it in the form of books – which end up in the British Library.

Actively seeking out religious scandal gives one a slanted sense not just of the clergy, but of those who have written about the clergy. Matthew in his introduction suggests that there is something in the Christian religion that encourages a confusion of the sacred and profane. Even the central rite of the Christian Church, the Eucharist, requires a belief that the spirit and the flesh meet and fuse and perhaps it is not surprising that all too often its ministers emulate this: Harold Davidson proselytising in Egyptian brothels and Oxford Street teashops, Giacinto Achilli raping girls in the sacristies of Viterbo, Henry James Prince claiming 'soul brides' in Somerset.

But if the church has drawn in and thrown up endless lurid and colourful characters, then it has inspired equally lurid and colourful denunciations. John White's *The First Century of Scandalous, Malignant Priests Admitted into Benefices by the Prelates*, William Benbow's *Crimes of the Clergy*, the demented, anti-Catholic rants of Titus Oates's and Cardinal Newman's times all enter into fascinated, often fantastic, detail. In the end one felt that those digging up this dirt were themselves drawn into the same dubious spheres of religious experience that attracted those denounced. It was an uncomfortable thought.

The old British Library had a subtle way of dealing with such readers: segregation. I started off in Panizzi's great Round Reading Room – airy, open, invigorating – leafing through general histories of the church. Soon I was exiled from this magnificent dome to the 'North Library', a more shadowy place – the home of rare and unusual books – and more often than not found myself on what is known variously as the 'Dirty Books Desk', or the 'Desk of Shame'.

Situated directly in front of the issue desk, under the watchful eye of librarians, it was here that one was permitted to read books otherwise kept locked up in separate cabinets. A great many of the books I needed to consult were deemed too dangerous to be permitted to be read elsewhere.

Who decided? What criteria were used? On the whole anything containing the word 'sodomy' in the title was black-marked – and so it was here that I read about the Bishop of Clogher, caught buggering a soldier in the back room of a London pub in July 1822. Bound with pamphlets on the Bishop of Clogher were others on the Reverend John Church (*Religion and Morality Vindicated against* Hypocrisy and Pollution; *or an account of the Life and Character of JOHN CHURCH the Obelisk Preacher, who was formerly a frequenter of Vere Street and who has been charged with UNNATURAL PRACTICES in various places*), which led me to another hoard of pamphlets, which also had to be read at the Desk of Shame. And bound with these pamphlets on John Church was that odd, undated newspaper cutting about Henry Timbrell, the Methodist minister who castrated his two apprentices in the hope that they would become singers at the opera. Through the resourcefulness of the Wiltshire Record Office I finally tracked Timbrell to Kemble, near Salisbury, 1764. But who had pasted this cutting there in the first place? What had prompted this person to gather these pamphlets in one volume and present them to the British Library?

Sitting permanently at the Desk of Shame one started to feel conspicuous, and mildly paranoid. This, it seemed, was the high security wing of the British Library: placed all together, we were contained, more manageable if collectively we began howling or tearing off our clothes. The message was clear: it was not just the books that were suspect, but those who chose to read them.

All too aware of the adage that you can tell a chap by the company he keeps, one would find oneself seated next to a man leafing through turn-of-the-century pornographic photographs. Another man, also a permanent fixture at this desk, kept calling up books on Satanism. (And how many books there are on that subject!) Frequently one would sit opposite grey-haired gentlemen with half-moon glasses reading *Lolita*. In such company one is somehow compromised. And the question grows, *Why are they reading these things?* And then, disconcertingly, *Why am I reading these things?*

But one never asked out loud: readers rarely talked to each other, and cast glances at each other only furtively. On the unusual occasion when I did see one reader voluntarily talk to another, who had a cold, it was to tell him to go outside and blow his nose. Many seemed to go there just to sleep, many were very elderly, and more than once I thought that the man sitting next to me, inert, might actually be dead, and considered gently prodding him to check – until at the end of the day, when the bell tolled, the crumpled body gathered itself together, returned its books, and shuffled away.

Readers, I say did not talk to each other in the old British Library – until Saturday 25 October 1997, the last day that the Round Reading Room was open. Many turned up, and discovered on their desks a note announcing that drinks would be served at the end of the day. Stoically we read our books, ignoring the quite unusual hum of chatter, or the anarchy of people running around taking flash photographs. And then, at the end, when we had obediently returned our book and drinks were served (from the issue desk), we talked! How we talked!

*What do you do here?* we asked each other, and to general surprise discovered that everyone else was entirely normal, if unusually well-read. Intimacies and telephone numbers were exchanged. We grew drunk, and reckless. One man lit a cigarette – perhaps the first to be smoked in that room in 150 years – and the effect would have made a splendid Bateman cartoon. We wallowed in nostalgia and regrets. In the splendid isolation of research there had, after all, been some sort of solidarity.

Late in the evening we dispersed, vowing eternal friendship. And for a month this routed army wandered – through Lambeth, the Bodleian, the red bricks of the North – and finally reassembled in St Pancras – where no one talks to each other, where eye contact is furtive, where old men sleep, and where this book will soon find a place, waiting to be discovered and prompt someone to wonder what on earth can have induced anyone to embark on such a peculiar quest.

I do hope that readers have not thought it all in vain.

*Nick Angel*

# ILLUSTRATION CREDITS

**Integrated illustrations:**

p2    Unidentified fourteenth century miniature, © Mary Evans Picture Library.

p10   The Pope's manliness being inspected, © Peter Stanford/William Heinemann Ltd.

p12   Illustrations from contemporary pamphlets, © British Library.

p15   Dissection of a murderer in Surgeons' Hall, from *The Newgate Calendar*, 1788, © British Library.

p21   Detail from the 1764 Wiltshire Assizes records, © Mary Evans Picture Library.

p23   John Ball depicted in Froissart's *Chronicles*, © Mary Evans Picture Library.

p63   Harold Davidson's cartoon history of his trial and conviction, courtesy of Mrs George Robertson, Stiffkey.

p67   William Dodd in his heyday, © Mary Evans Picture Library.

p71   William Dodd depicted on the front of a German pamphlet, © British Library.

p91   John Bull knocking on the portals of justice, from *John Bull*, © British Library.

p92   Handwriting from the Bull Hotel register, © *John Bull*.

p94   *John Bull* making an 'important announcement', © British Library.

p123  Frontispiece of a pamphlet denouncing the Ranters, © British Library.

p147  Percy Jocelyn at the point of his discovery, © British Library.

p151  Title page of contemporary pamphlet, © British Library.

p161  Frontispiece of contemporary pamphlet, © British Library.

p164  Frontispiece of John Church's autobiography, © British Library.

p187  Roderick Wright and Rupert Murdoch meeting in the *Guardian*, © Martin Rowson.

p198  Detail of Rowlandson's *A Theatrical Chymist*, 1786, © British Museum.

p220  Titus Oates in the pillory, © British Museum.

p233  Frontispiece of a contemporary satirical poem, © British Library.

p238  'The Theatrical Dispute, or the Parson Baited', 1776, © British Museum.

p239  'A Baite for the Devil', 1779, © British Museum.

**Picture section:**

Cruickshank's 'The Arse Bishop', 1822, © British Museum.

'The Vindication of James Byrne', 1822, © British Museum.

All Harold Davidson photographs © Norwich Record Office.

Dr Dodd leaving his wife on the morning of his execution, © Mary Evans Picture Library.

'A Sandwich', from Henry Angelo's memoirs, © British Library.

Pope Joan giving birth, © Mary Evans Picture Library.

The author in Lambeth Palace, © Nick Angel.

# SELECT BIBLIOGRAPHY

The following is not a comprehensive bibliography, but among the many books and works of reference consulted, it is worth mentioning a handful upon which we have particularly relied:

*A Full Report of all the proceedings on the trial of the Rev. William Jackson*, Dublin, 1795

Angelo, Henry, *Reminiscences of Henry Angelo*, Kegan Paul & Co., 1904

Barrow, Andrew, *The Flesh is Weak: An Intimate History of the Church of England*, Hamilton, 1980

Bate, Henry, *The Vauxhall Affray; or, the Macaronies defeated*, London, 1773

Benbow, William, *Crimes of the Clergy; or, the Pillars of Priest-Craft Shaken*, London, 1823

Bernard, Nicholas, *The Penitent Death of a Woefull Sinner; or, the Penitent Death of John Atherton executed at Dublin the 5. of December, 1640*, Dublin, 1641

Bird, Brian, *Rebel Before His Time: the Story of John Ball and the Peasants' Revolt*, Churchman,1987

Blythe, Ronald, *The Age of Illusion: England in the Twenties and Thirties, 1919–1940*, Hamish Hamilton, 1963

Chandos, John, *Boys Together, English Public Schools, 1800–1864*, Hutchinson, 1984

Church, John, *The Foundling, or, the Child of Providence*, London, 1823

Coppe, Abiezer, *A Fiery Flying Roll: A Word from the Lord to all the Great Ones of the Earth*, London, 1649

Cullen, Tom, *The Prostitutes' Padre: the Story of the Notorious Rector of Stiffkey*, Bodley Head, 1975

Dabney, Virginius, *Dry Messiah: The Life of Bishop Cannon*, 1949

Dixon, William Hepworth, *Spiritual Wives*, London, 1868

Finlanson, William Francis, *Report of the Trial and Preliminary Proceedings in the Case of the Queen on the Prosecution of G. Achilli v. Dr. Newman*, C. Dolman, London, 1852

Fitzgerald, Percy, *A Famous Forgery, being the story of the Unfortunate Dr Dodd*, London, 1865

Hibben, Paxton, *Henry Ward Beecher: An American Portrait*, New York, 1927

Howson, Gerald, *The Macaroni Parson: A Life of the Unfortunate Dr Dodd*, Hutchinson, 1973

Kearsly, G., *The Case and Memoirs of J[ames] H[ackman], and of his acquaintance with Miss M. Reay*, 1779

Kenyon, John, *The Popish Plot*, Penguin, 1984

Maccormick, George Donald King, *Temple of Love*, Jarrolds, London, 1962

Mander, Charles, *The Reverend Prince and His Abode of Love*, Wakefield, EP Publishing, 1976

McNamara, Jo Ann, 'The Nun of Watton', in *Magistra*, Volume I, Number I, Peregrina Publishing Co.,1992

Murphy, Annie, with Peter de Rosa, *Forbidden Fruit: The True Story of My Secret Love for Eamonn Casey, the Bishop of Galway*, Little, Brown and Company,1993

Newman, John Henry, *Letters, Diaries, and Notebooks*, edited by Charles Stephen Dessain, Thomas Nelson & Sons, 1961–1977

Outhwaite, R.B., *Scandal in the Church: Dr Edward Drax Free, 1764–1843*, Hambledon, 1997

Schwieso, Joshua, *Deluded inmates, frantic ravers and communists, a sociological study of the Agapemone, a sect of Victorian apocalyptical millenarians*, University of Reading PhD unpublished thesis,1990

Shaplen, Robert, *Free Love and Heavenly Sinners: The Story of the Great Henry Ward Beecher Scandal*, Andre Deutsch, 1956

Stanford, Peter, *The She-Pope: A Quest for the Truth Behind the Mystery of Pope Joan*, Heinemann, 1998

Symonds, John Addington, *The Memoirs of John Addington Symonds*, edited by Phyllis Grosskurth, Hutchinson, 1984

*The Bishop!! Particulars of the charge against the Hon. P. Jocelyn*, J. Fairburn, London, 1822

Treherne, John, *Dangerous Precincts: the Mystery of the Wakeford Case*, Cape, 1987

Tyerman, Christopher, *Who's Who in Early Medieval England (1066–1272)*, Shepheard-Walwyn, 1996

# INDEX